Substance
Abuse
in Canada

Substance Abuse in Canada

Marilyn Herie
Wayne Skinner

ISSUES IN CANADA

OXFORD
UNIVERSITY PRESS

OXFORD
UNIVERSITY PRESS

8 Sampson Mews, Suite 204, Don Mills, Ontario M3C 0H5
www.oupcanada.com

Oxford University Press is a department of the University of Oxford.
It furthers the University's objective of excellence in research, scholarship,
and education by publishing worldwide in

Oxford   New York

Auckland Cape Town Dar es Salaam Hong Kong Karachi Kuala Lumpur Madrid
Melbourne Mexico City Nairobi New Delhi Shanghai Taipei Toronto

With offices in

Argentina Austria Brazil Chile Czech Republic France Greece
Guatemala Hungary Italy Japan Poland Portugal Singapore
South Korea Switzerland Thailand Turkey Ukraine Vietnam

Oxford is a trade mark of Oxford University Press in the UK and in certain other countries

Published in Canada by Oxford University Press

Library and Archives Canada Cataloguing in Publication

Herie, Marilyn, 1963–
Substance abuse in Canada / Marilyn Herie, Wayne Skinner.

(Issues in Canada)
Includes bibliographical references and index.
ISBN 978-0-19-543387-6

1. Substance abuse—Canada. I. Skinner W. J. Wayne, 1949– II. Title. III. Series: Issues in Canada

HV5000.C3H47 2009   362.290971   C2009-904265-7

Cover image © istock.com/nico-blue

1 2 3 4 -- 13 12 11 10

In memory of H David Archibald and in recognition of our mentors and colleagues from the Addiction Research Foundation, the organization he founded, and the clients with whom it has been our privilege to work over the years.

Contents

List of Illustrations

List of Tables

Abbreviations

AA	Alcoholics Anonymous
AADAC	Alberta Alcohol and Drug Abuse Commission
ADHD	Attention Deficit Hyperactivity Disorder
AIDS	Acquired Immune Deficiency Syndrome
APA	American Psychiatric Association
AUDIT	Alcohol Use Disorders Identification Test
BAC	Blood Alcohol Concentration
BAT	British American Tobacco Company
CAMH	Centre for Addiction and Mental Health
CARBC	Centre for Addiction Research of British Columbia
CAS	Canadian Addiction Survey, published by the Canadian Centre on Substance Abuse
CBC	Canadian Broadcasting Corporation
CBT	Cognitive Behaviour Therapy
CCJA	Canadian Criminal Justice Association
CCRTR	Canadian Coalition for Responsible Tobacco Retailing
CCSA	Canadian Centre on Substance Abuse
CCTC	Canadian Council for Tobacco Control
CDC	Centers for Disease Control and Prevention
CECA	Canadian Executive Council on Addictions

CFDP	Canadian Foundation for Drug Policy
CHD	Coronary Heart Disease
CINA	Clinical Institute Narcotic Assessment
COPD	Chronic Obstructive Pulmonary Disease
COPE	Coalition of Progressive Electors
CPR	Cardiopulmonary Resuscitation
CTUMS	Canadian Tobacco Use Monitoring Survey, published by Statistics Canada
DSM	Diagnostic and Statistical Manual of Mental Disorders
DTs	Delirium Tremens
FAS	Fetal Alcohol Syndrome
FASD	Fetal Alcohol Spectrum Disorder
FCTC	Framework Convention on Tobacco Control, treaty under the World Health Organization
FUBYAS	First Usual Brand Young Adult Smokers
HIV	Human Immunodeficiency Virus
LSD	Lysergic Acid Diethylamide
MAOI	Monoamine Oxidase Inhibitors
MHCC	Mental Health Commission of Canada
MI	Motivational Interviewing
NA	Narcotics Anonymous
NGO	Non-Governmental Organization
NIAAA	National Institute on Alcohol Abuse and Alcoholism
NIDA	National Institute on Drug Abuse
NRT	Nicotine Replacement Therapy
NSRA	Non-Smokers' Rights Association
OCAT	Ontario Campaign for Action on Tobacco
OTRU	Ontario Tobacco Research Unit
RBH	Rothmans, Benson & Hedges Tobacco Company
RCMP	Royal Canadian Mounted Police
RJR	R.J. Reynolds Tobacco Company
THC	Tetrahydrocannabinol
UNAIDS	Joint United Nations Programme on HIV/AIDS
UNICEF	United Nations Children's Fund
UNODC	United Nations Office on Drugs and Crime
WHO	World Health Organization

Introduction

What is it about psychoactive drugs that—literally—captures our imagination? Unlike other kinds of drugs, they interact with our brains' chemistry in ways that alter our thoughts, feelings, and sensations. This unique ability is also the critical factor that makes psychoactive substances liable to abuse. It is rare that anyone would use other kinds of medications on a recreational basis—there is no "upside," since they do not stimulate the parts of the brain associated with pleasure, reward, and reinforcement. People abuse drugs that make them feel good.

Psychoactive drugs are the most efficient way to reliably and consistently activate the brain's reward pathway. In some respects they allow us control over our brains—depending on the substance taken, we can decide when to sleep or be wakeful, when to be excited or calm or euphoric. The power of these substances is such that in many cultures and periods of history they were reserved for ceremonial use and treated with great respect, even awe.

A few years ago, Thomas Homer-Dixon, a Canadian professor in the Faculty of Environment at the University of Waterloo, wrote a book called *The Upside of Down: Catastrophe, Creativity, and the Renewal of Civilization* (2006). The title of his book communicates the message that human progress has a significant downside, seen in the "tectonic stresses" underlying today's global order: diminishing energy sources, social inequities, population growth, and environmental impacts.

If we were to apply Homer-Dixon's premise to the development and distribution of psychoactive drugs, the "upside" is undeniable. The growth in medical science and pharmaceutical technology marks impressive progress on the prevention, diagnosis, treatment, and care of illness. From the hypodermic needle to the transdermal patch, the toolkit for identifying and addressing disease has grown in quantum proportions. It seems reasonable to expect continuing advances in our understanding of health and illness and our ability to intervene and address problems.

However, in some ways, substance abuse might be considered the "downside of up." All of these amazing tools have a diversionary potential and can be turned to other ends. The economic costs of substance abuse in Canada have been calculated as just under $40 billion per year. That staggering figure does not include the incalculable costs of broken relationships, lost dreams, and human suffering.

In Canada we have access to a vast number of licit and illicit psychoactive drugs. Legal but restricted substances include alcohol, tobacco, and many prescription and non-prescription medications. While stories about illicit drug abuse involving heroin, cocaine, or methamphetamine are often sensationalized in print and television media, only a very small proportion of Canadians abuse these drugs. The highest prevalence of substance use and abuse is of the legal drugs—alcohol, tobacco, and prescription medication.

Legal drugs are intertwined with Canadian culture and society. Imagine if caffeine was banned overnight, and you woke up to find the coffee shop on the corner closed down. What would be the impact on socializing and celebrating if bars and retail liquor outlets were forbidden? And just under a fifth of the population would be in acute nicotine withdrawal if cigarettes suddenly became illegal. The impact on how many Canadians relax, socialize, celebrate, and self-medicate would be enormous if these substances were taken away.

Of course, in the beginning, people generally believe that they are in control of the substance they are taking. The trouble is that psychoactive drugs are so well-suited to our brains' neurochemistry that it does not take long for the brain to adapt as if the substance had always been there. Regular dosing of nearly all psychoactive drugs can result in dependence. The chain of substance use, leading to abuse, leading to dependence has been tragically chronicled in literature, film, and media. Yet the majority of people who use psychoactive drugs do not go on to abuse them, and not all people who abuse drugs progress to dependence.

Given that all human brains are "hard-wired" to become dependent on psychoactive drugs, why is it that most people who use substances, including illegal drugs, do so without problems? This is the question that continues to engage researchers and clinicians in the addictions field, and the answers are neither simple nor unequivocal.

Clearly the biological aspects of substance use and abuse are central to understanding addiction. However, biology is not the whole story. Psychological factors like impulsivity, socialization, internalized values and norms, and self-efficacy can also predispose a person to drug abuse. In addition, the broader social context in which substance use occurs can act as either a risk or a protective factor for abuse and addiction.

A holistic, integrated understanding of substance abuse needs to take into account these biological, psychological, and broader social-structural factors. This theory of addiction is called the *biopsychosocial model*, and is the most widely accepted explanatory framework among scientists working in the field of addiction. Biopsychosocial theory is appealing because it is able to capture the multiplicity of contributing factors and the complexity of addictive processes and behaviours.

There is, nonetheless, disagreement among researchers in the field about the relative weight and importance of the varying domains of biology, psychology, and society. Some posit that addiction is essentially a mental health problem originating in a combination of genetic predisposition and neuroadaptation. Others look primarily at personality factors as primary precursors of abuse and dependence. Still others emphasize family and community norms and values around substance use, social inequities, oppressive social structures, marginalization, and access to substances as key causal variables. The often slow and iterative progress of scientific knowledge-building means that it will probably be a long time before the puzzle of addiction is truly solved.

In the meantime the breadth and scope of substance abuse in Canada make it an issue that should concern all of us. Chapter 1 of this book gives a broad overview of the costs and prevalence of substance use and abuse in Canada, as well as how Canadian patterns compare with those of other countries. Chapter 1 also sets the stage for the rest of the book by offering definitions of substance use, abuse, dependence, and addiction, and briefly elaborating a theoretical model for understanding these concepts. Case examples drawn from the authors' clinical experience in addiction treatment help to ground the analysis and put a human face on the issues surrounding drug abuse. Finally, we offer answers to some "frequently asked questions," such as why some people become addicted and others do not; why some people are able to recover from addiction and others continue to struggle; and why some drugs are more addictive than others.

The following chapters focus on three of the most frequently used drugs of abuse and those that overall cause the greatest harm: Alcohol (Chapter 2), Tobacco (Chapter 3), and Opiates and Opioids (Chapter 4). These chapters hone in on each substance in detail, focusing on Canadian patterns of consumption and laws regulating use, the physical effects of the drug, tools for identifying problem use or abuse, and treatment options. We also consider harm reduction, a much-debated approach to minimizing the social and individual harms experienced as a result of substance abuse. Cultural and social justice issues are interwoven throughout our discussion, including Aboriginal experiences and perspectives.

The final chapter addresses Canadian policy-level responses to substance abuse in order to contextualize individual use and misuse within a broader framework of population-based strategies and approaches. This last chapter concludes with a compelling question: Is substance abuse a personal choice or a social problem? The discussion at the end of the book brings together the varying strands of conversation, controversy, and scientific knowledge.

People tend to have strong opinions about drug use and abuse. Often these are directly rooted in personal experience or are influenced by media and literary portrayals of the impacts of addiction. It is our intention to challenge some of the prevailing assumptions about substance abuse and address the many myths and misinformation surrounding this issue. We discuss research, treatment resources, and policy approaches from a Canadian perspective spanning a vast body of literature, and have tried to do so in an engaging, accessible way. The content will appeal to students in the addictions field, individuals who are experiencing the negative consequences of substance use directly or indirectly, as well as those who would simply like to know more about a topic that affects all Canadians.

Marilyn Herie and Wayne Skinner, July 2009

Chapter 1

An Overview of Substance Abuse in Canada

Introduction

Substance use—and abuse—has existed in virtually all cultures throughout human history. Wherever mind-altering drugs are available to be used, they will also be abused.

That is certainly the case in Canada. Print and television media consistently feature headlines about drug abuse by celebrities, artists, politicians, and others in the public eye. There is something about substance abuse that continues to fascinate people; although almost everyone has had some form of experience with it, directly or indirectly, the phenomenon itself remains poorly understood.

The rituals of having a cup of coffee in the morning or a glass of wine in the evening are benign examples of the human proclivity to use substances to wake up, to feel pleasure, or to relax. For a minority of people, however, substances become ends in themselves, where a person is trapped in a cycle of intoxication, withdrawal, and craving. Excessive use, or abuse, exacts an enormous toll on individuals, families, and communities. Even the language used to describe people who abuse drugs is telling: addict, junky, crackhead, bum, stoner—negative judgments attached to individuals with substance use problems.

The extent of the costs of substance use in Canada can be seen in a 2002 study that estimated total costs for all substance abuse at $39.8 billion, a figure equivalent to $1,267 for every man, woman and child in Canada (Rehm et al. 2006). Of the total costs, the top three are lost productivity (61 percent of the total, or $24.3 billion), health care (22.1 percent, or $8.8 billion), and law enforcement (13.6 percent, or $5.4 billion). Tobacco was the leading cause of mortality in 2002, accounting for 16.6 percent of all deaths in Canada. Alcohol is unique because it is associated with both costs (illness and death) and benefits (the heart-healthy effects of daily moderate drinking); this was addressed in the study by subtracting the number of deaths *prevented* from the number of deaths *caused* by alcohol, resulting in a net 1.9 percent of deaths in Canada attributable to alcohol. Finally, illicit drug abuse accounted for 0.8 percent of all deaths. These figures do not include the personal and social costs of substance abuse, such as the devastating consequences to relationships and families. In general, males—particularly those aged 24 and under—are more likely to report heavy use of alcohol and illicit drugs than are females or older age groups.

There are many different explanations for the phenomenon of substance abuse. Some people see it as a moral failing or a lack of willpower, others as a heritable disease over which the person has no control. Another outlook is that at least

How Much Is $40 Billion?

Substance abuse costs Canadians nearly $40 billion per year in lost productivity, health care, and enforcement, yet it is hard for the average person to visualize even $1 billion. J. Paul Getty, the American industrialist and the world's first billionaire, famously said, "If you can count your money, you don't have a billion dollars." That is because it would take the average person 100 years to count to a billion (including time for meals and sleep). By this calculation, it would take 4,000 years to count the cost of substance abuse in Canada *in a single year.*

some types of substance abuse occur in response to past experiences of trauma, deprivation, or oppression. A more all-encompassing perspective is that substance abuse happens within the larger context of an "addicted society," one of many expressions of compulsivity and excess. A spectrum of behaviours, including eating, exercising, working, having sex, watching television, shopping, Internet surfing, and video gaming, are all seen as having the same addictive potential, particularly in a society preoccupied with commodification, advertising, and consumption.

In fact, even seemingly innocuous behaviours have been problematized, as in Judith Wright's 2003 book, *There Must Be More Than This: Finding More Life, Love, and Meaning by Overcoming Your Soft Addictions*. The author argues that seemingly innocuous behaviours can become "soft addictions" when they are used to "zone out or avoid feelings" (25). Examples of "top soft addictions" include things like reading only one type of fiction (e.g., romance, mystery), checking the weather or news, bargain hunting, listening to the radio, gossiping, or doing crossword puzzles. Such an expansive definition would suggest that no one is free of addictions; yet most experts in the addiction field would be unlikely to place bargain hunting in the same category as heroin addiction.

With all these conflicting ideas about substance abuse and other compulsive behaviours, it is perhaps not surprising that the topic is surrounded by so much controversy. There is no clear consensus on definitions. Do the so-called behavioural addictions involve the same neurobiological mechanisms and processes as substance abuse? And even if they share common biological pathways, there is clearly a range of psychological, interpersonal, and societal factors that shape these phenomena.

No area exemplifies this more strikingly than problem gambling. There is good emerging evidence that gambling disorders manifest similar neurobiological patterns as the use of cocaine or stimulants. An in-depth exploration of this issue (that is, the issue of whether substance abuse and other non-substance-related compulsive behaviours represent different aspects of the same underlying pathology) is beyond the scope of this book. But it is worth keeping in mind that our discussion will take place in disputed terrain. The multiple definitions and explanations reflect the incredible complexity of the causes, nature, and consequences of substance abuse. And a given person's perspectives on some very basic issues shape not only his or her understanding of substance abuse but also what needs to be done.

One promising theory of substance abuse and addiction is the *biopsychosocial model*. This model integrates aspects of all of the preceding explanations (with the exception of the "moral failing" viewpoint), acknowledging that biological/genetic factors, psychological factors, and social factors all play a part in the development of substance abuse. Social factors can be expanded to include cultural, spiritual, and even broader structural elements, such as societal inequality and oppression of marginalized groups. The very human drive to enhance pleasure and avoid pain through use of mind-altering substances is affected by biology, personality, family experiences, culture, religion or spirituality, society, and the properties of different drugs themselves. By exploring and integrating these many factors, this book will address some of the most mysterious and compelling questions about substance abuse:

> Why do some people develop problems with drugs and others don't?
> How is it that some drugs are more addictive than others?
> How do I know if a person has a problem with substance abuse?
> Why do some people manage to quit using substances, while others just can't seem to change?
> Which drugs cause the most harm?

Although this book offers some answers to these questions, it also raises new questions that have no straightforward answers. It is also worth noting that some of the material here may conflict with prevailing attitudes, values, and beliefs about substance abuse and commonly used drugs.

Why Do People Abuse Drugs?

Not all drugs are equally likely to be abused. In fact, most prescribed medications have little or no abuse liability. For example, people do not steal, cheat, or lie in order to purchase acetaminophen; injectable insulin for people with diabetes is not diverted into a "black market"; and physicians have difficulty convincing their patients to take a full course of antibiotics. Addictive drugs are unique in that they act on the brain's natural reward system in ways that are highly reinforcing and memorable. It is this interaction with the brain's reward system that, at a biological level, determines why some drugs are abused and others are not.

Substance abuse can only occur if and when a drug has a psychoactive effect. That is, drugs must act on the brain in ways that affect people's moods and perceptions. To accomplish this, these drugs must be able to cross the *blood-brain barrier*, an internal membrane that protects the brain from harmful chemicals and bacteria.

Psychoactive drugs act on the brain through the brain's own neurotransmitters, altering the production of naturally occurring chemicals in the brain. The most addictive drugs act directly on the brain's reward system—the part of the brain that also governs highly reinforcing behaviours critical to human survival (such as eating and sex). These drugs also act on regions that govern learning, memory, and emotion. There is increasing evidence to show that repeated drug administration actually changes the brain itself (especially the reward system). It is still unclear whether these changes are permanent; however, these findings are opening a new understanding of the biological basis for continued drug abuse, even when the abuse may devastate a user's life.

The route of administration also influences which drugs have the highest abuse liability. Substances that are smoked (e.g., tobacco, crack cocaine) or injected (e.g., heroin, amphetamines) reach the brain in a matter of seconds. Snorting a drug produces less rapid effects than smoking or injecting, but is faster than swallowing. Drinking alcohol on an empty stomach produces more rapid intoxication than drinking on a full stomach because the alcohol passes through the stomach first. Most is absorbed into the bloodstream through the small intestine (the presence of food in the stomach slows the alcohol from reaching the small intestine). In general, the faster a drug reaches the brain, the more powerfully reinforcing (or addictive) its effects.

Of course, only a minority of people who use psychoactive drugs become addicted or abuse them. This is true even in the case of highly addictive substances, such as opioids (synthetic narcotics). Patients experiencing severe pain (e.g., cancer patients or post-operative patients) are often prescribed morphine, and they may even take higher doses and develop more physical dependence than people addicted to heroin. Yet the vast majority of these individuals stop using the drug as soon as a doctor advises them that they are able to do so. How can this be the case? This suggests that biology alone is not sufficient to account for the fact that some people abuse drugs and others do not.

Social and environmental factors play a large part in accounting for different rates of substance use and abuse among diverse populations and communities. For example, although overall illicit drug use rates are low in Canada, drug abuse is more common among some populations. Examples of these groups are people who are homeless or under-housed, incarcerated, suffering from mental health problems, or living in communities with high rates of unemployment and other social problems. And this is also true in the case of legal drugs: alcohol and tobacco.

These social, environmental, and economic factors have been identified as *determinants of health*. These include having enough money for food, housing, and other costs, a network of supportive friends and family, access to education, good working conditions, a safe and healthy physical environment, access to health care, and freedom from racism or discrimination based on culture, ethnicity, gender, sexual orientation, ability, or age. The following story illustrates how complex and interconnected these determinants of health can be. For example, to say that poverty causes drug abuse would miss the many other contributing factors or issues, and

Determinants of Health: What Makes Canadians Healthy or Unhealthy?

This deceptively simple story speaks to the complex set of factors or conditions that determine the level of health of every Canadian.

Why is Jason in the hospital?
Because he has a bad infection in his leg.

But why does he have an infection?
Because he has a cut on his leg and it got infected.

But why does he have a cut on his leg?
Because he was playing in the junk yard next to his apartment building and there was some sharp, jagged steel there that he fell on.

But why was he playing in a junk yard?
Because his neighbourhood is kind of run down. A lot of kids play there and there is no one to supervise them.

But why does he live in that neighbourhood?
Because his parents can't afford a nicer place to live.

But why can't his parents afford a nicer place to live?
Because his Dad is unemployed and his Mom is sick.

But why is his Dad unemployed?
Because he doesn't have much education and he can't find a job.

But why ...?

Source: Public Health Agency of Canada 2001

does not explain why most people with lower incomes do not abuse drugs.

By taking a closer look at the various determinants of health, it is clear that a deficit in one or more areas can be a *risk* factor for substance abuse, while being surrounded by positive and healthy factors has a *protective* influence. The following examples show how risk and protective factors can interact, depending on the person and the situation.

Joy is going into grade 9, and can't wait until summer is over and she is back in school. Her home life has always been chaotic—she and her older brother and two younger sisters have always pretty much fended for themselves. There never seems to be enough food in the house, except for the couple of days a month when their mother goes to the local food bank. Strangers come and go at all hours of the day and night, and empty beer bottles and overflowing ashtrays litter the apartment. She and her siblings try to stay out of the way of their mother and her friends by going to a nearby park during the day, or keeping to the single bedroom she and her sisters share. She has learned to avoid making eye contact with the drug dealers that hang out in her building's stairwells and grounds. Joy loves school and sometimes people around her make fun of her because she always has her nose in a book. There is one teacher who makes a point of giving Joy books he thinks she'd enjoy, and talking to her about them. He's also shown her some websites of different university programs, and has offered to help her with applying for a scholarship in a couple of years. She would love to go somewhere far away, but she worries what would happen to her sisters and brother if she left.

Paul comes from a family of high achievers: his parents are both doctors and his older sister is a lawyer. He often feels like an outsider in his family, since he never did well in school, didn't go to university, and hasn't managed to hold down a job for more than a few months. His main memories growing up are of a series of caregivers, and in his older years coming home to an empty house. He started sneaking alcohol from his parents and smoking cannabis in grade 7, and quickly moved on to other drugs. It took his parents a long time to catch on, as they were always working and his sister was away at university. Paul has also struggled with his sexual orientation—he is attracted to other men, but hates the idea that he might be gay. He dreads the thought of how his parents would react, and has never disclosed his feelings to anyone. Currently Paul is living with his parents, where he generally keeps to himself; he always knows that they will help him out financially. When his father asks him what the problem is, Paul feels like there's nothing he can say. He knows he's had the best of everything, but somehow the only times he feels really alive are when he's high.

Joy is surrounded by alcohol and other drugs, yet she is determined to succeed. Paul grew up in an affluent household with many opportunities, but is struggling. In Joy's case, one powerful protective factor is her relationship with her teacher. Having a mentor or strong, positive adult role model has been shown to be key in preventing substance abuse problems from developing or progressing.

Paul, on the other hand, feels disconnected from family and school, and had lots of unsupervised time growing up. Lacking bonds to school, community, or religious institutions are risk factors, as are poor parental supervision and monitoring. Joy is academically gifted and enjoys her success in school, while Paul has always struggled with his studies and is not involved in sports or other activities at which he can succeed. Paul's ambivalence and worry about his sexual identity are happening in a family and culture with many negative stereotypes about being gay. He might also be suffering from an additional risk factor, like undiagnosed depression or some other mental health issue.

In summary, there is no single cause of substance abuse problems—a variety of interconnected risk and protective factors influence who will progress from normal teenage experimentation to abuse or dependence. Biology also plays an important role in vulnerability to substance abuse; as scientists' understanding of the brain becomes more sophisticated, the role of the brain's natural reward system in addiction is becoming clearer.

In addition to individual risk and protective factors, there are a host of other factors that influence rates of substance abuse at the population level. Research has shown that in communities with more liquor stores or points of sale, drinking rates are higher. Higher taxes on alcohol and tobacco reduce overall prevalence in the use of these substances. Strong social and educational programs reduce substance use and abuse at the community level, as do legislation and policies that limit use.

What's In a Name? Defining Substance Abuse

Despite the complexity surrounding the causes and consequences of substance abuse problems, at least the term "substance abuse" itself appears to be pretty straightforward: it implies using substances to excess or in inappropriate ways or settings. However, such a definition fails to capture the meaning of "excessive" or "inappropriate" use. The following case examples illustrate some situations in which the people using drugs see their use as non-problematic, at least at the beginning, while others in their lives take an opposing view.

Azim is nearing the end of his second year of university. He lives at home with his parents, his three younger siblings, and his grandmother. His family is proud of his academic success, and sees him as setting a good example for his younger sister and two brothers. Azim grew up in a strict Muslim household, where alcohol use is forbidden. Lately he has been questioning some of the rules that he has always taken for granted. He has started going out on weekends to bars with two of his friends from university, who have been putting pressure on him to drink. Azim has begun to join his friends in sharing pitchers of beer when they go out, and often "overindulges"—though his grades have not been affected. Last weekend he came home intoxicated, and his parents found out that he had been drinking. His father has threatened to kick him out of the house and cut off all financial support if he "so much as touches another drop."

Emily started smoking cannabis with her boyfriend of three years. She finds that it helps her relax after a hard day, and prefers getting high to drinking alcohol. All of her friends smoke too, and there is always a joint circulating at parties. Over the past year Emily has been smoking cannabis almost daily. She considers herself a "social user," noting that only occasionally has it ever interfered with her work or other commitments. A few times she has tried to cut back just to "prove I can." She and her boyfriend are planning a trip to visit her boyfriend's family in a small town in the US—she is afraid to bring any drugs across the border, but she is wondering about what it will be like if they can't smoke during their two-week visit. Although her boyfriend doesn't seem worried about not being able to smoke any cannabis while they are away, Emily is thinking of backing out of the trip.

Connie works in advertising as a production assistant. Almost everyone she works with smokes cigarettes and likes to drink and use other drugs at parties and social events. When she is offered cocaine she really likes how alert and talkative she feels after snorting a couple of lines. When a good friend comes to visit her from out of town, she invites him to a party, where they share a joint that is offered to them. Later, she is surprised and embarrassed at her friend's angry reaction when he sees her using coke. She tries to explain that she rarely indulges, but he tells her that she is getting into "dangerous territory," and that he is worried about her. He says that he's just not comfortable being around someone who uses "hard" drugs.

Jeff has been driving long hauls for a major trucking company for the past seven years. He has an excellent driving record, and prides himself on his professionalism and safety. Jeff notes that fatigue is one of the biggest risk factors in his job: late at night, driving long stretches of highway with few distractions, he sometimes feels his eyes closing. A warehouse worker Jeff knows has been selling him prescription stimulants—Jeff isn't sure where they come from, but he's glad to use them. His own physician is quite conservative about prescribing medication, and Jeff feels sure that he wouldn't be able to get these drugs any other way. After he delivers his shipment, when he is ready to sleep, Jeff drinks alcohol to "come down." He is happy with his system of coping with a difficult job, and believes that ultimately he is protecting himself and other drivers from the risk of falling asleep at the wheel.

Emile started drinking when he was 11 years old. He has been a heavy daily drinker ever since, when he hasn't been in jail, in hospital, or in addiction treatment programs. Now that he is in his early 40s, a devastating family breakup that cost him his wife and children, a failed suicide attempt, and early stage diabetes have led to what he calls "my epiphany"—that he is an alcoholic. This was brought about when a friend in recovery dragged him to a meeting of Alcoholics Anonymous, an experience he had actively avoided until then. Hearing the stories and seeing the people there, he realized that he was one of them, and if they could make something of a life of failure, maybe he should give it a try. Even so, it has not been easy.

Substance abuse can mean different things to different people. Someone from a cultural or religious background prohibiting alcohol use may regard any drinking to be problematic. A woman who often smokes cannabis to relax and socialize is starting to wonder if her drug use is becoming too important in her life. A young adult sees his use of "soft" drugs (such as drinking alcohol or smoking cigarettes and an occasional joint at a party) as recreational, while classifying a friend's use of "hard" drugs (such as cocaine) as high-risk. A long-haul truck driver uses prescription stimulants that he buys from a friend to keep him awake on long trips, although he would be disciplined by his employer if his drug use came to light. A father who has abused alcohol virtually all his life doesn't see the need for change until he lost nearly everything. The common thread linking all of these examples is the different definitions applied to substance abuse depending on a person's context and standpoint.

All of the above cases could potentially be seen as substance abuse, or as substance use—the question is, who gets to decide? Should it be an addiction treatment professional? The legal system? The person using substances? Or people in the person's life? As it turns out, there are some fairly well-defined criteria that can help distinguish use from abuse. These provide a good starting point.

The fourth edition of the *Diagnostic and Statistical Manual of Mental Disorders (DSM)* is a comprehensive manual with guidelines for diagnosing different mental health disorders, including substance abuse and dependence.[1] Published by the American Psychiatric Association (APA), the *DSM* gives key criteria that can help us to better understand, from a clinical perspective, what constitutes abuse. Having a common assessment framework has allowed for standardized language and a formal shifting of substance abuse and dependence into the domain of health—that is, a recognition that these are disorders that qualify those with them for health care. This has helped move substance abuse and other problems that are grouped under the concept of addiction from the moral domain to that of health. (And while illness is less stigmatizing than moral weakness, it is important note that even so, substance abuse—along with its close cousin, mental illness—is subject to prejudice and misunderstanding.)

According to the *DSM*, substance abuse is defined as

a maladaptive pattern of substance use leading to clinically significant impairment or distress, as manifested by one or more of the following, occurring within a 12-month period:

> recurrent substance use resulting in a failure to fulfill major role obligations at work, school, or home (e.g., repeated absences or poor work performance related to substance use; substance-related absences, suspensions, or expulsions from school; neglect of children or household)

> recurrent substance use in situations in which it is physically hazardous (e.g., driving an automobile or operating a machine when impaired by substance use)

> recurrent substance-related legal problems (e.g., arrests for substance-related disorderly conduct)

> continued substance use despite having persistent or recurrent social or interpersonal problems caused or exacerbated by the effects of the substance (e.g., arguments with spouse about consequences of intoxication, physical fights)

Source: APA 2000, 198–99

In other words, a person whose substance use (over the last year) has substantially interfered with work, school, or family;

who uses substances in unsafe situations; who has had legal problems as a result of substance use; and/or who has had negative social consequences—all of these would be said to be abusing substances. The *DSM* also distinguishes between substance abuse and substance dependence. Substance abuse can precede the development of dependence, or it can occur on its own and never progress.

Substance dependence is defined by the *DSM* as at least three of the following within the last 12 months:

> ❯ increased tolerance (needing to use more of a drug to get the same effect that one had when first started using the drug)
> ❯ withdrawal (physical symptoms resulting from the drug leaving the body)
> ❯ using more of the drug than intended, or for longer than intended
> ❯ persistent desire or efforts to control use of the drug
> ❯ considerable time spent obtaining, using or recovering from use
> ❯ reducing or abandoning important work, school or family activities
> ❯ continuing to use the drug despite negative consequences (social, legal, physical, etc.)

Source: APA 2000, 197–98

Note that tolerance and withdrawal, the classic criteria for addiction, are neither necessary nor sufficient in this model to meet criteria for substance dependence. A person has to meet at least three criteria, which could be other than these two features. This implicitly supports the integrative biopsychosocial model being employed here.

Notice also that the *DSM* uses the terms "substance abuse" and "substance dependence" instead of "addiction." "Addiction" as a concept tends to draw attention to those with extreme problems, while some argue that it needs to be seen as a continuum (Maté 2008), but the stigmatizing images for "addicts" and "addictions" are quite stereotypically set. The *DSM* allows for a less severe diagnosis of substance abuse disorder, as well as substance dependence; but it has been criticized for defining a categorical paradigm rather than describing a continuum.

The term "addiction" itself has both problems and advantages. On the problem side, addiction has been used in a variety of ways and with many different meanings, and tends to have negative connotations (as in one's different reactions to hearing about a person who *is an addict* versus a person who *has a substance dependence problem*). "Addict" stigmatizes the whole person, while "dependence" specifies a problem resulting from one's behaviour. This may seem like a minor difference, but language both reflects and shapes people's perspectives, and individuals with substance abuse problems already contend with many negative stereotypes and assumptions. Another issue is that the word "addiction" implies that a person either has it or doesn't have it. There is little room here for "in-between" states. But it is clear that substance use, abuse, and dependence can occur along a continuum of severity, where people can be said to be mildly, moderately, or severely dependent on substances. While the term addiction is probably here to stay, it is important to understand why "dependence" is often preferred.

It is also worth noting (and respecting) that for many people it has become vitally necessary to self-identify with and use the terms "addict" and "addiction." Mutual aid organizations drawing on the 12-step model first articulated by Alcoholics Anonymous (AA) see admission of people's own vulnerability as a required first step to getting their lives back in order (Humphreys 2004). These are typically individuals who meet diagnostic criteria for substance dependence, and who have turned to mutual aid fellowship and peer support as the key to recovery. It is important to take note of the language that people use to talk about substance use problems, and to use terms that are non-judgmental, as open to health and change as they are to illness and habit. The case example of Emile illustrates the powerfully transformative effect that fellowships like AA can have on a person's life.

A final note on diagnosis is that a person can abuse substances without being dependent on them, and similarly can be classified as being dependent without necessarily abusing substances. A 2004 study by Hasin and Grant in the US found that approximately one-third of people who met the *DSM* criteria for substance dependence did not meet criteria for abuse—particularly women and people from specific ethnocultural groups. For example, a person who is dependent on alcohol could experience tolerance (needing to drink more to feel high or drunk) and withdrawal (having severe hangovers the morning after drinking heavily) and repeatedly try to quit drinking (persistent attempts to control use); but the same person may have no legal, work, or family problems and never drink in unsafe situations. This research was carried out on a clinical population already diagnosed with dependence; in the general population a higher proportion of people abuse substances than are dependent.

Returning to the five case examples outlined earlier, it is possible to see where each person might fit within diagnostic criteria for substance abuse and/or dependence. Keep in mind that making accurate diagnoses can be challenging, particularly in the area of mental health disorders. For this reason, attempts to classify each case represent a "best guess" that would need to be supported by a comprehensive assessment. Also, in Canada only certain disciplines are legally permitted to make formal diagnoses. Other health and counselling professionals often refer to the *DSM* as a set of guidelines.

Azim, the university student who has begun to drink socially, would likely fit the criteria for substance abuse. His use is causing problems with his family (negative social consequences) even if his grades are not suffering and his drinking is in line with his friends' level of consumption. Emily, on the other hand, is at high risk for both abuse and dependence: her use is having some impact on outside responsibilities, she has some concerns about her regular use of cannabis (attempts to cut down), and is thinking of backing out of an important trip with her boyfriend (limiting activities due to substance use). A more in-depth assessment of her cannabis use might reveal other behaviours or consequences that would point to dependence.

Connie's situation doesn't immediately point to abuse or dependence, though her friend's concern that her behaviour is risky is probably accurate. Has she ever used more than she intended? Has she ever missed work because of too much partying the night before? Will her drug use affect their friendship? These are signals that Connie may be abusing substances. Jeff's case is an example of a person who has not yet experienced any negative consequences to his drug use, and would likely be surprised, puzzled, or angry if someone suggested that he has a problem. Nonetheless, his illicit use of prescription medication carries serious safety and legal concerns, so it is probably accurate to identify him as having a substance abuse problem.

Finally, Emile is someone who has many of the markers of substance dependence and who would meet entry criteria for the most intensive addiction programs. However, he is also someone who—until he had a transformative experience, perhaps—will not be inclined to take any sustained action to deal with problems that have serious consequences for those he cared most about, as well as for himself. Still, the lack of positive coping skills means that he struggles with substance abuse as he works to make some basic changes in his life.

These examples highlight the challenges in identifying substance abuse and dependence, as well as some of the criteria used by professionals to diagnose these problems. It is notable that all of these individuals do not see their substance use as out of the ordinary. In the cases of Azim, Emily, and Connie, others around them seem to use substances in the same way, and Jeff regards his use as a positive coping strategy in a challenging job. Emile always associated with other heavy drinkers, and sees himself as an ordinary guy. It is not unusual for people who use and misuse substances to hang around with people who have similar patterns of use, giving the impression that everyone uses in the same way they do. This makes the substance use seem "normal" and less problematic than they might otherwise perceive. It also can make it harder for a person to acknowledge that he or she has a problem.

To put substance use patterns in a larger perspective, the next section provides an overview of substance use in Canada. Before reading further, consider some of your ideas and assumptions about substance use. Which substances are the most commonly used and abused, and by which groups of people? Which cause the most problems? How does substance use and abuse vary by province? Canadian researchers have collected recent data that can shed some light on these questions.

Who, What, and Where?
Substance Use Patterns in Canada

In December 2003, the Canadian Centre on Substance Abuse launched the Canadian Addiction Survey (CAS). This telephone survey was carried out with 13,909 Canadians aged 15 and older between 16 December 2003 and 19 April 2004. Subjects in the survey were randomly selected, meaning that every household with a telephone (and every respondent in each randomly chosen household) had an equal chance of being contacted by researchers. The results of this survey represent the most comprehensive and up-to-date Canadian information about substance use patterns, consequences, and public opinion. Changes over time in Canadians' use of various substances were examined by making the CAS questions the same as previous questions in other national surveys.

Alcohol

Alcohol continues to be the most commonly used psychoactive drug in Canada. Four out of five Canadians aged 15 and older consume alcohol (79.3 percent), most drinking in moderation. The survey defines *light* drinking as fewer than five standard drinks per occasion for men, or four drinks for women; *heavy* drinking consists of five or more drinks per occasion for men, and four drinks for women. (See below for an explanation of what is meant by a standard drink.) The survey also defines *infrequent* drinking as less than once a week, and *frequent* drinking as once a week or more (Adlaf, Begin, and Sawka 2005).

Of the 79.3 percent of people who drink, approximately four out of ten (38.7 percent) are classified as "light infrequent drinkers" and another 27.7 percent report "light frequent

What Is a Standard Drink?

What do we mean by a drink? People consume a variety of alcoholic beverages in different amounts, mixtures, and sizes, so it is important to have a common understanding of a *standard drink*. Figure 1-1 shows standard drink conversions for different types of alcohol, with each beverage containing 13.6 grams of absolute alcohol. Note that a standard drink might not be the same as what a person would typically pour into a glass and consume. For example, someone drinking 10 ounces (280 ml) of wine from a large glass is actually consuming the equivalent of two standard drinks, while another person drinking a 12 ounce (341 ml) bottle of higher alcohol (7 percent) beer is drinking the equivalent of 1.4 standard drinks.

1 standard drink = 13.6 grams of alcohol

 = =

| 12 oz. Beer | 5 oz. Wine | 1.5 oz. Liquor |
| (5% alcohol) | (10–12% alcohol) | (40% alcohol) |

Figure 1-1 What Is Standard?
Source: adapted from CAMH 2008c

drinking." A much smaller proportion of drinkers report heavy infrequent alcohol use (5.6 percent) or heavy frequent alcohol use (7.1 percent). Of the remaining 21 percent of Canadians, 14 percent are former drinkers and 7 percent are lifetime abstainers (never drink).

These different patterns of alcohol use occur along a continuum, with no use of alcohol at one end and heavy, frequent use at the other end, as shown in Figure 1-2. The continuum of use corresponds with a continuum of risk: in other words, as the quantity a person drinks as well as the frequency increases, so does the abuse and dependence. This concept—that the severity and risk of substance use problems occur along a continuum—represents an alternative to thinking about addiction as an "either/or" phenomenon.

As the previous data from the Canadian Addiction Survey (CAS) illustrate, a small minority of people do not use alcohol (abstainers and former drinkers, no or low risk); the majority of people who use alcohol do so without problems (light infrequent drinkers, low risk); a large minority experience some negative consequences (light frequent drinkers and heavy infrequent drinkers, higher risk); and a small minority of people experience severe consequences (heavy frequent drinkers, highest risk).

If we were to classify only those who occupy the extreme end of the continuum (those at the highest severity and risk) as being "addicted," chances are we would miss the much larger

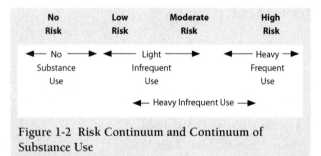

Figure 1-2 Risk Continuum and Continuum of Substance Use

group who abuse alcohol and/or are mildly to moderately dependent. This is important because the costs to society of so-called "problem drinkers" (from the groups who report light frequent drinking and heavy infrequent drinking) are actually much higher than those who are more severely dependent (the heavy frequent drinkers). In other words, the majority of the health, legal, social, and economic problems caused by alcohol are not due to people who could be described as alcoholics, but rather by the larger group of problem drinkers. Alcohol abuse will be explored in greater detail in Chapter 2, but the notion of a continuum relates to all substances—not just alcohol—and can improve our understanding of why the costs of social or recreational drinking (and other substance use) may be much greater than for severely dependent patterns of use.

The CAS (Adlaf, Begin, and Sawka 2005) found some interesting differences across Canadian provinces and among different groups. Quebec has the highest percentage of alcohol use (82.3 percent); however, people from Quebec are the least likely to engage in high-risk drinking (defined as consuming five or more drinks on one occasion). Prince Edward Island has the lowest percentage (70.2 percent) of alcohol use, and people from Newfoundland and Labrador have the highest risk of heavier, more risky patterns of drinking.

More men than women report past-year drinking (82.0 percent versus 76.8 percent), weekly drinking (55.2 percent versus 32.8 percent) and heavy drinking (23.2 percent versus 8.8 percent). Heavier and more frequent drinking are also more common among young adults aged 18 to 24, while older adults (aged 65 to 74) are more likely to report no drinking in the last year. People who are divorced, separated, or widowed, those with higher levels of education, or those with higher income levels are all more likely to report drinking in the previous year. The number of drinks consumed per day decreases with higher levels of formal education.

Tobacco

Tobacco is the second most commonly used psychoactive drug in Canada, with 18 percent of Canadians 15 years of age and older reporting current smoking. Rates of tobacco use have been declining in Canada since the 1990s, the result of a variety of federal, provincial, and municipal policies and programs. Comparing use of tobacco to alcohol, a much larger number of Canadians report never smoking (53 percent) and having quit smoking (29 percent). British Columbia has the lowest rate of tobacco use (15 percent), while Manitoba has the highest provincial rate (21 percent). People with lower incomes and lower levels of formal education are more likely to report daily smoking. Smoking is also more likely among males overall (20 percent, versus 16 percent for women), and especially among young men aged 23 to 24 (34 percent; Health Canada 2008).

Before the late 1970s, women smoked at much lower rates than men; however, it takes about 20 years for the health impacts of smoking to become evident. Therefore, as smoking rates have increased among women, so has mortality—from 1985 through 1996 there was a 77 percent increase in smoking-related deaths among women, while males' deaths from smoking remained constant (Physicians for a Smoke-Free Canada 2003). At a global level, the difference in smoking rates among boys and girls is smaller than the difference between adult men and women; this suggests that in the future, overall female prevalence will continue to rise (Shafey et al. 2009).

Although tobacco use will be discussed in detail in Chapter 3, it is worth pointing out some important differences between patterns and consequences of use for alcohol and tobacco. While only a small proportion of the roughly 80 percent of people who drink are severely alcohol dependent, the majority of people who smoke would qualify as having severe dependence (frequent heavy use).

One simple physiological measure of dependence is the amount of time after a person wakes up in the morning before he or she uses a drug. Only a very small subset of frequent heavy drinkers report morning drinking, while 58 percent of daily smokers have their first cigarette within 30 minutes of waking (Health Canada 2008). In addition, one in two smokers die from smoking-related diseases, and one in five deaths in Canada are due to smoking, the equivalent of wiping out a town of about 40,000 people every year. In fact, the rate of deaths due to smoking is five times the rate of deaths due to car accidents, suicides, other drug abuse, murder, and HIV *combined*.

Illicit drugs

While cigarette smoking has declined in Canada, cannabis use has been steadily increasing and is by far the most popular illicit drug used by Canadians. The CAS (Adlaf, Begin, and Sawka 2005) reports that lifetime cannabis use (that is, whether a person has ever used cannabis in his or her life) was 23.2 percent in 1989, increasing to 28.2 percent in 1994 and to 44.5 percent in 2004. Canadians' past-year cannabis use (use during the 12 months prior to the survey) also rose from 6.5 percent in 1989 to 14.1 percent in 2004. British Columbia and Alberta have the highest rates of lifetime cannabis use, and Ontario, Newfoundland and Labrador, and Prince Edward Island have the lowest rates. Among people who report past-year use of cannabis, roughly one-third report failing to control their use and having a strong desire to use. Men, younger people, and currently single people are more likely to report lifetime and past-year use of cannabis. Lifetime use rates also generally increase with level of formal education, from 34.9 percent among those not completing high school to 52.4 percent among those with some post-secondary education, and then declining to 44.3 percent among those with a university degree.

Other illicit drug use in Canada is extremely low, with only 1.9 percent of the population reporting past-year cocaine use, and 1 percent or less using other illicit drugs (inhalants, heroin, steroids, and intravenous drugs) during the past year. Lifetime use of drugs other than cannabis is also low, and includes hallucinogens (11.4 percent), cocaine (10.6 percent), speed (6.4 percent), and ecstasy (4.1 percent). Among the small proportion of Canadians with past-year illicit drug use, 42.1 percent report symptoms that suggest the need for substance abuse treatment or other health or counselling interventions. The rates of both lifetime and past-year illicit drug use are highest among men, young adults, and single people; provincially, rates are highest for residents of Quebec and British Columbia.

The Bigger Picture: International Rates and Patterns of Substance Use

How do Canadian rates of substance use compare with other countries around the world? Perhaps surprisingly, this is not an easy question to answer.

Each country has its own way of collecting information, making direct comparisons difficult. For example, if the items on a questionnaire about illicit drug use are worded differently, it is less valid to directly compare the data gathered. Within countries, different government ministries or research organizations may be focused on different substances. Tobacco is classified as an agricultural product in most countries, including Canada, while alcohol is legally regulated under food and beverage legislation. Illicit drugs are the responsibility of enforcement bodies. Many surveys of substance use omit tobacco and often alcohol, focusing only on illicit drugs. Finally, countries with large rural or remote populations—with limited telephone access, or where the majority of people consume homemade alcohol— present challenges in obtaining accurate population samples or consumption data. So, with these limitations in mind, below is a brief overview of alcohol, tobacco, and illicit drug use rates and trends around the world.

Alcohol

Although alcohol is widely used worldwide, there is only one source—*World Drink Trends 2005*, now out of print— that gathers and publishes global alcohol consumption data (Commission for Distilled Spirits 2005). Forty-five countries are ranked by per capita consumption of litres of pure alcohol consumed in 2003. The book also compares alcohol consumption with other beverages, such as juice and pop. The dubious honour of the highest consumption is attained by

Luxembourg (at 12.6 litres per capita), followed by Hungary, the Czech Republic, the Republic of Ireland, and Germany. Canada (7.0 litres) is ranked 23rd, just behind Greece (7.7 litres) and Australia (7.2 litres). The US comes in at number 26 (6.8 litres), ahead of Japan at 29 (6.5 litres). Brazil ranks 41 (4.2 litres), China is 42 (4.0 litres), and Mexico ranks lowest at 45 (3.1 litres).

Data on international rates of alcohol *consumption* do not, however, reveal the rates of alcohol *abuse* in any given country. As discussed earlier, patterns of use (quantity and frequency) are more important indicators of alcohol-related problems than overall per-capita consumption. While there is no comprehensive international data available, some European studies have shown how different drinking patterns in a given country and culture can lead to different kinds of problems at the population level.

In Ireland and England, for example, alcohol is often consumed with less frequency but in greater quantities (binge drinking). Problems such as public drunkenness, assault, impaired driving, alcohol-related personal injury, and workplace accidents are often associated with this type of drinking. In France, Spain, and Italy, on the other hand, people drink with more frequency (generally with meals) but in lower quantities per drinking occasion. Although this pattern of consumption does not tend to result in high levels of intoxication, France has one of the highest rates of liver cirrhosis in the world. This is the result of greater frequency of consumption over time, demonstrating that even countries like France with lower rates of alcohol abuse are not immune from alcohol-related problems.

Tobacco

In contrast to the lack of global data on alcohol consumption and problems, worldwide data on tobacco are readily available. This is due in large part to a well-organized response to the massive and devastating public health consequences of what has been termed a "tobacco epidemic." International organizations, partnerships, and collaboration among researchers and scientists have been focused on tobacco control since the 1960s. The 2009 *Tobacco Atlas*, published by the American Cancer Society (Shafey et al.), provides an excellent overview of worldwide rates, patterns, and consequences of tobacco use. Most of the tobacco data relate to cigarettes, as they comprise 96 percent of the world's tobacco products.

Around the world, one billion men and 250 million women are daily smokers. Overall, 35 percent of men in developed countries and 50 percent of men in developing countries are daily smokers (compared with 20 percent of Canadian men and 23 percent of American men). Female rates are lower, with 22 percent in developed countries, and 9 percent in developing countries (compared with 16 percent of Canadian women and 19 percent of American women). Lower rates for women can largely be accounted for by cultural norms proscribing smoking among women, particularly in developing countries. Tobacco companies have not been slow to seize on this issue as a powerful marketing tactic, equating female emancipation with tobacco use. As advances in women's rights are achieved, there is concern that female smoking rates in many developing countries are also rising, leading to "an unmitigated global public health disaster" (Shafey et al. 2009, 24). For this reason, the authors of the *Tobacco Atlas* point to preventing increased smoking among women as having a greater impact on world health than any other single intervention.

Rates of male smoking in China are among the highest in the world: 60 percent of men in China are daily smokers. China also consumes 37 percent of the estimated 6.3 trillion cigarettes that will be produced annually by tobacco companies by 2010 (this figure is equivalent to over 900 cigarettes per year for every man, woman, and child on earth). Again, tobacco companies have been aware of marketing opportunities for some time. An internal document from Philip Morris in 1989 stated, "our objective is to limit the introduction and spread of smoking restrictions and maintain the widespread social acceptability of smoking in Asia" (Shafey et al. 2009, 64).

Even if tobacco-control efforts are successful in drastically reducing the numbers of young people starting to smoke,

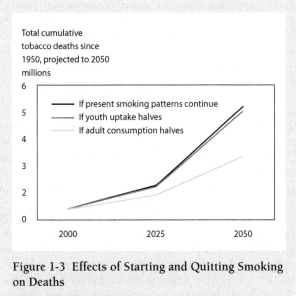

Figure 1-3 Effects of Starting and Quitting Smoking on Deaths

Source: Mackay 2006

these prevention efforts alone will not appreciably decrease death, disease, and health costs in this generation. That is because the negative effects of smoking take a long time to develop. Figure 1-3 shows how deaths due to smoking will not change by 2025 even if youth uptake is cut in half. Only a focus on persuading adult smokers to quit can affect smoking-related mortality in the coming years. If cessation (as opposed to prevention) efforts are not successful, it is estimated that 10 percent of the current world population—650 million people alive today—will die due to tobacco use, half of them in middle age.

Illicit drugs

Of all illicit drugs, cannabis is the one that is the most widely produced, trafficked, and consumed, with 4 percent of the world population reporting cannabis use in the past 12 months. Amphetamines, ecstasy, cocaine, and opiates account for a much smaller proportion of use. Table 1-1 summarizes annual world prevalence data for illicit drug use. The United States is currently the world's largest market for cocaine, although 2002 student survey data show a 15 percent drop in use since 1998, and a 60 percent drop since 1985, suggesting that cocaine use may be beginning a decline in that country. Most Western European countries, on the other hand, have shown increased rates in cocaine use over the last decade. Global use of heroin and opium has been stable since the late 1990s, but the growth of opium production in Afghanistan has led to a regional shift in use from Western Europe to Eastern Europe, Russia, and Central Asia.

International use of illicit drugs is much lower than that of alcohol and tobacco, but still accounts for significant health, law enforcement, and social costs. The United Nations Office on Drugs and Crime (UNODC) points to opiates, especially heroin, as being the major problem, followed by cocaine. This is due to high rates of injection heroin use, and the attendant high rates of HIV and hepatitis C infections. Treatment demand (meaning information on patients entering treatment for problem drug use) varies across substances and regions. Opiates account for 62 percent of treatment demand in Europe and Asia, and 47.1 percent in

Table 1-1   Estimated Annual Global Prevalence of Illicit Drugs 2003–2004

	Number of People (millions)	Global Population, Ages 15–64 (%)
cannabis	160.9	4.0
amphetamines	26.2	0.6
ecstasy	7.9	0.2
cocaine	13.7	0.3
opiates	15.9	0.4
heroin	10.6	0.23
all illicit drugs	200	5.0

Source: adapted from United Nations Office on Drugs and Crime 2005

Oceania (Australia, New Zealand, and adjacent islands). In South America cocaine accounts for 59 percent, and in Africa cannabis accounts for 64 percent. North American treatment demand rates are split between cocaine (28.6 percent) and cannabis (28.3 percent; United Nations Office on Drugs and Crime 2005).

Some shifts in treatment demand can also be seen as areas of drug cultivation and distribution migrate globally. Cannabis abuse and dependence are increasingly being seen by treatment centres in the Americas, Oceania, Europe, and Africa. Treatment demand for cocaine is decreasing in North America and increasing in many European countries, and stimulant use (primarily speed and ecstasy) is a growing problem in Asia, Europe, North America, and Africa.

This overview of worldwide substance use and abuse shows Canada as being roughly in the middle with respect to alcohol use (at least among countries where alcohol data is gathered), and having low overall rates of tobacco use (especially for males) and illicit drug use. These lower rates can be attributed to concerted efforts on the part of different levels of government, as well as social programs and accessible, high-quality health care. Nonetheless, substance abuse in Canada remains a major problem, particularly among youth and vulnerable populations. Contrary to media reports sensationalizing the harms of illicit drug use, alcohol and tobacco have been shown to be the most significant problem substances with respect to social, legal, and health costs. This does not negate the impacts of illicit drug use, but it does reflect how legal drugs are one of Canada's most pressing public health issues.

Earlier in this chapter, the strong reinforcing effects of all psychoactive drugs were discussed. The powerful biological, psychological, social, and cultural imperatives to use, abuse, or abstain from substances make substance abuse and dependence difficult to overcome. The next section of this chapter will address the roles of ambivalence and motivation in how and why people choose to (or choose not to) change their substance use behaviour.

Motivation and Behaviour Change

Just as the factors contributing to substance use and dependence are complex, so are the reasons and processes for changing one's use of substances. Prochaska, Norcross, and DiClemente are psychologists who started out by exploring how people made and maintained a decision to quit smoking. They developed a "stages of change" model (Prochaska and DiClemente 1984; Prochaska, Norcross, and DiClemente 1992) that has been generalized to behaviours as diverse as applying sunscreen, eating a healthy diet, effecting organizational change, and recovering from all types of drug addiction (see Figure 1-4). They have termed their model a "transtheoretical" approach because it does not subscribe to any single theory of behaviour change; rather, people are said to progress through different stages of the change process regardless of the causes

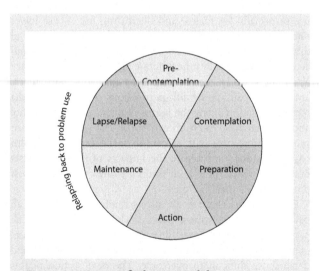

Figure 1-4 Stages of Change Model
Source: Prochaska and DiClemente 1984

or consequences of the problem behaviour or condition. The underlying premise of the stages of change model is that if a given individual has a better understanding of his or her particular stage of change, this knowledge can foster increased motivation to change.

The first stage in the transtheoretical model is called *precontemplation*. This stage is akin to the idea of "denial," where a person believes that his or her substance use is not a problem. As English critic, novelist, and poet G.K. Chesterton said, "It isn't that they can't see the solution. It is that they can't see the problem."

By becoming aware of one's defensive stance through information or negative consequences of substance abuse, one moves to the next stage, *contemplation*. In this stage a person wants to give up substance use but at the same time cannot bear the thought of being without drugs. The ambivalence so characteristic of the contemplation stage can continue for a long time—months, or even years. In many cases, people remain contemplators indefinitely. However, at some point many people are able to resolve their ambivalence and make a firm commitment to change: the *preparation* stage. Preparation means having a clear idea of the steps needed to make a change during the subsequent action stage in the change process. During action, a person is taking concrete steps to address and resolve his or her substance use problem. This might be accomplished by attending a treatment program, going to self-help meetings, or through individual change-oriented activities.

After a period of time engaged in the action stage—Prochaska and DiClemente suggest six months or longer—a person is said to be in the *maintenance* stage. This means using ongoing coping skills and other strategies to sustain change efforts in the longer term. The final stage in the change process is *termination* (if no relapse back to substance use occurs) or *recycling* (learning from a slip or relapse). In the termination stage, the person's problem has been resolved, with no risk of relapse.

Note that the stages of change model is shown as a circle, rather than as a straight line. That is because people can cycle backwards and forwards across different stages as motivation and life events fluctuate. Some iterations of the stages of change model present it as a spiral, in order to suggest that change is an ongoing process of successively identifying and dealing with problematic behaviours.

An important contribution of the model to the substance abuse field has been to normalize denial (precontemplation) and ambivalence (contemplation) as stages that are characteristic of all behaviour change. In this view, changing one's use of substances involves the same processes as making other life changes, such as starting an exercise program or cutting back on junk food.

The transtheoretical model has been widely used in the substance abuse field and beyond. It has, however, been criticized by researchers who argue that the different stages are not empirically distinct and that people do not necessarily progress through every stage before making a change. In a 2002 review of 87 studies of the stages of change across a variety of different behaviours, two researchers (Littell and Girvin) concluded that there is "scant evidence" that people

Listening for the Stages of Change

What do the different stages in the change process sound like? According to Prochaska, Norcross, and DiClemente (1994), people speak differently in different stages of change. The stages of change are applicable to a variety of behaviours, as illustrated in the examples below. Think about a behaviour that others have suggested you change, or one that you have been considering. Read the following statements and try to identify which stage you are in at this time.

Precontemplation
I don't understand why others are telling me I should do this—they are the ones that need to change!

My life is great right now. Why should I fix something that's not broken?

I drink the same as my friends, and none of them are alcoholics.

Contemplation

I know that fried foods are bad for me, but I love them.

Things have been pretty stressful lately—I just can't add to all the pressure by making this change.

I should cut back on the beer, but how else am I going to relax at the end of a hard day?

Preparation

I'm tired of living on the street. It's time to get a real life.

I've come to the conclusion that there is never going to be an ideal time to quit smoking, so I'm going to start on the nicotine patch tomorrow.

I've made an appointment to get a stress test, and then my doctor and I will come up with a treatment plan.

Action

I've started going for a walk in the evening, and it's really made a difference in my energy level.

Going to these group counselling sessions has helped me stay away from drinking and using drugs.

Now that I pack a lunch for work I am saving a lot of money and eating healthier too.

Maintenance

Yesterday I saw one of my former drug dealers—it was tough to say no, but I reminded myself of how hard I've worked to get to this point.

It's not always easy to get up early and make it to the gym, but I know that afterwards I'll feel great.

I'm not going to counselling sessions any more, but when things start to get overwhelming it helps to check in with my therapist once in a while over the phone.

Termination

I remember when I first started jogging—I could barely make it to the end of the block. I know that physical activity will always be part of my life.

I quit smoking so long ago I don't even remember the last time I had a craving for a cigarette when I saw another person light up.

Being vegetarian is so much a part of who I am now—I could never go back to eating meat.

move sequentially through discrete stages. Another article by Callaghan, Taylor, and Cunningham (2007) questioned the assumption that understanding the stage of change a person is in can be helpful in predicting the likelihood of change (for example, that people in the precontemplation or contemplation stages would be less likely to change, and people in the action stage more likely to change). The authors analyzed data from a large study of alcohol-dependent subjects (Project MATCH), and found that people in the action stage of change did not necessarily end up drinking less than those in the precontemplation and contemplation stages. In addition, they found that people in the "pre-action" stages were able to make significant improvements in their alcohol use. The general consensus in the research literature seems to be that the stages of change model can be a reasonable, informal indicator of where a person is at with respect to change, but should not be used as a basis for providing care or treatment. It should be noted, however, that despite critiques of the stages of change by researchers, the model remains widely applied in substance abuse and other treatment and health settings.

Despite the empirical shortcomings of the transtheoretical model, it articulates quite nicely the important concepts of ambivalence and motivation in behaviour change. Miller and Rollnick (2002) developed a clinical approach to addiction treatment called *motivational interviewing*: this is partly based on the idea that people in different stages of the change process benefit from different kinds of counselling interventions. Miller and Rollnick note that motivation is not an unchangeable character trait (as may be expressed by treatment professionals, employers, or family members who refer to the substance abuser as "unmotivated"). Rather, motivation is a *state* that fluctuates partly in response to the way that another person (health professional, counsellor, family member, etc.) engages with him or her. In the precontemplation stage, the task is to raise the person's awareness of the negative consequences of his or her substance use and elicit doubt and concern. In the contemplation stage, directing people to change when they are feeling ambivalent usually has the paradoxical effect of cementing a person's resolve to stay the same. Instead, Miller and Rollnick suggest reflecting the two sides of the person's ambivalence in a process of helping to explore and resolve barriers to making a decision to change.

The philosophy and techniques of motivational interviewing are in stark contrast to the more traditional confrontational approaches for treating people with substance abuse problems. Emphasizing personal choice and control, "rolling with resistance," and supporting a person's self-efficacy (confidence in one's ability to change) all present an alternative to arguing, debating, and persuading. It should be remembered that all change is a process rather than an event, and that people with substance abuse problems are not unique in this respect. The stages of change and motivational interviewing approaches provide a starting point for understanding the process of changing all kinds of behaviours.

Summary

We posed a number of common questions about substance abuse at the beginning of this book. We will address these questions more fully in the following chapters, but much of the information presented so far has gone some way towards answering them. Below are the questions again, along with some preliminary ideas based on the material that has already been covered.

Why do some people develop problems with drugs and others don't?

Biological, psychological, and social/cultural factors all play a part in determining who will develop substance abuse problems (known as the *biopsychosocial model* of addiction). The presence of risk and protective factors can point to areas of particular vulnerability or resilience, even in extremely advantaged or disadvantaged settings. The determinants of health illustrate how these complex and interacting factors can contribute to the development of substance abuse problems.

Legislation and social policy also play a role, influencing substance patterns at the population level.

How is it that some drugs are more addictive than others?
Psychoactive drugs have special properties that allow them to cross the blood-brain barrier and directly change the brain's neurochemistry. The most addictive substances, such as opiates, cocaine, and nicotine, have a particular affinity for the area of the midbrain that controls pleasure (the reward system). Other factors, such as the route of administration, the dose taken, and the setting in which a drug is taken, also determine its addictive liability. Thus, people who take opioid medications prescribed to manage pain are much less likely to develop a substance abuse problem than individuals who use illicit opioids to get high.

How do I know if a person has a problem with substance abuse?
Conflicting perspectives (between the substance abuser, peers, family members, employers, health professionals, and others) about the role and consequences of substance use in a person's life can make it challenging to reach agreement as to whether or not there is cause for concern. The *Diagnostic and Statistical Manual* (*DSM*) provides some concrete criteria for the diagnosis of substance abuse and substance dependence; however, a comprehensive assessment is an important step in gathering relevant information and determining the existence or extent of a person's problem. A major issue in treating substance abuse is that even though others may be certain that an individual is abusing or dependent on substances, the person using substances may not be willing to acknowledge the existence of a problem.

Why do some people manage to quit using substances, while others just can't seem to change?
Change is a process, and people can take months or years to successfully change any behaviour, including substance abuse. The stages of change model offers a way to understand

the process of change as people move from not thinking about change (precontemplation), to being in a state of ambivalence (contemplation), and onward to preparation, action, and maintenance. Relapse is part of the process and can provide individuals with valuable learning about what went wrong and what to do differently next time. Motivational interviewing is an approach to counselling that builds on the stages of change model, and avoids confrontation and persuasion in favor of eliciting the person's own best reasons for change. This philosophy and style of counselling can enhance motivation and help people to resolve their ambivalence about change.

Which drugs cause the most harm?

Of all drugs of abuse, alcohol and tobacco cause the most harm. Although alcohol is used by a higher proportion of people in Canada (four out of five Canadians), tobacco is by far the most harmful drug: tobacco accounted for 16.6 percent of all deaths and $17 billion dollars in lost productivity and health-care costs in 2002. Alcohol accounted for 1.9 percent of all deaths, with $14.6 billion in costs. Finally, illicit drugs resulted in 0.8 percent of all deaths, but proportionately high total costs, $8.2 billion (Rehm et al. 2006). It should be noted that the majority of deaths due to illicit drug use involve younger people, resulting in significant losses in years of life.

Overview of the book

Building on the groundwork of information and examples provided in this chapter, the rest of the book will examine some of the major drugs of abuse in Canada in more detail. Alcohol, the most commonly used psychoactive drug, is the subject of Chapter 2. Topics include major physical effects and consequences, as well as a few brief questionnaires specific to alcohol that can help identify whether someone has a drinking problem. Guidelines for lower risk drinking are also discussed, along with different treatment options and referral information. Finally, cultural considerations related to alcohol use and abuse are addressed. Case examples help to illustrate the information and concepts covered in this chapter.

Tobacco (the drug that causes the most death and disease), and cannabis (the most widely used illicit drug), are addressed in Chapter 3. The sections on tobacco use examine some of the myths about cessation treatment, including the use of nicotine replacement therapies and other smoking cessation medications. Alternative approaches, such as hypnosis and acupuncture, are also discussed, with a review of the most evidence-based tobacco cessation interventions including the debate relating to smokeless tobacco products and harm reduction strategies. The use of tobacco among Aboriginal populations, both for ceremonial purposes and recreationally, is also addressed in this chapter. The question of whether cannabis use represents a low-risk alternative to cigarette smoking or the abuse of "hard" drugs is discussed at the end of the chapter.

Opiates, including heroin and prescription opioids used illicitly, are the subject of Chapter 4. Patterns of opiate use in Canada and treatment implications are covered, along with pharmacological and psychosocial treatment approaches specific to injection drug use. Court diversion programs and such harm reduction initiatives as needle exchange programs and safe injection sites are addressed from both sides of the debate about their effectiveness and utility.

Chapter 5 moves the discussion from individual level risk factors, consequences and treatment approaches to the policy level, exploring impaired driving legislation, tobacco control efforts, and policies to reduce drug-related harm. The final section of this book will bring together these various strands in addressing the question of whether substance abuse is a personal choice, a medical disability, or a social problem.

Chapter 2

Alcohol

Introduction

Alcohol consumption is woven into the social, cultural, and economic fabric of Canadian society. Its relaxing effects and intoxicating properties make it a desirable offering at celebrations and informal gatherings. Regardless of their personal views or cultural norms, virtually all Canadians are inundated with alcohol advertisements and have easy access to alcohol. The coded images used in advertising often equate alcohol consumption with youth, sex appeal, affluence, and style.

The active ingredient in beverage alcohol is ethyl alcohol, or ethanol, a central nervous system depressant. Ethanol is different from non-beverage alcohol, called methyl alcohol, methanol, or "wood alcohol" (because it was originally processed from wood, though it is now manufactured synthetically). Methanol is a toxic poison, leading to such severe consequences as blindness or death if consumed. It is often added to ethanol in industrial products, such as aftershaves, colognes, and cleaning products. Methanol (along with other additives and chemicals) makes these products dangerous to consume, although a small proportion of people with severe levels of dependence will resort to non-beverage alcohol sources if nothing else is available.

Alcohol use among human civilizations goes back to earliest recorded history.[1] People have been brewing and consuming alcohol for at least seven thousand years; it was likely first discovered through the accidental fermenting of fruit, grain, or honey left standing for several days or weeks. The word for fermented honey, "mead," has been traced back to ancient Greek and Sanskrit languages, and clay tablets from the Babylonians in 5000 BCE show that they considered beer a gift from the gods, incorporating it into their religious ceremonies.

The eighth-century Arabic chemist Jabir ibn Hayyan (better known as Geber) developed methods for alcohol distillation still in use today. He named the distilled wine he created *al kuhul*, or "alcohol." The invention of distilled spirits meant that consuming a smaller quantity of alcohol produced a greater effect. Later scientists in thirteenth-century Europe viewed distilled liquor as "a water of immortality" that could cure all diseases: "It prolongs life, clears away ill humours, revives the heart and maintains youth" (de Villeneuve, in Fleming 1975, 12). The importance given to the supposedly curative powers of alcohol are reflected in the term it was known by: *aqua vitae*, or water of life.

Given its long history and unique properties, alcohol is associated with various traditions and expressions—many of which survive today from earlier times. The custom of clinking glasses arose from medieval Christians who believed

An Ancient Recipe for Instant Beer

The ancient Egyptians were avid beer brewers and drinkers. Alice Fleming (1975) describes how Egyptian beer, known as *hek*, was made from crumbled barley bread and water in clay jars. Once the beer was ready, the liquid was strained off and consumed. The fermented bread crumbs at the bottom of the jars were kept for long journeys across the desert. When the travelers reached an oasis, they simply added water to the jars, making instant beer.

that intoxication resulted from the Devil entering people's bodies when they opened their mouths to drink—the clinking sound supposedly frightened the Devil away. Seventeenth-century celebrations were known as "ales" (since cakes and ales were served). A wedding celebration, or a "bride's ale," gives us the term "bridal." The expression "mind your Ps and Qs" comes from English pub keepers who needed to track the *pints* and *quarts* that they served to their customers so that they did not lose any money. Early American whiskey makers shipped their products in barrels, not bottles. The distiller's name was burned on the head of the barrel, and came to be called the "brand name," a term used now by manufacturers to identify both their products and the lifestyles they are meant to represent.

Expressions such as "good health" and "cheers" are called toasts, deriving from a time when it was customary to put a piece of toasted bread into wine or beer to improve its flavour. The contemporary tradition of a host taking the first sip of wine before guests are served was originally a way of reassuring them that the wine was not poisoned, a common practice in the Middle Ages. Also, before the use of corks, pieces of hemp dipped in oil were used to seal bottles of wine; taking the first sip showed the host's consideration in ensuring that guests did not taste any of the residual oil left on top of the wine.

These historical customs and traditions illustrate the extent to which alcohol use has been integrated into day-to-day life and culture. This remains true in modern society, as most Canadians associate drinking with hospitality, celebration, and relaxation. Today, most Canadians drink alcohol, the majority without problems. However, a significant minority experience negative consequences that vary in their severity. These consequences range along a continuum, with minimal consequences at one end to more severe at the other, roughly corresponding to how much and how often a person consumes alcohol. Note that quantity and frequency are good indicators of the likelihood of risk, but alcohol abuse and dependence result from multiple interrelated causes and contexts (the biopsychosocial model discussed in Chapter 1).

Even though alcohol use is so widespread, there remain many misconceptions and misunderstandings about the effects of alcohol, and about alcohol abuse and dependence. This chapter will outline how alcohol affects the body and provide some brief and well-researched screening tools that can help identify who is at risk for alcohol abuse and dependence. Information about different treatment options as well as a discussion about moderate drinking versus abstinence will show that there are multiple paths to recovery from alcohol problems. The concluding section on cultural diversity and alcohol use puts this information into a broader Canadian context and illustrates how social and environmental factors influence drinking patterns and consequences at both individual and societal levels.

The Physical Effects of Alcohol Use

Beverage alcohol is a depressant drug, and diminishes the activity in parts of the brain and spinal cord in direct proportion to the amount of alcohol in a person's bloodstream. Short-term effects appear rapidly after a single drink, and can include slight euphoria, enhanced confidence and relaxation, decreased inhibitions, slightly impaired judgment, and decreased alertness. The effects of higher doses are more pronounced than those outlined above, and include drowsiness, dizziness, flushed face, slurred speech, clumsiness, and impaired vision. These effects disappear within hours; the total length of time depends on the amount consumed. Long-term effects appear following repeated use over an extended period. These effects are much more serious: metabolic disturbances, impaired responses to infection, impairment of the body's ability to absorb and use dietary nutrients, obstructive sleep apnea, as well as dependence, injury, and diseases of the gastrointestinal, nervous, cardiovascular, and respiratory systems (Brands 2000).

When a person takes a drink, the alcohol passes through the stomach into the small intestine, where most of it gets absorbed into the bloodstream. Roughly 20 percent of alcohol is absorbed through the stomach and 80 percent through the small intestine. Having food in the stomach slows the rate of alcohol's absorption, as this means that the alcohol takes longer to reach the small intestine. Other factors also affect absorption: the alcohol in wine and beer is more diluted than distilled spirits and is less quickly absorbed. On the other hand, the carbon dioxide bubbles in champagne or other sparkling wines lead to faster absorption.

Once alcohol enters the bloodstream, the liver is the primary site where it is processed (metabolized) into acetaldehyde, and then to acetate, water, and carbon dioxide. The liver breaks down alcohol at a steady rate of approximately two-thirds of a standard drink per hour. The more and the faster alcohol is consumed, the more alcohol is left circulating in the blood waiting to be metabolized by the liver. Although heavy drinkers can have almost double this rate of metabolism (Kahan 2000), the resulting damage to the liver will ultimately decrease its capacity to metabolize alcohol.

In a sense, the body is like a funnel—a person can consume a great deal of alcohol, but it can only be eliminated at a steady rate. That is why so-called strategies to speed up metabolism are ineffective; cold showers, caffeine, a short nap, or a jog around the block do not influence the liver's alcohol-metabolizing action. Individuals might subjectively feel more alert or sober after a coffee and a shower, but their blood alcohol level is only affected by the passing of time. Also note that because liquids pass more quickly than food from the stomach into the small intestine, additional liquids don't slow the rate of alcohol's absorption to the same degree.

Alcohol is eliminated from the body mainly through urine, but small amounts of alcohol are excreted through perspiration and breath. That is why an individual's blood alcohol level can be accurately assessed through testing blood, breath, or saliva. People's blood alcohol levels rise and fall in fairly predictable ways, and vary based on gender, weight, body type, the presence of other medications, and how much or little a person has eaten.

Alcohol and the Brain

Alcohol is able to cross the blood-brain barrier, meaning its effects are psychoactive. So, it is important to ask: How does alcohol affect the brain? First, alcohol acts on neurons in the brain, cells that communicate with other parts of the brain, spinal column, and peripheral nerves. Since alcohol is a depressant, it slows the communication between nerve cells and affects behaviour. In fact, if the dose is high enough, this slowing effect can be neuron-toxic, meaning alcohol can actually kill brain cells. Alcohol also acts on the part of the brain that controls consciousness, so that high amounts of alcohol can make someone pass out. The same dampening effect in another part of the brain—the cerebellum—affects balance and coordination. This is one of the key markers of alcohol intoxication. Going further, it can slow down heart rate and breathing, to the point of inducing coma. This is a risk that young people face drinking for the first time, or in social "drinking contests" to see who can drink the most. Every year there are deaths due to alcohol poisoning among college students at initiation parties largely because of alcohol's depressant effects on the body (Brands, Sproule, and Brands 1998).

Alcohol also affects the hippocampus, the part of the brain that coordinates memory. Alcohol can impair memory, and the blackout is a classic phenomenon of chronic heavy drinking. But the most common effect is the one that most people value: disinhibition. What happens in the brain is that alcohol works on the frontal lobes, which regulate judgment and emotional control—the executive functioning centre of the brain. Alcohol dampens those executive functions so that people tend to act and respond based on emotions versus judgment, for better or for worse, without the usual filters and controls to mediate their expression (Valenzuela and Harris 1997).

George Bernard Shaw observed that "alcohol is the anesthesia by which we endure the operation of life," a viewpoint that may explain in part why its use is so common. Just under 80 percent of Canadians drink, 44 percent at

Can a Person "Trick" Roadside Breathalyzer Tests?

People suspected of impaired driving can be pulled over by the police and may be asked to provide a breath sample (Breathalyzer test) to determine their blood alcohol concentration. The Criminal Code of Canada sets the "legal limit" for alcohol use and driving at .08 blood alcohol concentration (the measure of grams per decilitre in the blood), but impairment occurs at lower blood alcohol concentrations as well. Because the consequences of an impaired-driving conviction are severe—including a criminal record, driver's licence suspension, fines, possible jail sentence, and possible requirements to complete an education or treatment program—most people are motivated to heed the law. However, some may think they can drink and drive, and be able to "trick" the test into finding a falsely low reading.

The myths surrounding breath testing arise from an incomplete understanding of how alcohol affects the body. For example, sucking on breath mints before testing can mask alcohol's odor in the mouth, but has no effect on blood alcohol level measured by a breath test. (This may work when an officer sticks his head in your window and asks you at close range if you have been drinking, hoping to smell your breath, but it won't reduce your blood alcohol level). Using mouthwash (some brands contain over 25 percent alcohol) can, in the short term, actually *raise* levels measured by a Breathalyzer. Some people also think that sucking on pennies or other coins, or licking tinfoil can help lower one's reading—this is untrue.

Another tactic is to stall—to try to wait as long as possible before submitting to a Breathalyzer. This is wrong on two counts: first, breath test readings can be extrapolated backwards and forwards in time, based on alcohol's steady and predictable pattern of absorption and metabolism (called the *blood alcohol curve*); second, if a person has had a drink shortly before being stopped by police, his or her blood alcohol level may increase over time as the alcohol gets absorbed into the bloodstream.

Taking a deep breath before blowing into a Breathalyzer has been shown to increase readings. Hyperventilating (taking several quick in-and-out breaths) may lower readings somewhat; however individuals are typically observed by police for some time prior to providing a breath sample. Lastly, subjective perceptions of sobriety ("I don't feel drunk at all") can have little or no relationship to blood alcohol concentration. People with high levels of tolerance might consume enough alcohol to be legally impaired (and even beyond the legal definition of impairment) but *subjectively* feel sober. Alternatively, people who rarely drink are likely to feel intoxicated when their blood alcohol level approaches .08, because of their lower levels of tolerance to the effects of alcohol.

In short, the only way to register a zero-to-low reading on a Breathalyzer is to not consume alcohol, and not drink and drive.

least once a week (Adlaf, Begin, and Sawka 2005). However, alcohol consumption is more than a means to endure life; it is about celebration and the experience of being high. This brief description of alcohol's effects on the brain represents only a quick glimpse of what happens when one is under the influence of the most popular intoxicating substance in the Western world, and beyond.[2]

Alcohol use and pregnancy

Adverse pregnancy outcomes and fetal abnormalities are among the harms caused by alcohol use among pregnant women. Alcohol can cause defects in fetal organs and skeletal structure (teratogenic) and cause harmful effects on the growing fetus and child long after exposure in the uterus (fetotoxic). Because alcohol readily crosses the placenta, it can reach similar blood concentrations in both the fetus and the mother. It is the leading preventable cause of neurological, developmental, and physiological harms to infants in Canada (CAMH 2007b).

The overarching term *fetal alcohol spectrum disorder* (FASD) describes the range of effects in people exposed to alcohol during pregnancy. FASD most often presents as cognitive deficits or behavioural problems, with no outward physical signs. The most severe form of FASD, *fetal alcohol syndrome* (FAS) includes specific facial abnormalities, retarded growth, central nervous system deficits, and cognitive and/or behavioural problems.

Because no "safe" threshold for alcohol consumption during pregnancy has been identified, no alcohol use whatsoever is strongly recommended to improve pregnancy outcomes. However, alcohol use during the few days between fertilization and implantation of the ova (female egg) has not been shown to have teratogenic effects (CAMH 2007b).

Alcohol use while breastfeeding should also be avoided, as it can disrupt the child's sleep patterns and motor development, and reduce the mother's milk production. Breastfeeding women who choose to drink alcohol can plan ahead by expressing (pumping) their breast milk prior to drinking, and waiting until their blood alcohol level is close to zero before breastfeeding again.[3]

The phenomenon of tolerance

Another important concept in understanding how alcohol affects the body is *tolerance*. This refers to the way our bodies adapt to the repeated administration of different drugs, where after a while a person needs more of the substance to get the same psychoactive effect as when the drug was first taken. People who drink infrequently typically have low levels of alcohol tolerance—they start to feel its effects after just one or two drinks. On the other hand, drinking several days a week builds up tolerance to alcohol's effects. The expression about people who can "hold their liquor" does not mean they are immune to the effects of alcohol; rather, they have just built up a higher resistance to its immediate effects.

Tolerance to one drug can also extend to tolerance to other drugs in the same class. For example, heavy drinkers may also exhibit tolerance to benzodiazepines and barbiturates (other central nervous system depressants) even if they have never taken these drugs (Kahan 2000). This is called *cross-tolerance*. Taking two drugs of the same class at the same time can have effects well beyond those if the drugs are taken separately. Known as *potentiation*, this means that even modest amounts of alcohol consumed in combination with other depressants (e.g., benzodiazepines or some over-the-counter medications) can result in high levels of intoxication and impairment.

The following three cases illustrate different levels of alcohol tolerance:

Jolinda is a high school teacher and sole parent of two teenage boys. She almost never drinks at home with her family, but occasionally on weekends she gets together with a group of female friends for wine, dinner, and conversation. On the rare occasions when she has more than one or two glasses of wine she says that she feels drunk and dizzy, while it seems that her friends can easily have three or more drinks with no ill effects. Jolinda is known among her social group as the one who "can't hold her liquor," and is sometimes the subject of friendly teasing among the group.

Alex loves to entertain and socialize with friends and family. His dinner parties are legendary for their fine food and wine, and creating new recipes and shopping for hard-to-find ingredients is one of his favourite hobbies. When Alex is not entertaining at home, he loves to dine out at new restaurants. If he were asked to quantify his drinking, Alex wouldn't know where to start—alcohol is very much a part of his life, yet he has a successful career, a reasonably happy marriage, and a close relationship with his adult children. Although he drinks a lot on many occasions, his friends have only rarely ever seen him drunk.

Josef has been living on the street and in shelters for the past eight years. At one time he had a well-paying job as an accountant and was married with one daughter. His father was a heavy drinker, and Josef remembers the financial hardship in his family growing up because his dad could never hold down a job. For a long time Josef thought he had escaped the same fate as his father, but over the years his drinking steadily increased. His marriage broke down mainly because of his alcohol use, and his daughter stopped speaking to him. He began to drink at lunchtime in his office, then in the morning when he woke up, then throughout the day and into the night. After he lost his job he started missing rent payments on his apartment, and after borrowing thousands of dollars from friends and family members, they also broke off contact. Eventually Josef was evicted with nowhere to go and no one left to ask for help.

Josef's life now revolves around getting his next drink. He hates what his life has become, but he says that alcohol is the one thing in his life that he can always depend on.

In the first example, it is likely that the women in Jolinda's social circle are frequent drinkers. Even though Jolinda's response to alcohol is labelled as different or unusual, it is mainly her pattern of infrequent, light drinking that makes her more susceptible the few times she exceeds one or two glasses of wine. On the other hand, Alex's friends have rarely or never seen him "drunk" despite his frequent, heavy alcohol use. Even though Alex would be puzzled or angry at the idea that his drinking is excessive, his daily heavy drinking could have negative health consequences in the longer term. It is Alex's high tolerance that allows him to drink so much without feeling any effects, while Jolinda's very low tolerance makes her feel "drunk" after just three glasses of wine.

Josef's tolerance is extremely high after a lifetime of heavy drinking. The amount he consumes in 24 hours (anywhere from 14 to 20 standard drinks) could be enough to kill someone with a lower tolerance level. In fact, it may be dangerous for someone like Josef to suddenly stop drinking because of the possibility of severe alcohol withdrawal syndrome. This can include hallucinations and disorientation (known as delirium tremens, or DTs), seizures, agitation, severe hand tremors, extreme sweating, and headache. For people with high levels of alcohol dependence it is important for alcohol withdrawal to be managed by a physician trained in addiction medicine.

Alcohol's effects on women

These case examples also highlight some important differences between males and females. Overall, women tend to drink less than men: in the most recent Canadian Addiction Survey, a higher proportion of males than females reported past-year drinking (82 percent versus 77 percent), weekly drinking (55 percent versus 33 percent), and heavy drinking (23 percent versus 9 percent; Adlaf, Begin, and Sawka 2005). However, when men and women do drink in similar quantities blood alcohol levels are generally higher in women than in men, even at the same weight. This is because women typically have a higher proportion of body fat. Since alcohol is dissolved in the bloodstream (or "body water"), having a higher proportion of fat means less total body water and a higher concentration of alcohol. In addition, women's bodies are not as efficient in metabolizing alcohol because women have less of the liver enzyme dehydrogenase that helps process alcohol. Some research has found that hormones can also affect alcohol's absorption and elimination, especially premenstrually when intoxication may be more likely due to slower alcohol elimination time. The estrogen in birth control pills can also slow down alcohol metabolism. The mechanisms by which hormones might influence alcohol absorption and elimination are unclear, and conflicting findings make this an area where further research is needed (Cha et al. 2006; Mumenthaler et al. 1999).

The graph below demonstrates how being male versus female can influence blood alcohol level. A man and woman, both weighing 145 pounds, have three standard drinks. Thirty minutes after finishing their last drink, the man's blood alcohol concentration is .08 (the legal limit for impaired driving in Canada) while the woman's is .097 (see Figure 2.1).

Note that in the above graph, the female's BAC is higher than the male's, yet both take approximately six hours to return to zero. This is because the liver burns alcohol at the same steady rate, regardless of how much or how little is consumed. In the above examples, both people have had three standard drinks. If either person had consumed more alcohol the elimination time would be proportionally greater. Keep in mind that how much and how fast a person drinks, and whether a person has eaten, will affect peak blood alcohol level, but alcohol elimination occurs at the same steady rate of roughly three quarters of a drink per hour.

Female drinkers not only get drunk faster than male drinkers, they also experience negative health consequences sooner. Liver disease, various cancers, heart disease, and brain damage associated with alcohol use happen at a younger age and with

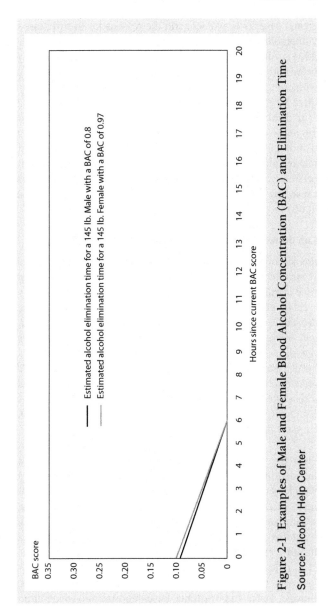

Figure 2-1 Examples of Male and Female Blood Alcohol Concentration (BAC) and Elimination Time

Source: Alcohol Help Center

greater severity to women, and the reasons for this increased vulnerability are not well understood (Harrison and Ingber 2004). Although these differential effects have historically been mitigated by overall lower rates of alcohol use among women, recent data suggest that this pattern may be changing. Over 40 percent of women aged 18 to 24 report consuming four drinks or more at least once per month, with 18- and 19-year-old women reporting more frequent heavy drinking (Ahmad, Poole, and Dell 2008; see page 57 for definitions of relative alcohol consumption). This is of additional concern because young people generally are more vulnerable to harms caused by alcohol than older people (Adlaf, Begin, and Sawka 2005).

Can drinking in moderation promote health?

Rosario lives by the adage, "all things in moderation." A group of men, including his brother and three cousins, make a batch of wine together every year. He has a glass or two of red wine every evening, and was delighted when he read in the newspaper that drinking is good for the heart. Rosario is conscious of his weight, and enjoys working in his garden, going for walks, and playing squash twice a week. On Sunday mornings after church he and his extended family, including his siblings, in-laws, children and grandchildren, go to a local café, where the men have espresso and a shot of Grappa (an Italian grape-based brandy). Rosario notes that in his youth he was "a little wild" with respect to his drinking, but those days are far behind him.

Over the past decade there has been much media interest in scientific findings linking moderate alcohol consumption with lowered risk of coronary heart disease (CHD). Given that heart disease is the number one cause of death in Canada, widespread adoption of any measure that can reduce risk would have potentially high payoffs in years of life saved and health costs. However, in the case of alcohol, there are some clear risks as well as benefits.

Research studies across over 20 countries in North America, Europe, Asia, and Australia have reported anywhere from

20 to 40 percent reduction in CHD among drinkers versus non-drinkers (NIAAA 1999). These studies have found that moderate drinkers (1 to 2 drinks per day for men, 1 drink per day for women) have the lowest risk of death due to heart disease compared with both heavy drinkers and non-drinkers (abstainers).

The research in the area of alcohol and CHD risk is robust and persuasive. In addition to multiple retrospective studies, where subjects are screened for the presence of CHD and asked to estimate their past alcohol use patterns, there have been a number of large-scale prospective studies. Prospective studies ask research subjects to give information about their drinking patterns *before* any onset of disease, and then follow up subjects over long time periods. In all, over one million men and women of diverse ethnicities have participated in prospective research trials, with an average follow-up time of 11 years, and the longest follow up 24 years (NIAAA 1999). There is now little doubt that moderate alcohol consumption is associated with reduced CHD risk in both men and women.

So does this mean that all adult Canadians should drink daily? As with most scientific and medical findings, there are some important caveats to the research support for the potential health benefits of alcohol. The first is that *moderate* use is associated with lowered risk. Heavy drinking, ranging from 3 to 6 drinks daily, surpasses alcohol's heart-healthy benefits due to increased risk of cancer, cirrhosis, and accidents. For women, drinking from 3 to 3.5 standard drinks per day increases the risk of breast cancer by almost one-third, with almost double the risk for higher levels of drinking (Collaborative Group on Hormonal Factors in Breast Cancer, 2002). Note too that the risk of CHD begins over the age of 45, and so moderate drinking among younger adults has not been shown to have an impact.

Even where there is evidence of benefit in one health vector (say, heart disease) there is countervailing evidence that drinking increases other risks (cancer, for example). The zone in which the benefits might balance or outweigh the risks appears to be very small—restricted to less than

2 drinks per day, and no more than 9 drinks per week for women or 14 per week for men. For people with moderate to heavy drinking patterns, that appears to be tantamount to not drinking at all!

In addition, research studies only show an *association* between moderate alcohol use and lowered risk; they do not conclusively show that alcohol is solely or even primarily responsible. For example, few of the studies have examined the level of physical activity among subjects, even though CHD and exercise are strongly related. In addition, there is some evidence that moderate and heavy drinkers are more likely to engage in regular physical activity than non-drinkers. There is also data to suggest that moderate drinkers consume lower amounts of fat and cholesterol than both heavy drinkers and abstainers. Finally, people who prefer wine to other alcoholic beverages also tend to smoke less, drink less, and eat a healthier diet (NIAAA 1999). The possibly confounding variables of exercise and diet point to a need for further research into the role of alcohol in reducing CHD risk independent of other variables.

Some animal studies with mice have suggested that a substance in red wine called resveratrol might have independent or additional benefits for heart health. Resveratrol is found in the skins and seeds of grapes, as well as in peanuts, blueberries, and cranberries. Although these findings are promising, evidence that red wine is superior to other types of alcohol has been mixed—a number of large studies with humans have not found a difference among different types of alcohol consumed (NIAAA 1999). Other research with mice has pointed to compounds in red wine called polyphenols that potentially reduce the buildup of toxic protein fibres in the brain. These fibres are deposited as plaques, destroying brain cells, and are thought to be associated with the cognitive decline typical of Alzheimer's disease (Ono et al. 2008). Polyphenols are also found in teas, nuts, berries, cocoa, and other plants; however, like the research on resveratrol, clinical applications of polyphenols in treating Alzheimer's will likely take much time to develop.

The case illustration of Rosario at the beginning of this section typifies the type of person for whom some alcohol use may be the most beneficial: he is male and over age 45 (and thus at higher risk of heart disease), he drinks moderately, pays attention to his diet, and exercises regularly. Until there is more conclusive evidence for association between drinking and lower CHD risk, it is not recommended that non-drinkers should start drinking. The addictive potential of alcohol along with the other risks outlined above can outweigh any benefits. Some populations, such as pregnant women, those who already have some form of heart disease, those who are on prescription medications, and others for whom any alcohol use is contraindicated, should avoid alcohol entirely.

Screening for Alcohol Problems

Although most Canadians drink without experiencing any problems, one-quarter of former and current drinkers in Canada report that alcohol has caused harm in their lives, and 33 percent of Canadians report harm in the past year as a result of someone else's drinking (Adlaf, Begin, and Sawka 2005). In particular, younger people, single men, and people with lower incomes have the highest prevalence of negative consequences due to alcohol. That said, alcohol problems reach across the spectrum of age, sex, gender, income, culture, and ability.

Given that many "problem drinkers" do not view themselves as different from "social drinkers," how is it possible to decide which is which? There are a number of well-researched screening tools that can identify whether a person's drinking should be a cause for concern. It is important to note that screening is not the same as assessment and diagnosis: screening simply means a "red flag," that it is possible or likely that someone has a problem with alcohol. A formal assessment would then explore specific drinking patterns and consequences, other substances and medications used, as well as social, occupational, medical, cultural, and other circumstances to confirm the existence and severity of alcohol abuse or dependence. Any health or allied health professional can and should screen for alcohol problems as a routine part of intake and assessment. More intensive assessments are typically carried out in specialist addiction treatment settings.

A common screening method involves asking a few questions about the quantity and frequency of an individual's alcohol consumption. It is useful to frame questions in terms of standard drinks: 12 ounces of beer, 5 ounces of wine, and 1.5 ounces of distilled spirits each have equivalent amounts of ethanol. The following are examples of quantity/frequency questions (Cooney, Zweben, and Fleming 1995, 47–48):

> ❯ How many days per week did you drink over the last month?
> ❯ On a day when you drink alcohol, how many drinks do you have?
> ❯ How many times during the last month did you drink more than five drinks (binge drinking)?

A person's answers to these questions are then looked at in the context of known levels of risk. See below for a description of Canadian low-risk drinking guidelines for women and men. Individuals whose drinking exceeds two drinks on any day are at risk for developing alcohol related health problems. Some individuals are recommended not to consume any alcohol.

Another popular brief screening tool for alcohol dependence is the CAGE questionnaire (Mayfield, McLeod, and Hall 1974), an acronym for four questions about lifetime drinking:

C Have you ever felt the need to Cut down on your drinking?
A Have you ever felt Annoyed by someone criticizing your drinking?
G Have you ever felt bad or Guilty about your drinking?
E Have you ever had a drink first thing in the morning to steady your nerves and get rid of a hangover (Eye opener)?

Low-Risk Drinking Guidelines:
Maximize Life, Minimize Risk

> Zero drinks = lowest risk of an alcohol-related problem
> No more than 2 standard drinks on any one day
> Women: up to 9 standard drinks a week
> Men: up to 14 standard drinks a week

One Standard Drink =13.6 g of alcohol

> 5 ounces (142 ml) of wine (12% alcohol)
> 1.5 ounces (43 ml) of spirits (40% alcohol)
> 12 ounces (341 ml) of regular strength beer (5% alcohol).

Note: Higher alcohol beers and coolers have more alcohol than one standard drink.

> If you don't already drink, don't start for health reasons.
> If you do drink, avoid getting intoxicated or drunk.
> Wait at least one hour between drinks.
> Have something to eat. Drink non-alcoholic beverages, such as water, soft drinks or fruit juice

The Low-Risk Drinking Guidelines are for people of legal drinking age. The guidelines *do not apply* if you

> have health problems such as liver disease or mental illness
> are taking medications such as sedatives, painkillers, or sleeping pills
> have a personal or family history of drinking problems
> have a family history of cancer or other risk factors for cancer
> are pregnant, trying to get pregnant, or breastfeeding
> will be operating vehicles such as cars, trucks, motorcycles, boats, snowmobiles, all-terrain vehicles, or bicycles
> need to be alert; for example, if you will be operating machinery or working with farm implements or dangerous equipment
> will be doing sports or other physical activities where you need to be in control
> are responsible for the safety of others at work or at home
> are told not to drink for legal, medical, or other reasons

If you are concerned about how drinking may affect your health, check with your doctor.

Tips for following these Guidelines

> Know what a standard drink is.
> Keep track of how much you drink, daily and weekly.
> Never drink and drive, or ride with a driver who has been drinking.
> Don't start drinking for health reasons. To keep your heart healthy, eat better, exercise more, and don't smoke.
> Don't drink if you are pregnant or planning to become pregnant.
> Be a responsible host—encourage your guests to follow these guidelines.
> Talk to your kids about alcohol.
> Find out about programs and policies that support low-risk drinking.
> Develop an alcohol policy for your home, workplace, school, or community organization.

Note: These are "low-risk" guidelines. They are not "no-risk" guidelines.

Source: adapted from CAMH 2008c

A major challenge in developing screening tools for all kinds of health and mental health problems, including alcohol, lies in balancing *sensitivity* with *specificity*. The sensitivity of a test refers to how good it is at detecting all of the people screened who actually have the target problem or condition, or "true positives." A test's specificity refers to the opposite—how good it is at detecting those who do not have the target problem or condition, the "true negatives."

Reports on the sensitivity of the CAGE range from 40 to 95 percent, meaning that if 100 people with drinking problems are asked the above four questions, the CAGE will identify between 40 and 95 people—a considerable amount of variability. A number of factors can affect the questionnaire's accuracy, including the definition of dependence used, assessment of lifetime versus current drinking, varying the cut-off from one to four positive responses, and population differences (e.g., cultural group, age, gender; Cooney, Zweben, and Fleming 1995). Because the CAGE does not address current problems, consumption levels, or binge drinking, it is recommended that it be used along with quantity/frequency questions. Combining the CAGE with questions about how much and how often a person drinks increases its sensitivity and specificity in screening for alcohol problems.

Like much early research on alcohol and drug screening and assessment tools, the CAGE questionnaire was originally validated with men. Subsequent researchers have developed screening tools more suited to the drinking patterns and consequences experienced by women. One of the best known is the TWEAK questionnaire (Russell 1994), a modification of the CAGE:

T How many drinks can you hold (3+ drinks suggests **T**olerance)?

W Have close friends or relatives **W**orried or complained about your drinking in the past year?

E Do you sometimes take a drink in the morning when you first get up (**E**ye-opener)?

A Has a friend or family member ever told you about things you said or did while you were drinking that you could not remember (**A**mnesia or blackouts)?

K Do you sometimes feel the need to **K**/cut down on your drinking?

The TWEAK is scored by assigning two points for a "yes" response to the first two questions, and one point for a "yes" response to each of the last three questions. A score of two or greater indicates the likelihood that the person has a drinking problem and should be assessed further. The TWEAK has a sensitivity of 79 percent, and a specificity of 83 percent.

A variety of other screening tools have been developed, but the quantity/frequency method, the CAGE, and the TWEAK are among the best researched and validated. Because many individuals may not even be aware that they have an alcohol problem, it is important that screening questions are posed in a non-judgmental, matter-of-fact way, avoiding labelling and lecturing (Miller and Rollnick 2002).

Individuals who are identified as at risk for having alcohol problems should be referred for a more detailed assessment. This includes a comprehensive psychosocial, legal, and treatment history, a more detailed exploration of the amount and frequency of alcohol and other drugs used, and some indicator of the severity of alcohol and drug dependence. A list of assessment and treatment resources in Canada is provided at the end of this chapter.

The case examples of Jolinda, Alex, and Josef introduced on page 48 can help to illustrate how the quantity/frequency questions and the CAGE/TWEAK are applied and interpreted. Their responses are given below, with an overall summary at the end of this section.

Case Examples of Alcohol Screening
Quantity/Frequency Questions

How many days per week did you drink over the last month?
Jolinda: 2 days = 3 drinks
Alex: 30 days = 140 drinks (approximately 35 drinks per week)
Josef: 30 days = 392 drinks (approximately 98 drinks per week)

On a day when you drink alcohol, how many drinks do you have?
Jolinda: 1–2 drinks
Alex: 5 drinks
Josef: 14 drinks

How many times during the last month did you drink more than five drinks (binge drinking)?
Jolinda: 0
Alex: 8
Josef: 30

TWEAK Questionnaire: Jolinda	CAGE Questionnaire: Alex and Josef
T How many drinks can you hold? Jolinda: 2 drinks	**C** Have you ever felt the need to **C**ut down on your drinking? Alex: No Josef: No
W Have close friends or relatives **W**orried or complained about your drinking in the past year? Jolinda: No	**A** Have you ever felt **A**nnoyed by someone criticizing your drinking? Alex: Yes Josef: Yes
E Do you sometimes take a drink in the morning when you first get up (**E**ye-opener)? Jolinda: No	**G** Have you ever felt bad or **G**uilty about your drinking? Alex: No Josef: Yes
A Has a friend or family member ever told you about things you said or did while you were drinking that you could not remember (Amnesia or blackouts)? Jolinda: No	**E** Have you ever had a drink first thing in the morning to steady your nerves and get rid of a hangover (**E**ye opener)? Alex: No Josef: Yes
K Do you sometimes feel the need to **K**/cut down on your drinking? Jolinda: No	

Summary and Recommendations

Jolinda: No or low risk: well within recommended guidelines, TWEAK score = 0.
No recommendation of a follow-up assessment.

Alex: High risk: considerably in excess of recommended guidelines, CAGE score = 1.
Recommend follow-up assessment.

Josef: Extremely high risk drinking pattern, CAGE score = 4.
Recommend for medically supervised withdrawal management and assessment.

In Jolinda's case, even though she occasionally drinks to the point where she feels somewhat intoxicated, her overall pattern of very light, infrequent drinking places her at no or minimal risk for alcohol-related problems. The example of Alex illustrates how the combination of quantity/frequency questions and the CAGE questionnaire is preferable to either screening tool alone. If the CAGE were used by itself with a "cut point" of two (meaning that two "yes" responses are needed to indicate a concern), Alex would screen as a "false negative," since his drinking patterns place him at high risk but he would not be screened as such. The quantity/frequency question responses indicate that he is well in excess of recommended low-risk drinking guidelines. For Josef, both screening tools show high severity. Since he drinks throughout the day, Josef always has alcohol in his system, and assessment findings have been shown to be less valid if the person being assessed has a blood alcohol level of .03 or greater. Therefore, Josef would need to be medically supervised in order to safely withdraw from alcohol before he could be accurately assessed.

One additional screening questionnaire to highlight is the AUDIT (*Alcohol Use Disorders Identification Test*; Babor et al. 2001). The AUDIT goes beyond the quantity/frequency questions of the CAGE and TWEAK by screening for the level of severity along a continuum (that is, identifying hazardous drinking, harmful use, or alcohol dependence). The AUDIT has been used in a variety of settings and populations, such as general hospitals, people with mental illness, acute care settings, general medical practice, under-housed or homeless populations, prison inmates, military personnel, workplace employee assistance programs, and the legal system. This brief ten-item questionnaire has also been researched across gender, age, and diverse cultural groups, and can be administered as part of a clinical interview, or in "paper and pencil" or computerized formats.

A Canadian scientist, John Cunningham, led the design and evaluation of an online, personalized screening tool that incorporates the AUDIT within a longer series of 18 questions (Cunningham, Humphreys, et al. 2006). After the questions are electronically answered and submitted, users receive a detailed summary of how their alcohol use patterns compare with people of the same age and sex in Canada or other countries, as well as a summary of risks, consequences, and areas of concern.[4] The online feedback is applicable to drinkers across the risk continuum, including the infrequent heavy drinkers for whom traditional screening tools may be less suitable. It is also an excellent option for individuals who prefer the anonymity of online interaction and feedback, although it is not a replacement for a full clinical assessment.

Alcohol Treatment and Recovery

Although alcohol abuse affects roughly one in ten Canadians, only one out of every three people with problems ever seeks formal treatment (Cunningham and Breslin 2004). Issues of access, stigma, ambivalence about changing, and cultural or other barriers mean that the majority of people resolve their substance abuse issues independent of professional, specialized assistance. Mutual aid or self-help groups comprise the most easily accessed support for alcohol recovery, and of those the most popular and ubiquitous is Alcoholics Anonymous (Humphreys 2004).

A major challenge for individuals suffering from alcohol and other drug problems lies in the many and often-competing philosophies underlying self-help and professional treatment programs. Alcoholics Anonymous, some other self-help models, and many formal treatment programs regard abstinence as the only effective path to recovery. Others view moderation as an acceptable and achievable alternative to abstinence for many people, particularly those with lower levels of dependence. Clients attending different programs can be caught in the middle of an ideological battle and given competing or contradictory advice. Family members and friends may also experience confusion, frustration, anger, and disappointment when treatment recommendations don't match their own expectations or experiences of recovery.

This section will outline some of the various recovery options and approaches to alcohol abuse and dependence.

Self-help approaches

Alcoholics Anonymous (AA) may be the world's leading example of a successful self-help group. Founded in 1935, AA has helped countless alcoholics achieve sobriety. Alcoholics Anonymous is a fellowship of individuals who provide mutual support within a specific framework of beliefs and philosophies. Al-Anon and Alateen are offshoots designed to help families and the teenage children of alcoholics.

It is important to remember that AA was founded by people who self-identify as being alcoholic. They see loss of control over drinking—and through that, loss of control over their whole lives—as being at the core of their problems. The goal they embrace, or at least struggle to achieve, is abstinence; not just now, but as a lifelong project. And the solution comes from accepting that you cannot succeed at this on your own. Instead, you need the support of the fellowship and the belief in a higher power, however you define that. Although the 12 steps mention God a number of times, the notion of a higher power is not exclusively religious (Alcoholics Anonymous 1976).

The widespread availability of AA groups throughout Canada and internationally makes it an accessible resource for people who want to get help with their alcohol use. AA meetings can be open to the public or closed to those in recovery. The emphasis on mutual support and the clear guidelines implicit in the 12 steps are helpful for many people who struggle with how to go about achieving abstinence from alcohol. While this approach is endorsed by people who see themselves as alcoholics, it is not hard to see why AA and other such fellowships do not appeal to people whose lives have not been derailed by substance abuse, even if they acknowledge that they are having problems.

The organization Women For Sobriety is an alternative source of help and support designed specifically for women. Unlike AA, which asserts that "once an alcoholic, always

Alcoholics Anonymous: The 12 Steps

1. We admitted we were powerless over alcohol—that our lives had become unmanageable.
2. Came to believe that a Power greater than ourselves could restore us to sanity.
3. Made a decision to turn our will and our lives over to the care of God *as we understood Him*.
4. Made a searching and fearless moral inventory of ourselves.
5. Admitted to God, to ourselves and to another human being the exact nature of our wrongs.
6. Were entirely ready to have God remove all these defects of character.
7. Humbly asked Him to remove our shortcomings.
8. Made a list of all persons we had harmed, and became willing to make amends to them all.
9. Made direct amends to such people wherever possible, except when to do so would injure them or others.
10. Continued to take personal inventory and when we were wrong promptly admitted it.
11. Sought through prayer and meditation to improve our conscious contact with God, *as we understood Him*, praying only for knowledge of His will for us and the power to carry that out.
12. Having had a spiritual awakening as the result of these steps, we tried to carry this message to alcoholics, and to practice these principles in all our affairs.

Source: Alcoholics Anonymous 1984

an alcoholic," Women For Sobriety states that it is possible to fully recover from alcohol dependence through personal control and empowerment. The 13 statements of Women For Sobriety comprise a "New Life Acceptance Program," and emphasize autonomy and personal competence.

Other self-help approaches include Rational Recovery and Moderation Management. Rational Recovery is based on the principles of "Rational Emotive Therapy" (Ellis and Dryden 2007) and focuses on rational choice—as opposed to spirituality and faith—and the development of self-esteem to maintain abstinence (McCrady and Delaney 1995). Kishline (1995), a former problem drinker, began Moderation Management as an alternative to abstinence-based self-help programs. Moderation Management is not intended for severely dependent, chronic drinkers or others for whom alcohol is contraindicated (such as those with health or medical problems), and outlines "nine steps toward moderation and positive lifestyle changes" (Kishline 1995; Rotgers, Kern, and Hoeltzel 2002).

Even professionals whose concepts and theories of addiction differ from those of AA or other self-help groups generally consider them to be an excellent resource for alcohol-dependent individuals. Combining self-help with formal treatment approaches can provide extra support, encouragement, and motivation for change.

Formal treatments for alcohol dependence

Substance abuse treatment is often presented in the media as inpatient "rehab" or residential counseling. However, this approach constitutes the minority of a wide array of treatment services offered in Canada. Just as the majority of people with physical health problems are not hospitalized, the majority of people with substance abuse problems are treated on an outpatient basis in their own communities.

The concept of "stepped care" suggests that a person should start with the least intrusive type of treatment (for example, the one that has the least impact on other work, family, or social obligations), and the treatment should be "stepped up" if it is found to be ineffective. An analogous example is a patient with high blood cholesterol: he or she would not generally be given medication right away—let alone be hospitalized—as a first-line treatment. Rather, a physician likely would recommend dietary and lifestyle changes and would continue to monitor blood cholesterol levels to see if these strategies are effective. Medication would be prescribed only if the person is unable or unwilling to make such changes, or if the changes to diet and lifestyle alone are not working. Similarly, a person with alcohol dependence might initially be referred to attend weekly outpatient group counselling sessions, with the therapist monitoring to see whether the person is making changes to his or her drinking. If weekly sessions aren't working, then sessions may be scheduled more often. Residential treatment is seen as a last resort reserved for people who are most severely dependent or socially unstable, and/or who have few community supports or resources. The overarching principle is to reserve the most intensive treatment spaces for those who need them the most.

The issue of which clients benefit most from what treatments is still being investigated by researchers in the addiction field. No single treatment approach is superior to all others for all populations, and certain treatments may be more helpful to some specific client groups. In general, people with greater psychosocial stability, strong support networks, and lower substance use severity do well in brief, outpatient interventions, while people with greater severity and less stability may benefit more from more intensive treatments. However, there is considerable research that supports the use of more cost-effective outpatient or day treatment options, even for people with more severe levels of dependence (Health Canada 1999). In addition, people with mental health problems tend to require longer-term treatments that address both substance use and mental health issues in an integrated way.

Some of the different kinds of substance abuse treatment include the following:

> Brief outpatient interventions (lasting eight sessions or fewer): generally in a group format, one to two hours per week.
> Outpatient treatment (lasting more than eight sessions): longer outpatient treatment programs are also typically offered in groups, but incorporate additional training in coping with "high-risk" situations when a person is strongly tempted to drink alcohol or use other drugs.
> Day treatment (where the person attends a variety of individual and group therapy sessions, lasting all day for up to four weeks): these programs often

incorporate a variety of individual and group therapies and activities, such as coping skills training, relapse prevention, educational sessions on healthy lifestyle, stress management, etc.

› Residential (live-in) treatment (where the person attends a variety of individual and group therapy sessions, lasting all day for three to four weeks and stays overnight at the treatment facility): these programs are often attended by day treatment clients as well. However, additional support in finding stable housing or employment is often needed, as are essential health or medical services.

› Long-term residential treatment (generally lasting three to six months): clients attending longer term residential programs are typically the least stable and most in need of intensive support for multiple, chronic issues related to substance abuse, housing, employment, and other health problems.

› Recovery homes and therapeutic communities (where the person lives in a supportive housing complex or single home, with staff and other people recovering from addictions): recovery homes provide long-term support allowing individuals to learn to live in a community setting where they can receive ongoing support, encouragement, and assistance in a variety of areas related to intrapersonal, interpersonal, occupational, and recreational domains.

› Aftercare (offered to those who have completed an outpatient or residential program): treatment to help people integrate back into the community and to offer supportive continuing care.

› Treatments geared to specific populations: these may include programs focusing on the traditional healing approaches of Aboriginal peoples, programs for other culturally diverse groups, programs based on sexual orientation or identity, woman-specific programs, treatments geared towards youth or older adults, programs for differently abled people, concurrent disorders treatment, forensic treatment and rehabilitation programs (for people found not criminally responsible for offences committed due to mental health issues), programs for impaired drivers, and substance-specific program options.

❯ Self-guided treatment (self-help groups or books, or interactive online websites): generally helpful for people with lower levels of alcohol use severity and high levels of social support and coping skills.

There are a variety of specialized therapy models (often used in an eclectic combination) in both outpatient and residential settings. These include cognitive-behavioural therapy (CBT), motivational interviewing (MI), narrative therapy, solution focused therapy, structural family therapy, interpersonal group therapy, and mindfulness meditation therapy, to name some of the more popular approaches. It is impossible to do justice to each of these models of treatment here; however, Appendix A summarizes the major premises and techniques of each along with some suggestions for further reading.

Harm reduction approaches

Recent programs and interventions aimed at harm reduction have provided additional fodder for debate among providers, clients, policy makers, and media. The issue of harm reduction for opioid users is discussed in depth in Chapter 4; however, the concept is equally relevant to alcohol, especially for individuals with severe levels of dependence. Many people with alcohol problems will continue to drink. This inclination is not unique to individuals with substance abuse problems: in the general population, people make a variety of risky or harmful health and lifestyle choices in spite of negative or undesired consequences, or exhortations from loved ones, health professionals, or media.

Because of the stigma and marginalization that people with substance abuse problems experience, access to mainstream health and social services can be limited or blocked. This is especially true for the most severely dependent individuals, like Josef (whose case was discussed earlier in the chapter).

For example, supportive housing programs with strict rules regarding abstinence often evict clients for even mild or moderate alcohol consumption (Tsemberis, Gulcur, and Nakae 2004). This can result in chronic homelessness, poverty, vulnerability to abuse or assault, health problems, and mistrust of health and human service professionals. The adverse physical and mental health consequences for people can be severe, and are frequently the first "level of harm" that needs to be addressed (Mueser and Drake 2003).

Many people who are homeless may not have regular access to medical care, and can be experiencing undiagnosed problems ranging from urinary tract infections to cancer (HCH Clinicians' Network 2003). Community-based outreach services that are "low-threshold" in terms of health insurance or other access requirements are most effective for people who are unwilling or unable to access mainstream services. A premature focus on treatment can actually undermine both the therapeutic relationship and a person's motivation for change—alcohol or other drug treatment is likely not a priority for individuals experiencing a myriad of other problems. Thus, where a discussion of substance use is undertaken, this is done in the context of assessing harm to the individual or to others. Some examples of areas for assessment of drug-related harms include symptoms of a co-occurring mental illness, other health problems, and ongoing issues of poverty, poor nutrition, isolation, homelessness, and criminal offences (Edwards et al. 2003).

A number of accessible services aimed at harm reduction in people with more severe mental health and addiction issues have been developed and implemented, though they are most often available in larger urban centres. These include mobile or storefront dental clinics; outreach or 24-hour walk-in crisis counselling; street outreach mobile units with interdisciplinary clinical teams providing food, condoms, needle exchange, foot care, and other essential needs; and supportive housing tailored to the needs of people with severe mental illness and addiction. Such resources offer a humane and pragmatic approach that respects these individuals' most immediate and pressing needs, and leads to improved mental health and substance use outcomes, as well as enhanced overall functioning and stability (Pickett-Schenk, Banghart, and Cook 2003).

It is important to remember that change is a process that can occur over years or decades, and it may be unrealistic to assume that professional intervention is sufficient to effect wholesale alterations to lifestyle or behaviour. Instead, the primary task with severely dependent, marginalized populations who continue to use substances is the development of trust—a critical first step that can take years to accomplish (Carey 1996).

Ethnocultural Considerations in Alcohol Abuse

Alcohol use patterns and perceptions about drinking differ among various cultures and communities. In some groups alcohol is strictly prohibited, while others view moderate or even heavy drinking as a normal accompaniment to social celebrations and interactions. In addition, specific populations may be subject to negative and stigmatizing stereotypes surrounding alcohol use.

It is important to remember that there is great heterogeneity within diverse groups, and society's perceptions or judgments can obscure the individual differences and social factors that contribute to, or cause, alcohol problems. The two interviews in this section highlight cultural factors related to alcohol use and abuse among Canadians from diverse communities, as well as the broader social/structural factors that affect Canada's Aboriginal peoples.

An interview with Branka Agic, MHSc, PhD (Cand.)
Centre for Addiction and Mental Health and University of Toronto

Branka Agic received her Masters of Health Science degree in Health Promotion at the University of Toronto and her medical degree from the University of Sarajevo, Bosnia and Herzegovina. She is working towards her PhD in Health and

Behavioural Sciences at the Department of Public Health Sciences, Faculty of Medicine, University of Toronto.

She has extensive experience in research, counselling, program planning, and community development with immigrants and refugees. Agic is currently working as a Community Health and Education Specialist with the Centre for Addiction and Mental Health (CAMH) in Toronto. She is also a course instructor for the Women and Gender Studies department at the University of Toronto.

Agic conducted a study looking at the diverse perspectives towards alcohol use among different cultural groups in Toronto, Canada (Agic 2005). She conducted seven focus groups with members of the Polish, Portuguese, Punjabi, Russian, Serbian, Somali, and Tamil communities in Ontario. In general, qualitative research allows for an in-depth understanding and description about subjective attitudes, beliefs, and experiences. These views are not necessarily representative of the attitudes, beliefs, and experiences of all members of these communities or of other diverse ethnocultural groups. The interview was held in October 2008; below are her responses to three questions about perceptions of Canadian low-risk drinking guidelines, what constitutes "normal" drinking, and consumption of homemade alcoholic beverages.

The Canadian low-risk drinking guidelines (no more than 2 standard drinks on any day, and no more than 9 standard drinks per week for women, or 14 standard drinks per week for men) were developed based on health risks, and don't take into account how they might be perceived or implemented by diverse cultural groups. What has your research revealed about cultural dimensions in understanding and applying these guidelines in day-to-day life?

We found significant differences in the participating communities' perceptions of "low-risk drinking." For example, participants from the Russian community provided a very liberal interpretation of low-risk drinking, describing it as "consuming reasonable amounts of alcohol and not every day," "being able to control drinking and stop once you feel relaxed and happy," "understanding individual reactions to alcohol and knowing your limits," or "drinking red wine to maintain good health." In contrast, Punjabi men noted that "low-risk drinking means 'you drink very little.' Little drinking will not harm you."

The concept of a "standard drink," a conceptual cornerstone of the low-risk drinking guidelines, was unfamiliar and confusing to almost all of the participants because of different types of alcoholic beverages they use, the different sized glasses or different drinking habits. For some, the concept of a standard drink was confusing because alcohol consumption was viewed as an individual preference or depended on the specific beverage being served rather than a way to approximate equivalent amounts of alcohol across different beverage types. Counting and measuring drinks is not a habit in any of the participating communities. As one of the Serbian participants put it, "People do not care about comparisons or what a standard drink is. If they want to drink, they'll drink."

Focus group participants stated that alcohol is consumed in different-sized glasses, making quantifying a standard drink a challenge. For example, in the Portuguese community the size of the glasses in which wine is usually served varied from 5 ounces to 12 ounces. The "standard drink" in the Punjabi community was described as being equal to a drink three times the size of the low-risk drinking guidelines' measurement of a standard drink. This is because of expectations that a good host is one who serves larger drinks as a sign of his generosity: "The host's obligation is to 'satisfy' guests by pouring 'bigger' drinks. The bigger the drink is, the more 'generous' the host is." Focus group participants stressed that "alcohol should not 'run out.' The host MUST have enough alcohol in his home. God forbid, if the host runs out of drink, it will be the talk of the town."

A number of focus group participants from the Somali community noted that most people drink out of the bottle and very few use "standard drink" size glasses, while others found the guidelines culturally inappropriate because both their religion and culture prohibit the use of alcohol. These participants expressed concern that disseminating low-risk drinking guidelines would lead some people to believe that the Somali community would tolerate alcohol consumption. "It is possible that some people may translate (the low-risk drinking guidelines) as a permission to drink a cup or two as if it is not against our culture and religion." They stressed that the only culturally acceptable message is the one promoting total abstinence from alcohol consumption.

Participants from the Punjabi community noted that although alcohol use is prohibited in the Sikh religion, and the only culturally appropriate messages are those focusing on abstinence, "reducing the consumption may also be good for health and well-being of individuals." The men's group also suggested adding the following message: "If you are an alcoholic, you should abstain from drinking rather than trying to engage in low-risk drinking."

Similarly, all participants from the Tamil community felt that it would be better to encourage abstinence than low-risk or social drinking. However, the majority of the participants, both community members and key informants, felt that the information on low-risk drinking is important for their community: "When the message of total abstinence is no more possible, the message about low-risk drinking is better than no message."

The notion of what constitutes "normal drinking" is pretty elastic across different groups and communities. What does your research tell us about people's varying ways of understanding what normal drinking means to them?

Moderate, non-problematic drinking is the norm in most cultures. Yet, what is considered "non-problematic," "socially acceptable," or "binge drinking," and attitudes towards intoxication vary from culture to culture. Not surprisingly, our study revealed great differences in the perceptions of "normal" or socially acceptable drinking levels among seven participating ethnic communities.

Drinking is a gender issue across cultures. Male drinking is socially acceptable within a certain degree even in the communities where alcohol is prohibited by religious norms, such as Punjabi and Somali. Being intoxicated is generally unacceptable, but occasional intoxication is considered acceptable for men, but not for women.

Descriptions of "normal" or "acceptable" drinking can include up to 0.5 litres of vodka in the Russian community. In the Tamil community social drinking may be accepted as long as the number of drinks taken is limited, while some of the Punjabi participants noted that in their community there is no acceptable level of drinking and others found occasional intoxication to be acceptable.

In the Portuguese community, participants described the socially acceptable amounts consumed on one occasion as four to eight beers, but "a bartender is the only one who can say when it's too much." Four or more drinks with a meal are acceptable "as long as a person does not misbehave." The number of drinks consumed on one occasion again depends on the occasion and situation. "People generally do not count their drinks or notice how much others drink until somebody shows inappropriate signs of intoxication."

The number of drinks commonly consumed on one occasion in the Serbian community was also difficult to determine. Community members explained that this depends on the type and length of the occasion, the company, and other circumstances. "It is often three, four drinks or more. However, people usually do not count. One can drink as long as he doesn't bother others." This was considered "socially acceptable" and "sensible" drinking.

Alcohol policy interventions like restricting the number of stores that sell alcohol, limiting hours of sale, and monitoring liquor licences in bars and restaurants can help to reduce alcohol-related harm at the population level. Where does homemade wine and beer fit into

this, and what do you think are some of the possible impacts?

For some ethnocultural groups, consumption of homemade wine, beer, or distilled spirits is the norm. For example, it seems that a large proportion of wine consumed in the Portuguese community in Toronto is homemade or purchased "under the table" from local merchants. The actual alcohol content of this wine is unknown, but is generally considered to be higher than 12 percent alcohol content.

Different Canadian municipal alcohol policies may outline things that people holding events on city property should do to prevent problems associated with alcohol use. However, it is almost impossible to limit and monitor production of homemade wine, beer, and distilled spirits made for personal consumption. The most effective way to reduce alcohol-related harm associated with homemade beverages is to increase community knowledge of the health and social problems associated with it.

The findings from my research do not imply that members of the ethnocultural communities in the study are necessarily heavier drinkers. In fact, immigrants other than those who have lived in Canada for at least 30 years have lower rates of alcohol dependence than the Canadian-born population. However, several factors should be emphasized: immigrants arrive from countries that may have different drinking customs and alcohol regulations. Their culturally acceptable drinking levels, as well as perceptions of potential harm, may put them at risk. New immigrants may not understand health and safety messages due to linguistic and cultural barriers. Certain subgroups, such as those who have suffered severe pre-migration trauma due to war or displacement, or who experience adaptation problems resulting from culture conflict, discrimination, or lack of personal resources, are at an increased risk of developing substance use problems, especially during the first few years. Furthermore, acculturation can lead to changes in drinking patterns, in the direction of either increasing or decreasing one's consumption.

The research findings from Agic's study illustrate the challenges in disseminating consistent general guidelines and health messages about alcohol (and other drugs). Varying cultural norms, translation into different languages, attitudes, and beliefs all influence consumption and perceived risk or consequences. Although the study looked at just a small subset of the many ethnocultural groups in Canada, these examples emphasize the complexity in addressing alcohol abuse and risk.

An interview with Jeff D'Hondt, MSW, RSW
Centre for Addiction and Mental Health

Jeff D'Hondt is the manager of the Aboriginal Service at the Centre for Addiction and Mental Health, and has 15 years experience working in mental health and addictions, gained at hospitals, homeless shelters, the correctional system, and Aboriginal communities and organizations. D'Hondt is also the author of the novel *Spiderbones* (2008), which deals with the impacts of racism on mental health. This email interview was conducted in November 2008 and addresses some of the major contemporary and historical oppression and inequities to which Canada's Aboriginal people continue to be subjected, and how these injustices relate to alcohol and other drug abuse.

There have been numerous media accounts of the high rates of alcohol and other drug abuse among Aboriginal communities. Why do some of these communities seem to be disproportionately affected by substance abuse?

As an Aboriginal person, my first instinct is to point out that "Aboriginal" is a broad term, including citizens/members of First Nations, the Inuit, the Métis, people labelled as treaty/status "Indians" (an arcane term still used in the racist legislation governing indigenous affairs in Canada), people labelled as non-status/treaty "Indians," on-reserve people, off-reserve people, and people with Bill C-31 status (Bill C-31, passed by parliament 28 June 1985, is an *Act to Amend the Indian Act,* aimed at removing discriminatory rules for registration, Band membership, funding, and self-government). Each of these categories of identities has unique concerns and histories.

The term Aboriginal also includes different genders, sexualities, political beliefs, spiritual beliefs, socio-economic statuses, languages, histories, and cultural teachings. A heterosexual, Anglophone lawyer born and raised in Toronto and married to a non-Aboriginal woman may proudly identify himself as Aboriginal, as could a Cree-speaking lesbian community nurse with a status card, working at her reserve's health centre.

With all of these variables in place, generalized statements about alcohol and other drug abuse in Aboriginal communities become very difficult to make—the same explanations may not apply in all settings. In fact, how does one define "Aboriginal communities?" Reserves are the most typical example of such communities, but what about off-reserve housing developments for Aboriginal people, such as Project Amik[5] in Toronto? What about the clientele of Native Friendship centres spread throughout Canada? Or the residents of urban areas with high Aboriginal populations, such as Toronto, Winnipeg, or Saskatoon? Or Canada's three northern territories? Or urban/rural areas with Métis settlements?

Answering these questions is often difficult, and fraught with tension, both between Aboriginal and non-Aboriginal peoples, and within Aboriginal communities themselves (however they're defined). Aboriginal identity is often complex and contentious, as can be expected in when so many groups and places are included in an single category of identity.

However, there are issues that affect many Aboriginal people. Wherever Aboriginal people live, or which group of Aboriginal people are being discussed, there are readily available stereotypes of Aboriginal drunks. I can easily picture an Aboriginal person passed out on a street corner, or on a reserve, or up north—everywhere in Canada, essentially.

The "drunken Indian," the label given to the images of intoxicated Aboriginal people suffering throughout Canada (it's applied to Métis and Inuit people, even though they don't self-identify as Indians), or the "high Indian," is something I'm all too familiar with as an Aboriginal person. Yet I know dozens of Aboriginal people who don't use substances at all, or drink socially, with little impact on their lives.

Great strength and resiliency exist in the Aboriginal community, though there are people who suffer from punishing substance abuse issues.

What are the reasons that many, not all, Aboriginal people misuse substances? There isn't one explanation, but rather an interacting series of possible explanations. For example, I've known a middle-class, Vancouver-based Aboriginal person with a cocaine problem. His/her reasons for using were far different from those of a teenaged Aboriginal prostitute who got addicted to crack while working the sex trade in Edmonton.

So, here are many of the explanations that I've heard for Aboriginal substance use throughout my 15-year career as a social worker, and throughout my life as an off-reserve, urban (sometimes rural) Aboriginal person:

> "Alienation" of Aboriginal peoples from Canada, whereby their traditions and styles of life are significantly different from, and not accommodated by, the patterns of Canadian society.
> Poverty, unemployment, poor health, low educational levels, low or absent community economic development; substance misuse becomes a coping strategy for these issues.
> Negative residential school experiences and other imposed actions which served to break apart families or relocate whole communities; substance misuse becomes a coping strategy for these issues.
> Aboriginal peoples have an inherent genetic and biological basis for alcohol addictions.
> Alcohol is a cultural-based attempt to seek "visions" in altered states of consciousness.
> Social pressure.
> Cultural loss.

> Defiance against the perceived on-going cultural oppression of Aboriginal peoples.
> Boredom due to a lack of adequate Aboriginal recreational opportunities on- and off-reserve.
> Peer group pressure.
> Family pressure.

In other words, Aboriginal people are often blocked from accessing their historical and cultural teachings and from having meaningful access to the social determinants of health. In lieu of this, they're often given easy access to another culture, that of the "suffering Aboriginal," or the "drunken Indian/Métis/Inuit/Eskimo."

Aboriginal substance abuse rates remain unjustly high, reflecting the impact of the numerous concerns listed above. Again, each is often a factor, but not all of them may be relevant in a given context. No one reason makes Aboriginal people drink, though some general trends have been noted.

"Intergenerational trauma" is a term used by academics in reference to Aboriginal peoples. What exactly does it mean, and how does it connect to substance abuse?

"Intergenerational trauma" refers to ongoing impacts of painful, oppressive historical acts that have occurred but have not been resolved, such as genocide and cultural oppression. Because the issues remain unresolved, their impacts are transmitted from one generation to the next.

In Canada, Aboriginal people survived or continue to deal with the effects of residential schools, the Sixties Scoop (when the Canadian government forcibly removed children from their parents and placed them with white families during the 1960s, 1970s, and early 1980s), ongoing poverty, racism, and persistently low access to the social determinant of health— centuries of oppression. Although the federal government has apologized for residential schools, and implemented programs to compensate the victims of such schooling, much work is still required to rebuild the families torn apart by those legacies.

However, the Canadian government has yet to apologize for racism and poverty (though social programs do exist to deal with these issues), and residential schools remain only one part of the systemic oppression faced by Aboriginal people.

How is intergenerational trauma significant to Aboriginal people? People suffering from the effects of intergenerational trauma have incredibly high rates of substance abuse, as substances can be used to cope with trauma, lack of family structure, and so forth.

In other words, substances replace love and health. This fact remains one of the most insidious impacts of intergenerational trauma in Canada's Aboriginal communities.

Why do Aboriginal peoples need unique approaches to substance abuse treatment? What are some examples of how these are delivered and what they look like in practice?

Aboriginal people have unique identities, histories, cultures, languages, levels of access to the social determinants of health, and so forth, which often differ from those of non-Aboriginal Canadians. This uniqueness can make it very difficult for some Aboriginal people to respond to non-Aboriginal types of treatment.

Sweat lodges, drumming, traditional arts and crafts, seven grandfather/mother teachings, medicine wheel teachings, and numerous other cultural healing practices often reach people who otherwise did not benefit from non-Aboriginal treatment programs.

Poundmaker's Lodge near Edmonton, Alberta, remains the most commonly cited example of Aboriginal substance abuse treatment programming that is designed, implemented, and evaluated by Aboriginal people.[6] There are also federally funded treatment centres and substance abuse workers in programs throughout Canada.

These programs are often underfunded, and do not always have access to the same level of well-trained, experienced professionals that may be available in non-Aboriginal substance abuse treatment settings, but consistent, and adequate, provincial and federal funding in Aboriginal health human resources and treatment centres could address these issues.

Jeff D'Hondt's commentary relates the cumulative and intergenerational impacts of government policies, social stereotypes, and institutionalized racism on Canadian Aboriginal peoples. When viewed through a broader lens of structural inequity and oppression, substance abuse emerges as an adaptive response for some individuals and communities. However, he also points out that negative stereotypes obscure the positive examples of the ways in which Aboriginal cultures are being reclaimed and remembered, and individuals and communities are healing from centuries of colonialism and marginalization. The intersecting diversities of culture, gender, age, sexual orientation, language, social location, geographical place, and lived experience are reminders that the term "Aboriginal" is itself a label encompassing multiple realities, lives, and histories. Substance abuse treatment approaches that use traditional approaches to healing and recovery represent an integral alternative to mainstream treatment approaches or programs, but broader reforms and system-level changes are also critical.

Conclusion

In this chapter, we have examined some of the ways in which alcohol has been part of nearly every human culture throughout history, and many customs related to alcohol use survive today. We have also looked at how people drink, and suggest that a binary definition of alcohol problems (that is, alcoholic versus non-alcoholic) fails to capture the nuances in risk and drinking patterns. Consumption patterns occur along a continuum of risk and severity, and are influenced by a range of biological, psychological, and social/structural/historical factors.

A number of well-validated screening and assessment tools can help determine whether a person might have a problem with alcohol. Further assessment by specialist addiction treatment services can identify the types of treatment that best fit an individual's specific needs. A menu of treatment options can range from brief outpatient interventions to intensive residential programs. In addition, self-help can be a useful stand-alone treatment or complement to other treatment. In short, there are many paths to recovery from alcohol and other drug problems.

A better appreciation of the cultural dimensions to alcohol use, as well as how society has affected different cultural groups, can contribute to more appropriate and inclusive policies, prevention, and treatment initiatives. Challenging our attitudes and beliefs as well as the negative and destructive stereotypes we may hold are also key to reversing the stigma and oppression of diverse populations and communities.

Chapter 3

Tobacco

Introduction

When people hear the term "substance abuse," tobacco is not usually the first drug that comes to mind. Smoking is generally considered to be a lifestyle choice or unfortunate habit rather than a health or addiction issue, a perspective that tobacco companies have successfully disseminated through advertising campaigns over the last several decades. Yet the economic costs of smoking are estimated at $17 billion annually (Rehm et al. 2006) and tobacco kills 50 percent of all people who do not quit smoking (West and Shiffman 2007). Roughly one in five Canadians continues to smoke despite well-known (and well-publicized) health impacts (Health Canada 2008).

Federal governments have passed increasingly restrictive legislation on tobacco advertising, and provincial and municipal governments have prohibited smoking in virtually all indoor public places and limited where tobacco can be sold. Smoking bylaws have been passed in response to research demonstrating that second-hand smoke (also called environmental tobacco smoke) is even more toxic than inhaled smoke. With each cigarette smoked, hazardous gases and particulates are released into the air, and adhere to walls, upholstery, and clothing. The "off-gassing" of these particles from different surfaces is, in itself, harmful and has been termed "third-hand smoke," because this off-gassing continues to occur long after a cigarette is extinguished. In fact, ingestion of third-hand smoke particles by small children (from playing near, crawling on, or mouthing contaminated surfaces in indoor smoking environments) has been associated with cognitive deficits (Winickoff et al. 2009).

It may be more accurate to say that only the first weeks of cigarette smoking constitute an active choice. The nicotine in tobacco smoke is what makes cigarettes so addictive, a fact that has long been known to tobacco manufacturers. The chairman of British American Tobacco (the third-largest tobacco company in the world) noted that, "We're in a kind of business where we know that people would much rather cut down on other areas of discretionary spending before they decide to down-trade or cut down on their overall daily cigarette consumption" (du Plessis, in Shafey et al. 2009, 47). Far from being a lifestyle choice, tobacco dependence is more akin to a chronic disease, with the majority of smokers continuing to smoke for years or decades and cycling through multiple periods of remission and relapse (Fiore et al. 2008; Jarvis 2004).

The short half-life of nicotine also plays a role in its addictive potential. The half-life of a drug refers to the time in which a drug's concentration in the body falls by half. Nicotine has a half-life of two hours in the bloodstream—thus, dependent smokers are motivated to smoke on an approximately hourly basis. During sleep, blood concentrations of nicotine may fall to the level of non-smokers, so the first cigarette of the day is smoked within 30 minutes after waking by about 70 percent of smokers (West and Shiffman 2007).

In addition to the addictive nature of the drug nicotine, there is another reason why cigarettes have such a high dependence liability. The route of administration, smoking, gets nicotine to the brain faster than injecting a drug: with each inhalation of smoke a bolus of nicotine is delivered to the brain via the arteries within 10 to 16 seconds. The faster that a drug can be delivered to the brain, the more immediately and powerfully reinforcing it is, and the higher its addictive potential. The slower delivery and lower concentrations of pharmaceutical nicotine (in the form of transdermal patch, nicotine gum, lozenge, or inhaler) makes these forms much less likely to induce or maintain dependence.

Another factor in dependence liability relates to the design of the cigarette itself. Although most people regard cigarettes as simply blended tobacco rolled in paper, they are one of the most sophisticated drug delivery system ever conceived. A drug's "capture rate" refers to the proportion of people who, once exposed to a psychoactive substance, go on to develop dependence. Research has shown that the capture rate for cigarettes is comparable to crack cocaine (Henningfield, Cohen, and Slade 2009).

The millions of dollars that tobacco companies have devoted to research and development over the years have resulted in products that can be targeted to different groups of smokers and potential smokers (such as adult males, women, youth and young adults, blue collar workers, etc.). Wayne and Connolly (2002) analyzed internal tobacco company documents to explore how changes in the design of Camel cigarettes coincided with their "Smooth Character" advertising campaign in the late 1980s. Industry documents referred to the product design preferences of "FUBYAS" ("first usual brand young adult smokers") to inform their modification of the cigarettes to reduce throat irritation while increasing or retaining nicotine impact through the use of additives and blends. For example, one quotation from the results of an RJR Tobacco committee meeting noted,

> smoothness is an identified opportunity area for improvement versus Marlboro, and sweetness can impart a different delivery taste dimension which younger adult smokers may be receptive to, as evidenced by their taste wants in other product areas. (Gemma 1985, in Wayne and Connolly 2002, 34)

Evidence of targeted marketing and research priorities on the part of tobacco companies has been made public through litigation and legal discovery in US tobacco industry court cases. The contents of other confidential tobacco industry materials from the 1950s through 1980s are now widely known as a result of an anonymous, unsolicited "donation" of a box of tobacco industry internal documents and memoranda to Professor Stanton Glantz at the University of California, San Francisco—the return address on the box read only "Mr. Butts" (Glantz et al. 1996).

How Cigarettes Work

Prior to the 1880s tobacco was used primarily as snuff or smoked in pipes, hand-rolled cigars or hand-rolled cigarettes. A tobacco worker could roll about three cigarettes by hand in one minute. In 1883 that changed when a Virginia teenager, James Bonsack, invented the first machine (the "Bonsack machine") to manufacture cigarettes, revolutionizing tobacco industry cigarette production (Roberts, 2007). In contrast, it is estimated that in 2010, 6.3 *trillion* cigarettes per year will be produced, and that the absolute number of smokers will continue to increase as the world population increases (Shafey et al. 2009).

What is it about cigarettes that makes them so attractive to so many people? Cigarettes are a potent and effective drug delivery mechanism over which users have "fingertip control." The release of internal tobacco company research and documents has provided a detailed picture of the close attention paid to tobacco formulation, additives, and cigarette design and modifications over the past several decades. A number of factors influence nicotine delivery, burn rate, taste, and smoking intensity, including tobacco formulation, type of filter and paper, and additives. In fact, tobacco companies spend more money on paper, filters, and packaging than on the actual tobacco itself (Mackay, Eriksen, and Shafey 2006).

Tobacco formulation

Cigarettes are classified as an *agricultural product* in Canada (as opposed to being regulated as a drug, over which much stricter controls and reporting requirements are applied by regulatory agencies). Tobacco companies have argued that this classification is justified because the nicotine in cigarettes is a naturally occurring component in tobacco. However, tobacco company documents demonstrate their long-standing awareness of the addictive nature of nicotine, especially when delivered via cigarettes (Kessler 1994). Tobacco companies manipulate the nicotine content in different brands of cigarettes in a variety of ways.

Nicotine content varies among different types of tobacco, and different parts of a tobacco plant contain different levels of nicotine. Tobacco types can be blended in various ways, along with reconstituted "sheet" tobacco and "puff" tobacco. Although Canadian cigarettes do not contain sheet or puff tobacco, American and illegal ("contraband") cigarettes often do.

Sheet tobacco is composed of the dust, stems, and tobacco scraps that prior to the 1940s were discarded as unusable. Since the 1940s the tobacco industry has had the capacity to reconstitute these materials in ways that lend themselves to the manipulation of nicotine levels and additives. "Puff" tobacco refers to tobacco that has been freeze-dried with ammonia and Freon to increase volume. Adding sheet and puff tobacco to the "tobacco column" in a cigarette reduces production costs. Since 1960, tobacco companies have used progressively less leaf tobacco per cigarette and higher proportions of sheet and puff tobacco (Mackay, Eriksen, and Shafey 2006).

Nicotine, in combination with levulinic acid (an organic acid used to hide the bitter taste of pure nicotine), can be sprayed as a salt on the tobacco blend to increase nicotine levels (Kozlowski, O'Connor, and Sweeney 2001). The pH content of tobacco can also be manipulated—this is important because pH levels influence the amount of nicotine that gets into the bloodstream. Modifying pH content thus controls the bioavailability of nicotine in a cigarette (Kessler 1994).

Since 2000, the Canadian government passed *Tobacco Reporting Regulations*, where tobacco companies are required to report to Health Canada 26 of the harmful chemical constituents in tobacco and 41 harmful chemical emissions in tobacco smoke. In addition, since 2001 tobacco packaging is required to contain information about three toxic emissions (in addition to the previously mandated information on tar, nicotine, and carbon monoxide levels). These three additional chemicals are benzene (an industrial solvent), formaldehyde (used to preserve human cadavers), and hydrogen cyanide (a component in chemical warfare agents). In all, 4,000 chemicals are released in cigarette smoke, which is why they have been characterized as "small toxic waste dumps on fire."

Some of the other chemicals in tobacco products include acetone (used in nail polish remover), aluminum, ammonia (used in cleaning products), arsenic (used as rat poison), cadmium (used in rechargeable batteries), carbon monoxide (found in car exhaust), copper, hexamine (barbecue lighter), lead, magnesium (used in flares), naphthalene (found in mothballs), nitrobenzene (a gasoline additive), polonium-210 (a radioactive compound), stearic acid (found in candle wax), toluene (an industrial solvent), and zinc—among many others. Because tobacco companies keep the formulations of each brand a secret, it is not possible to know exactly what is in each type of cigarette.

Type of filter and paper

The primary mechanism for reducing the amount of tar and nicotine a smoker inhales has been to introduce various filter ventilation technologies. Filter vents can be placed through electrostatic, laser, or mechanical perforation, and serve to dilute inhaled tar and nicotine with outside air. However the vent holes are generally placed where they tend to be covered, wittingly or unwittingly, by a smoker's fingers or lips, thus circumventing the dilution effect (Kozlowski, O'Connor, and Sweeney 2001).

So-called "light" or "mild" cigarettes were marketed in the past as being less harmful than regular cigarettes, because of tobacco companies' claim that smokers inhaled less tar and nicotine. This claim was based on findings from automatic "smoking machines" used by tobacco companies' internal researchers. Light and mild cigarettes have perforations in the filters or the cigarette paper, causing some smoke from a lit cigarette to be diverted before being inhaled. However, internal tobacco company documents reveal an emphasis on designing cigarettes that are "elastic" in their ability to allow for compensation of the vent holes by real smokers wishing to obtain higher levels of nicotine, yet at the same time show lower inhaled tar and nicotine readings by the smoking machines. Peer-reviewed research (that is, research not funded by tobacco companies) has shown that dependent smokers compensate for low yield cigarettes by blocking filter holes, increasing puff volume, and taking more frequent puffs (Kozlowski, O'Connor, and Sweeney 2001; West and Shiffman 2007).

Nicotine, flavourings, and other additives may be added to the tobacco, cigarette paper, and filter to manipulate taste and odour and to facilitate even burning. The weight, permeability, opacity, whiteness, and strength of paper used in cigarettes are carefully factored into cigarette design. Tobacco companies pay close attention to such aesthetic concerns as cigarette paper that will stay white throughout burning, and to filters that have minimal staining at the end after the cigarette is smoked.

Additives

Additives to tobacco and other components of the cigarette (the filter and paper) are key to manipulating nicotine and tar delivery, as well as smokers' subjective perceptions and preferences. Pharmacological additives increase nicotine transport to the brain; humectants keep tobacco and tobacco smoke moist, and menthol, sugars, and other flavours make smoke easier to inhale and improve the taste.

Additives such as sugar, cocoa, and licorice have been particularly effective in making cigarettes more palatable and appealing to youth. These products may not be harmful in and of themselves, but when combusted can form harmful compounds (Rabinoff et al. 2007). Of the 399 cigarette additives acknowledged by tobacco companies, Rabinoff and colleagues found that over 100 of these camouflage second-hand smoke, enhance or maintain nicotine delivery, potentially increase the addictiveness of cigarettes, and mask symptoms and illnesses associated with smoking.

Although Canadian cigarettes do not contain additives, they are as harmful as American cigarettes (Selby and Els 2004). This is true in large part because of the risks inherent in repeatedly inhaling a combusted substance containing tobacco-specific nitrosamines (a key cancer-causing agent in tobacco).

Aspects of Tobacco Dependence

Marjorie is 52 years old and works as a baker in a factory. She is married with three teenage children, none of whom smokes, and her husband of 17 years quit smoking six years ago. Marjorie has been smoking since she was 14 and has about 25 cigarettes per day. Marjorie has been recently diagnosed with chronic obstructive pulmonary disease (COPD), an incurable lung disease usually caused by smoking. Her husband and kids are furious with her for continuing to smoke and are constantly on her back telling her that she has to quit. Her doctor, the nurses at the COPD clinic, and her extended family are also putting pressure on her about her smoking. Marjorie feels angry and defensive about all of this, as she feels that smoking is her decision and no one else's business. Part of her wishes she had never started smoking, but she is adamant that this is something she really enjoys and is not willing to give up at this time. She hates being made to feel guilty every time she goes onto her back porch for a cigarette.

The case of Marjorie illustrates that tobacco use and dependence are not rational lifestyle choices. She has a long history of smoking, is experiencing serious health consequences as a result of her use of cigarettes, is experiencing conflict with loved ones, and is being pressured by family members, friends, and health practitioners to quit; yet, she is determined to continue smoking. Marjorie's reluctance to quit in the face of extreme social pressure and health consequences is formidable. What is keeping her from giving up the substance that is causing her harm, both physically and in her closest relationships?

Repeated exposure to tobacco smoke and nicotine results in psychological, behavioural, and physical aspects of dependence, making smoking cessation a challenge on three fronts (Nides 2008). Psychological aspects of dependence can be seen in the ways people use cigarettes to relieve stress or improve their mood, particularly negative affective states. The behavioural aspects of smoking dependence result from the continuous pairing of smoking with various other routine behaviours, such as driving, taking a break, or drinking coffee or alcohol. Over time these other behaviours become, in and of themselves, powerful smoking cues. Finally, the physical aspects of tobacco dependence include the effects of nicotine on the brain and the unpleasant withdrawal symptoms when nicotine levels in the brain drop.

West and Shiffman (2007) posit three key mechanisms underlying cigarette addiction: *habit*, *nicotine hunger*, and *withdrawal symptoms*. The habitual element in smoking is graphically described by Sante (2004) in his account of his own smoking history:

> I picture a tableau from some secondary Last Judgment, when all the cigarettes I have smoked shall be made whole again, all of them piled up like cordwood in a space the size of a hangar. Let's see, thirty years approximately, an average of two packs a day, that would be 438,000, give or take a few thousand. Nearly half a million, filtered and unfiltered, more than half of them hand rolled, all but a handful white papered. All of them passed through my mouth, my throat, my lungs. Smoked in every possible circumstance and setting. All of them utterly eradicated by fire. (20–21)

Sante provides a striking visual representation of the hundreds of thousands of cigarettes smoked over 30 years "in every possible circumstance and setting." Since the average person takes 10 puffs on each cigarette, Sante has logged roughly *four and a half million* hand-to-mouth repetitions over his 30 years of smoking. It is hard to imagine another human behaviour—besides breathing—that is so repetitive over time. The long term impact of pairing situational and behavioural cues with the activation of the brain's reward system results in a powerful and tenacious addiction.

Long-term smoking actually changes the structure and function of the brain's reward system. In other words, cigarettes essentially "hijack" the brain's reward system. Nicotine acts on the part of the brain associated with survival of the human species—the same part of the brain that governs eating and procreation. This important neural pathway, called the mesolimbic dopamine pathway, is located in the midbrain and runs from the ventral tegmental area to the nucleus accumbens. Nicotine acts directly on nicotinic acetylcholine receptors, inducing the release of dopamine in the nucleus accumbens. This is the same addictive process as in cocaine and other stimulants, and is thought to be a central feature of the biological mechanisms of addiction (Jarvis 2004).

The following paragraph highlights how altering the brain's natural neurochemistry influences behaviour:

> *Dopamine release in the [nucleus accumbens]* has been found to have a profound effect on animal and human behaviour—it is a *signal* that tells the animal or the person to notice what caused it and to try to *repeat* it. In the case of smoking, that action is smoking a cigarette. All of this goes on at an *unconscious level*. *Nicotine rewards smoking, causing it to be repeated.* It is important to note that smokers do not need to feel pleasure for this effect to occur—it is an automatic process. But this is just the start of the story. In many smokers *the nicotine alters the brain* so that smokers acquire a kind of *"drive"* to smoke, much like hunger. (McEwan et al. 2006, 45; emphasis in original)

Nicotine hunger is experienced when nicotine levels in the brain drop below a certain threshold. People who smoke are able to self-regulate nicotine levels within quite narrow parameters. Each person has an individual preference for a fairly specific nicotine level; this preference expresses itself early on and has been shown to be stable over time (Jarvis 2004). In other words, a person will naturally tend to smoke often enough to avoid withdrawal, but will avoid smoking to the point of nicotine overdose ("nicotine intoxication"). This individualized titration of nicotine is possible because of the sophistication of the cigarette as a drug delivery device, where users have "fingertip control" over the amount of nicotine they administer.

Tobacco withdrawal also plays a part in the intractability of cigarette smoking. Withdrawal symptoms are defined as the physical and mental changes that occur from an interruption, reduction, or cessation of tobacco use, and are the result of physical and psychological dependence. Symptoms include increased appetite, restlessness, depression, irritability or aggression, cravings, poor concentration, sleep disturbance, and lightheadedness (Jarvis 2004). Most of these symptoms last for two to four weeks; however some effects, such as increased appetite and cravings, can last ten weeks or longer (McEwan et al. 2006).

Recognizing the centrality of biological factors in nicotine dependence means acknowledging that smoking is not simply a lifestyle choice or a bad habit. An anti-smoking website funded by the Ontario government (www.stupid.ca) has been criticized for the implication that continuing to smoke is somehow related to a person's intelligence. Rather, smoking initiation is related to a variety of factors including savvy and youth-friendly marketing by tobacco companies, the way that cigarettes are designed to induce nicotine dependence, and adaptive changes in the brain that sustain dependence. This helps explain why even in the face of major health or other consequences, a person (like Marjorie in the case example above) may continue to smoke.

Smokeless Tobacco

Although smokeless tobacco products are less common than cigarettes, they have been a topic of increasing concern among tobacco control researchers due to their appeal to young people and tobacco companies' marketing them as a safe, convenient alternative to smoking (Stepanov et al. 2008; Ontario Tobacco Research Unit 2006; Severson and Hatsukami 1999). Smokeless tobacco comes in two basic forms. "*Chew*" tobacco is available as leafy tobacco sold in pouches, a brick form known as "plug" tobacco, or rope-like strands of "twist" chewing tobacco. Chew tobacco users put a "wad" of tobacco in the cheek pouch and mix it with saliva while chewing. In recent years the market share of chew tobacco has declined in favour of *oral snuff*. Oral snuff, also known as "dip" or "spit" tobacco, is a cured, finely ground powder tobacco sold as three types (dry snuff, moist snuff, and fine cut).

Each dose or "dip" of snuff (often packaged in small sachets similar to teabags) is placed between the cheek and gums for 30–60 minutes and then discarded. Traditional snuff causes excess salivation which the user must spit out, as swallowing tobacco-infused saliva generally leads to nausea, irritation of the esophagus, or vomiting, especially in less-experienced users. The Swedish version of snuff, called "snus," does not provoke excess salivation. This innovation has made "spit-free" snuff products more aesthetically appealing to a broader array of North American consumers, including young urban professionals or college and university students.

The overall prevalence of smokeless tobacco in Canada in 2005 was approximately 8 percent (ever used during lifetime) with less than 1 percent reporting recent use (in the last 30 days; Ontario Tobacco Research Unit 2006). US data for 2005 reports recent use by 4 percent of adult men and less than 1 percent of adult women (Fiore et. al. 2008), and 10 percent of male high school students reporting recent use (CDC 2005). However, general survey data do not reveal patterns of use among specific age groups, regions, and populations. In Canada, the use of spit tobacco has been found to be higher in the Prairies, in some Aboriginal populations, among athletes, and among rural males (AADAC 2007). For example, the Northwestern Ontario Student Drug Use Survey (Sieswerda, Starkes, and Adlaf 2006) found that 18 percent of grade 11 students and 21 percent of grade 12 students reported using snuff.

There are a number of reasons why smokeless tobacco is a concern to tobacco control researchers and health care providers. Newer types of smokeless tobacco are being formulated, packaged, and marketed in ways that are designed to appeal to specific market segments, particularly male youth (Wyckham 1999). The development of "spit-free" snus products, marketed under the brand names Taboka, Marlboro Snus, Camel Snus, and Skoal Dry, are being promoted by tobacco companies as a convenient (and discreet) alternative to cigarettes in settings where smoking is no longer permitted.

Tobacco companies can manipulate nicotine levels in smokeless tobacco through the actual nicotine level of the tobacco used in a particular brand, or by changing the pH level of a tobacco brand. The latter influences the amount of "bioavailable" nicotine, the amount of nicotine that can be absorbed by the body. Products with low pH levels reduce bioavailable nicotine to a greater extent than products with higher pH levels (the closer that tobacco pH levels are to the pH of the mouth, the more readily nicotine is absorbed). This is important because younger users who have not yet developed tolerance to nicotine would likely feel sick after using higher pH snuff or chew tobacco. In contrast, "starter brands" such as Skoal Bandits are sweeter and less potent than brands with a stronger tobacco taste and higher pH and nicotine levels (Stepanov et al. 2008; Wyckham 1999).

Candy-flavoured products, including apple, cherry, peach, vanilla, cinnamon, wintergreen, and spearmint, disguise the tobacco taste and likely account for why many youth try spit tobacco before the age of 12 (CDC 2007). In addition, the use of smokeless tobacco by young males has been shown to be an important predictor of later smoking, and most users of smokeless tobacco become dependent before the age of 18 (Haddock et al. 2001; Severson and Hatsukami 1999).

Because smokeless tobacco, by definition, avoids the negative health consequences associated with inhaling a combusted product, it does not affect long-term health to the same extent as cigarettes. Nonetheless, smokeless products are not risk-free. Chew tobacco and snuff contain varying amounts of carcinogens, including tobacco-specific nitrosamines (potent cancer-causing agents), formaldehyde, cadmium, polonium-210, arsenic, lead, cyanide, and benzene (National Cancer Institute 2003). A recent study examining toxicant and carcinogen levels in new versus traditional smokeless tobacco brands found widely varying levels of harmful agents, with reductions in major toxicants and carcinogens in some of the newer brands (Stepanov et al. 2008). In general, users of smokeless tobacco have an increased risk of oral cancers (cancers of the lip, tongue, cheeks, gums, and floor and roof of the mouth), pancreatic cancer, cardiovascular disease, and periodontal problems (National Cancer Institute 2003; Hatsukami and Severson 1999). Precancerous lesions in the mouth occur in up to one-third of regular smokeless tobacco users, and dental problems including gum recession and dental caries are not uncommon.

Smokeless tobacco as a harm reduction measure has become a topic of heated debate among tobacco control researchers and advocates (Gartner et al. 2007). The key question is whether people who are addicted to cigarettes would benefit from switching to lower-risk smokeless tobacco products. On one hand, proponents of smokeless tobacco as a harm reduction strategy point to the high prevalence of low-nitrosamine snus use in Sweden over the past several decades. Low smoking prevalence and health gains in the Swedish context have been attributed to former smokers switching to snus and new users opting for snus over cigarettes. Some harm reduction advocates suggest that smokeless tobacco should be recommended to North American smokers who are looking for safer sources of nicotine.

On the other side of the harm reduction debate, researchers argue that the Swedish context may be culturally unique and not transferable to North American preferences and patterns of tobacco use. Other concerns include the younger age of initiation among smokeless tobacco users, the risk of nicotine dependence in smokeless tobacco, smokeless tobacco as a "gateway" to cigarettes, and the combined risks of cigarette smoking and smokeless tobacco use (Gartner et al. 2007). In addition, pharmaceutical nicotine (such as that in nicotine patches, gum, inhalers, and lozenges) does not carry the same risks as smokeless tobacco, and has been proven effective in reducing smoking (Fiore et al. 2008). Therefore, the argument goes, why advocate for a tobacco product with known health risks (smokeless tobacco), when pharmaceutical options with minimal risks are widely available?

As tobacco control measures become increasingly restrictive, tobacco companies have a vested interest in promoting new products that can be used anytime, anywhere. The marketing slogan, "when you can't smoke, snus" demonstrates tobacco companies promoting the use of both cigarettes and smokeless tobacco (Gartner et al. 2007). These types of messages undermine tobacco control efforts to reduce prevalence and may appeal to new generations of potential users. Current clinical practice guidelines note that smokeless tobacco is not a safe alternative to smoking, and that there is no evidence that smokeless products are helpful in quitting smoking (Fiore et al. 2008).

Other Types of Tobacco

In addition to cigarettes and smokeless tobacco products, there are a number of other forms of tobacco available in Canada. These are mainly favoured by younger smokers attracted by their unique packaging or by perceptions that these products are less toxic or more "natural."

Cigars and cigarillos

Cigars come in many sizes and shapes, and are made of air-cured and fermented tobacco wrapped in leaf tobacco. The long aging and fermentation processes of cigar tobacco produces even higher concentration of carcinogenic toxins than what is found in cigarettes (Shafey et al. 2009).

Cigarillos, or mini-cigars, have become a popular choice for younger smokers. Although these products look like cigarettes, they are considered cigars because they are wrapped in tobacco. The federal government does not control aspects of the appearance, additives or packaging of cigarillos. Unlike cigarettes, they are sold individually in many provinces, and contain flavourings designed to appeal to youth. These include cherry, vanilla, chocolate, pina colada, grape, strawberry, peach, and so on. At this time there are no health warnings on individually sold cigarillos. Research shows that people are as likely to experiment with cigarillos as with cigarettes, with rates among youth three times that of adults (Physicians for a Smoke-Free Canada 2008). When smoke is inhaled, the health risks of cigar and cigarillo use are similar to those of cigarettes.

Kreteks (clove cigarettes)

Kreteks, or clove cigarettes, are imported primarily from Indonesia or Southeast Asia. They contain 60–70 percent tobacco, and 30–40 percent ground cloves, clove oil, and other additives (American Cancer Society 2009). Despite perceptions that these products are more natural and safe than regular cigarettes, they actually deliver more nicotine, tar, carbon monoxide, and other chemicals.

Bidis (flavoured cigarettes)

Bidis are imported primarily from India or other Southeast Asian countries and consist of tobacco rolled in tendu or temburi leaf tied with string at the end. They are generally cheaper than regular cigarettes, and many come in candy or fruit flavours. Like kreteks, bidis deliver more tar, nicotine, and carbon monoxide to the smoker. They are also thinner and more tightly packed with tobacco, requiring about three times as many puffs as do cigarettes (American Cancer Society 2009).

Hookahs (water pipes)

Hookahs originated in Asia and the Middle East, and can be used to combust and inhale a variety of psychoactive drugs, including opium, cannabis, hashish, and tobacco. The tobacco used in water pipes is generally pre-flavoured or mixed with honey, molasses, or dried fruit, and inhaled through a long hose (the tobacco mixture is called shisha). Some people believe that the water in a hookah filters out the harmful chemicals in tobacco smoke; however, this is a myth. Hookah smoke has been shown to have the same or higher concentrations of nicotine, tar, carbon monoxide, and heavy metals as cigarette smoke. In addition, hookah smoking is often done in groups, presenting other risks such as the spread of tuberculosis or hepatitis (WHO 2005).

Youth and Smoking

Jean was 12 years old when he tried his first cigarette. His father smoked at the time, so it was easy to take a couple of cigarettes from the pack in his dad's coat pocket. Although the first time he smoked he almost threw up, he was determined to be like a couple of the boys in his neighbourhood who were regular smokers. At 16 Jean is now smoking between four and eight cigarettes a day. He buys them from another boy at school and likes that they make him feel older and more mature. He's heard about the harm that tobacco can cause, but figures that if it was that bad the government would make smoking illegal. A year ago his dad quit after many attempts over the years, but Jean states that he can stop smoking any time and does not plan to be smoking after high school. His parents and younger sister haven't caught on that he smokes, but he knows that they would be upset with him if they found out.

The case of Jean illustrates some common themes among youth and tobacco use. Youth and young adults (especially males) are at the highest risk for smoking. Dependence becomes established fairly quickly, especially among people with a genetic predisposition for nicotine dependence. A positive family history of smoking (Jean's father was a smoker) constitutes the double risk factors of modelling smoking behaviour and a possible biological predisposition for dependence. Peer smoking, rebellion, and risk taking are also associated with teenage smoking.

The vast majority—90 percent—of people who become addicted to smoking do so before age 18. This has prompted researchers to term tobacco dependence a "pediatric disease" that carries over to adulthood (Fiore et al. 2008). In 2008, 18 percent of all Canadians aged 15+ were current smokers. Rates are higher among males, particularly young males: 27.4 percent of 18- and 19-year-olds are current smokers, with the highest proportion of smoking among males aged 20 to 24 (just under 33 percent; Health Canada 2008).

In Canada and in other countries, youth from lower socio-economic groups have higher tobacco use prevalence. In addition, role modelling from parents, peers, and media (including television and movies) is thought to influence smoking initiation (Golmier, Chebat, and Gélinas-Chebat 2007; Jarvis 2004). With increasing restrictions on tobacco industry advertising, movie placement has become an important mechanism by which positive images of smoking can be promoted: "the practice of product (or brand) placement has grown significantly during the past 20 years; marketers now frequently use placements as the basis for multimillion dollar integrated promotional campaigns" (Pardun, Brittain

McKee, and Karrh 2003, in Golmier, Chebat, and Gélinas-Chebat 2007, 4).

A number of factors have been identified as increasing the risk for smoking initiation in early adolescence. A prospective study (Brook et al. 2008) examined the smoking trajectories of 746 children between the ages of one to ten, taken from a randomly selected sample of US families from diverse socio-economic, geographic (both urban and rural), ethnocultural, and educational backgrounds. From 1975 until 2002 subjects were assessed for cigarette use and a variety of personality attributes. Five discrete smoking trajectory groups were identified: non-smokers (44 percent), occasional smokers (10 percent), late starters (20 percent), quitters (9 percent), and heavy/continuous smokers (17 percent). The heavy/continuous smoking group had an earlier average age of initiation (14 years) than the other groups. Heavy smokers were also significantly more likely than the other groups to have had emotional difficulties, childhood externalizing behaviours (aggression, delinquency, and hyperactivity), and lower educational aspirations. Occasional smokers and non-smokers, on the other hand, had the most positive patterns of emotional and behavioural characteristics.

The findings from Brook and colleagues' (2008) research point to the heterogeneity among adolescent and adult smokers, as well as the risk factors or areas of vulnerability for continuous heavy smoking. These risk factors are similar for other substances of abuse, but tobacco is somewhat unique in that it is most often the first drug started and the last to be relinquished. Their research data also demonstrate that a high proportion of adolescents who start smoking will continue to smoke into adulthood, whether as heavy or as occasional smokers. This is key because prospective studies have found that even light smoking (defined as fewer than ten cigarettes per day) has been found to be highly associated with increased morbidity and mortality. One study found that even smoking as few as one to four cigarettes per day was associated with a significantly higher risk of dying, particularly from lung cancer (in women) and ischemic heart disease (in both sexes; Bjartveit and Tverdal 2005).

One other point in Jean's case relates to his comment that "if it was that bad the government would make smoking illegal." This is a thorny issue for policy-makers, as on the one hand tobacco revenue from taxation is significant, but on the other hand this revenue is outweighed by the enormous health costs of tobacco use. For example, projected Ontario tax revenues for 2007–2008 totalled $1.127 billion, while tobacco-related diseases cost the Ontario economy $1.6 billion in healthcare, $4.4 billion in lost productivity, and accounted for at minimum 500,000 hospital days each year (Ontario Ministry of Health Promotion 2006). Furthermore, making tobacco illegal when one-fifth of the Canadian population still smokes would make such a measure difficult to enforce. Governments in Canada and elsewhere have chosen to address the tobacco problem by introducing measures to decrease the overall prevalence of tobacco use. Only when smoking prevalence approaches 5 percent or less might it be feasible for the government to consider making tobacco illegal.

Inside "Big Tobacco"

The tobacco industry in Canada is dominated by three companies: Imperial Tobacco Canada (which manufactures du Maurier, Player's, Matinée, and Peter Jackson), Rothmans, Benson & Hedges (RBH, which manufactures Craven A, Rothmans, Benson & Hedges, and Belvedere), and JTI-Macdonald Corporation (which manufactures Export A and Vantage). These companies are subsidiaries of large multinational corporations. Earlier incarnations of these three major companies have been in Canada for over 100 years.

Tobacco companies have used a variety of strategies to represent themselves as responsible corporate citizens. The tobacco industry funds "front organizations" that are designed to undermine tobacco control efforts or to give the perception of social responsibility. For example, the Fair Air Association, the Pub and Bar Coalition of Canada, Courtesy of Choice (hotels and restaurants), and the Canadian Coalition for Responsible Tobacco Retailing (CCRTR) are all funded by tobacco companies and have attempted to steer public discourse away from the health consequences of tobacco use, and instead place the focus on smoking as an issue of personal choice and rights (AADAC 2006). These organizations also sponsor enforcement programs, like the CCRTR-sponsored "Operation I.D. School Zone," which has been criticized by the Canadian Medical Association as focusing on individual choice and parental responsibility (versus emphasizing the health impacts of smoking).

The real agenda of tobacco companies—to increase market share and to recruit "replacement smokers" (young people to replace older smokers who are likely to die prematurely)—can be seen in the Guildford Depository and Documents. The Guildford Depository in Guildford, England, is one of the two collections of tobacco industry documents established by the order of the State of Minnesota in 1998. The second depository is located in Minnesota and consists of over 33 million pages of tobacco industry documents never intended for the general public.

These depositories were the result of litigation judgments in favour of Blue Cross and Blue Shield health insurance in Minnesota against British American Tobacco (BAT).

In September 1999, the United States filed a lawsuit against the major cigarette manufacturers and two industry-affiliated organizations. The case went before US District Judge Gladys Kessler of the US District Court for the District of Columbia. At the conclusion of a lawsuit against tobacco companies filed by the U.S. Department of Justice, the presiding judge had this to say:

> Over the course of more than 50 years, Defendants lied, misrepresented, and deceived the American public, including smokers and the young people they avidly sought as "replacement smokers," about the devastating health effects of smoking and environmental tobacco smoke, they suppressed research, they destroyed documents, they manipulated the use of nicotine so as to increase and perpetuate addiction, they distorted the truth about low tar and light cigarettes so as to discourage smokers from quitting, and they abused the legal system in order to achieve their goal—to make money with little, if any, regard for individual illness and suffering, soaring health care costs, or the integrity of the legal system.... In this case, the evidence of Defendants' fraud is so overwhelming

that it easily meets the clear and convincing standard of proof. The Findings of Fact lay out in exhaustive detail the myriad ways in which Defendants made public statements, often directly to consumers, which were flatly contradicted by their internal correspondence, knowledge, and understanding. (US Department of Justice 2006, 1500–01; 1565–66)

The millions of documents were submitted by BAT in the legal discovery process, and BAT was ordered by the Minnesota Supreme Court to maintain and operate the Guildford Depository for ten years. The Canadian Council for Tobacco Control (CCTC) and Health Canada are the Canadian hosts of the Guildford Depository, and access to the collection is available to the public.[1]

In Canada, a number of provinces are pursuing litigation against tobacco companies to recover the billions of dollars in health care costs for tobacco-related diseases; and some provinces have launched other lawsuits to recover the $9.6 billion in lost revenue due to tobacco companies' alleged complicity in smuggling contraband cigarettes in the 1990s (Sibbald 2005). Imperial Tobacco Canada Ltd., one of the parties named in the British Columbia Lawsuit, has noted that "BC can expect a long-winded and bad-tempered litigation" (Sibbald 2005, 1307).

Population-Based Approaches to Reducing Tobacco Use Prevalence

Population-based approaches refer to broad policy, legislative, and health promotion initiatives that have the potential to influence the overall population. These measures can be distinguished from "cessation approaches," which denote clinical tobacco cessation treatments offered to individuals. Both are key to tobacco control efforts; cessation treatment options and best practices are discussed in the next section of this chapter.

In an article titled "How to Prevent 100 Million Deaths from Tobacco," Frieden and Bloomberg (2007, 1758) make a compelling case for the importance of population-based tobacco control measures:

For the first time ever, the world's leading agent of death is a man-made substance–tobacco. If current trends continue, tobacco will kill 1000 million people prematurely during this century. Tobacco, which kills at least a third of people who use it, is also the largest single cause of health inequalities in some low-income populations. Millions of deaths can be prevented if we take urgent action based on available information.

Frieden and Bloomberg (2007) provide a comprehensive review of research evidence for the effectiveness of various population-based approaches, and articulate five evidence-based strategies. Although many countries including Canada employ some of these strategies, no country uses them all to their fullest extent. These approaches include the following:

> Price: Increase taxes and address illegal tobacco manufacture and smuggling.
> People with lower incomes and youth are the most "price sensitive" groups, but overall, taxation is the most effective way to reduce tobacco use. Contraband cigarettes represent a major threat to government taxation as a tobacco control measure, and need to be addressed in tandem with higher cigarette prices.

> Image: Legislate bans on both direct and indirect tobacco advertising, as this challenges the positive image of smoking promulgated by tobacco companies.
> These measures, in combination with anti-tobacco or warning messages in the media and on cigarette packages, effectively "denormalize" smoking. Denormalization challenges tobacco companies' portrayal of smoking as a normal and acceptable lifestyle choice. Frieden and Bloomberg (2007) note that tobacco companies in the US spend $50 *per person every year* on advertising and marketing.
> In 2003 Canadian tobacco companies spent $388 million on marketing and communications (AADAC 2006). Television, radio, and billboard advertising are already illegal in Canada, and there are tight restrictions

over print advertising. In addition, a number of Canadian provinces have outlawed "power walls" in retail displays (the large, colourful point-of-sale displays often placed near candy displays in convenience stores and other retail outlets). Indirect advertising venues—such as event sponsorship using tobacco brand names—are also banned in Canada.

Nonetheless, tobacco companies have found creative ways to subvert these marketing restrictions. For example, bar promotions sponsored by subsidiary companies (often held on college and university campuses) decorate venues with tobacco brand colours, give away branded t-shirts, lighters, and so on, and sponsor band contests or other events. Promotional websites focused on sports and music may offer free music downloads or other incentives (AADAC 2006). Cigarette packaging plays a key role in advertising and communicating a brand's image. Industry research ensures that packaging appeals to specific targeted groups, such as women and youth (Wakefield et al. 2002).

> Exposure: Establish smoke-free public places.
Smoking bans not only protect people from the toxic effects of second-hand smoke they also make it more likely that smokers will quit and raise people's awareness of the risks associated with smoking. These laws have been shown to encourage families to voluntarily make their homes smoke-free as well. Other legislative measures, such as banning smoking in cars where children are passengers and creating smoke-free apartment buildings, are offshoots of this strategy. One caveat noted by Frieden and Bloomberg (2007) is that partial smoking bans or allowing for designated smoking rooms undermines exposure strategies and does not prevent exposure to second-hand smoke. In Canada, smoke-free legislation has been passed in 9 of the 13 provinces and territories, and 3 others have smoke-free legislation enacted by municipalities within

those provinces (Canadian Council for Tobacco Control 2007).

> Monitoring: Evaluate the effectiveness of tobacco control efforts by monitoring prevalence and using research data to guide implementation.
> In Canada, there are a number of organizations devoted to tobacco control research, monitoring, and advocacy. These include the Canadian Council for Tobacco Control (CCTC), Non-Smokers' Rights Association (NSRA), Physicians for a Smoke-Free Canada, Canadian Lung Association, Canadian Heart and Stroke Foundation, and the Canadian Cancer Society. The Ontario Tobacco Research Unit (OTRU) at the Centre for Addiction and Mental Health is also an internationally recognized research enterprise focused on health and policy research related to tobacco use.

Frieden and Bloomberg (2007) state that the above four measures, in conjunction with evidence-based and accessible smoking cessation treatment services, will result in reduced tobacco prevalence. They note that if global prevalence can be reduced to 20 percent by 2020, a minimum of 100 million deaths from tobacco will be prevented.

An important global milestone in population-based tobacco control has been the ratification of the *World Health Organization Framework Convention on Tobacco Control* (WHO FCTC). This is an international treaty adopted by the 56th World Health Assembly in 2003. The main provisions of the WHO FCTC relate to regulating the contents, packaging, and labelling of tobacco products, prohibiting sales to minors, addressing illicit trade in tobacco products, and banning smoking in work and public places. The FCTC also focuses on reducing consumption through price and tax increases, enacting comprehensive bans on tobacco advertising, promotion, and sponsorship, and promoting cessation education, training, and public awareness about smoking cessation resources and assistance.

The FCTC is deposited at the United Nations Headquarters in New York and has been signed by 168 countries (signatories) as of March 2009. It is open to all member counties of the WHO and the United Nations. Canada signed the FCTC on 15 July 2003.

The following quotation from a 1990 document of the Philip Morris tobacco company illustrates the adversarial relationship between the tobacco industry and tobacco control researchers and advocates:

> What are we trying to accomplish? Prevent further deterioration of overall social, legislative and regulatory climate, and ultimately, actually improve the climate for the marketing and use of tobacco products. (In Mackay, Eriksen, and Shafey 2006, 63)

The FCTC measures introduce population-based tobacco control measures globally in order to counteract tobacco industry marketing and promotion.

Health Consequences of Smoking

We all know that smoking is bad for us—that message has been communicated effectively by media, government, and health advocacy groups. Less well understood are the *specific* health consequences and risks associated with smoking.

Tobacco is the leading cause of preventable death in the developed world. It is estimated that 45,000 Canadians die each year from smoking-related causes, and tobacco use is responsible for one out of every five deaths in Canada (CAMH 2008b). This is five times the number of deaths attributable to traffic accidents, suicides, homicides, drug abuse, and AIDS *combined* (Physicians for a Smoke-Free Canada 2003). One way to put the figure of 45,000 deaths each year in perspective is to imagine two jumbo jets crashing every week for one year—with no survivors. One in two people who smoke will die from smoking-related causes, making cigarettes the only legal product that kills 50 percent of all people who use it as intended.

Smoking causes heart attacks, stroke, and hardening of the arteries. Coronary heart disease and stroke are two to four times more common among people who smoke. Women who smoke and use birth control pills are at much higher risk of stroke or heart disease.

Thirty percent of all cancers are caused by smoking. Roughly 20 percent of people who smoke develop lung cancer, and more women die of lung cancer than from breast cancer. Smoking also causes cancer of the mouth, throat (pharynx, larynx, and esophagus), pancreas, kidney, and bladder, and smoking doubles the risk of cervical cancer in women.

Tobacco use is responsible for up to 90 percent of all cases of chronic obstructive pulmonary disease (COPD). Chronic bronchitis, emphysema, and pneumonia are all caused by smoking. Many people describe COPD as like trying to breathe through a straw.

Other risks of smoking include age-related blindness, deafness, and dementia; impaired fertility; and increased risk of fetal and neonatal death (West and Shiffman 2007). Fetal effects include low birth weight, risk of preterm premature rupture of membranes, and a two-fold risk of placental abruptions (separation of the placenta from the uterus, which can result in hemorrhage, maternal shock, and/or fetal death; CAMH 2007b).

Even light smoking—as few as one to five cigarettes per day—has been shown to increase a person's risk of dying from heart disease and other causes (Bjartveit and Tverdal 2005).

Benefits of Quitting
The benefits of quitting smoking start almost immediately, and increase with length of abstinence. Regardless of a person's age, smoking history or co-occurring health problems, quitting smoking leads to improved health.

Within 8 hours

> carbon monoxide level drops in your body
> oxygen level in your blood increases to normal

Within 48 hours

> your chances of having a heart attack start to go down
> sense of smell and taste begin to improve

Within 72 hours

> bronchial tubes relax making breathing easier
> lung capacity increases

Within 2 weeks to 3 months

> circulation improves
> lung functioning increases up to 30 percent

Within 6 months

> coughing, sinus congestion, tiredness and shortness of breath improve

Within 1 year

> risk of smoking-related heart attack is cut in half

Within 10 years

> risk of dying from lung cancer is cut in half

Within 15 years

> risk of dying from a heart attack is equal to a person who never smoked

Source: Health Canada 2007

Although people who smoke expect to feel better after quitting, many actually report feeling worse. Coughing, sore throat, respiratory tract infections and mouth ulcers are not uncommon, and are thought to result from a short-term negative impact on the body's immune system, likely the result of physical stress associated with smoking cessation (McEwan et al. 2006). These health effects are temporary, and can be seen as part of the process of the body beginning to heal itself from the effects of chronic tobacco use.

Quitting Smoking 101: Best Practices in Tobacco Cessation

Data suggest that 70 percent of smokers would like to quit, and between 32 and 44 percent report at least one quit attempt each year (Fiore et al. 2008; McEwan et al. 2006). The remaining 30 percent who do not report wanting to quit would likely choose not to start smoking if they had life to live over again, or would not want their children to start smoking. This chapter has outlined some of the biological, psychological, and social/environmental factors that reinforce smoking and can make quitting such a formidable challenge. This next section provides an overview of current research and best practices in smoking cessation, as well as some suggested resources that can increase a person's chances of success.

Among smokers who actively try to quit, only a small minority actually succeed, and most people do not seek outside support for quitting smoking. Part of the reason for low success rates may be due to a lack of information about the evidence and effectiveness of smoking cessation aids, which can increase a person's chances of quitting successfully. Almost four-fifths of cessation attempts are unassisted, and just 3 to 5 percent of people who attempt to quit on their own (that is, without receiving counselling or using medication) are successful (Fiore et al. 2008). In contrast, using medications and attending cessation counselling raises a person's chance of quitting to 20 percent (West and Shiffman 2007). The use of evidence-based cessation interventions yields outcomes that are comparable to those in the management of other chronic, relapsing diseases, such as type 1 diabetes, hypertension, or asthma.

Mark Twain, the famous American humorist and writer, once said, "It's easy to quit smoking, I've done it hundreds of times." This illustrates the unfortunate reality that most smokers relapse within the first week of quitting (Hughes, Keely, and Naud 2004). Key issues are how to prepare to quit, actually "do" the quit, and then sustain behavioural change in the longer term.

Developing a plan to quit

There is no "one size fits all" approach to quitting smoking. Developing an action plan should be based on at least six factors (Abrams et al. 2003):

> a person's motivation and confidence in being able to quit
> reasons for current smoking, pattern of smoking, and reasons for wanting to quit
> level of nicotine dependence and severity of nicotine withdrawal symptoms
> history of past quit attempts and reasons for relapse back to smoking
> social and environmental supports and obstacles to quitting
> the existence of any co-occurring medical, mental health, substance use or other issues

People with lower levels of motivation may benefit from attending a counselling session with a clinician trained in motivational interviewing skills (Miller and Rollnick 2002). Alternatively, making a list of the good things and "less good" things about smoking can be an illuminating experience and can help to increase motivation. Keeping track of the time, place, and feelings or thoughts associated with each cigarette smoked is also a powerful tool to understand reasons for smoking and the role that smoking plays in a person's life.

The level of nicotine dependence is another important consideration in coming up with a quit plan. Unlike most other addictive drugs, there is a wide variety of medications with demonstrated effectiveness that can increase a person's chances of success in quitting smoking. In general, people with higher levels of dependence would benefit from more intensive treatments than those with lower levels of dependence. People who smoke within 30 minutes of waking and who smoke more than an average of 25 cigarettes per day would probably do better in more intensive behavioural and pharmacological treatments (Abrams et al. 2003).

Myths and Facts about Stop-Smoking Medications

How much do you know about medications to help people quit smoking? Take this true-or-false quiz and find out (answers are at the bottom).

1. Nicotine is one of the harmful substances in cigarettes.
2. Nicotine addiction is equally likely whether the nicotine is obtained by cigarette, nicotine patch, gum, lozenge, or inhaler.
3. Nicotine patches, gum, lozenges, and inhalers carry significant health risks if used by people who smoke.
4. Smoking while on the patch causes heart attacks.
5. People with heart disease should not use nicotine replacement medications.
6. Pregnant women should never use nicotine replacement medications.
7. People under age 18 should never use nicotine replacement medications.
8. Stop-smoking medications should not be used in combination with one another.
9. People using nicotine replacement medications should not exceed the dose recommended on the medication package.
10. Stop-smoking medications are only appropriate for short-term use.
11. Nicotine replacement medications should not be used by people who just want to cut down on the number of cigarettes they smoke.

Answers

1. False: The thousands of toxins in tobacco smoke are harmful. Nicotine is not associated with cancers or chronic respiratory conditions. 2. False: Cigarettes are far more addictive than nicotine replacement, primarily because of how they deliver nicotine. 3. False: Nicotine replacement therapy is safe for smokers. 4. False: The use of nicotine replacement does not increase cardiovascular risk. 5. False: It is more dangerous for people with heart disease to continue smoking than to use nicotine replacement, and many such patients are not able to quit on their own. 6. False: Nicotine replacement is safer for the fetus than smoking, and is appropriate for pregnant women who are unable to quit using behavioural interventions. 7. False: Most daily smokers begin smoking

before age 18, and are already getting nicotine from cigarettes. Nicotine replacement should be considered for youth who are regular smokers who are unable or unwilling to quit using behavioural interventions. 8. False: The nicotine patch/gum/lozenge/inhaler can be used at the same time and/or in combination with bupropion (Zyban). 9. False: Smokers should be in control of how and how much they use nicotine replacement medications. 10. False: Nicotine replacement should be used for as long as needed to maintain or prolong tobacco abstinence. 11. False: Nicotine replacement can be used by people who are not ready to quit as a way to reduce their smoking, and progress towards a longer-term goal of abstinence.

Source: adapted from Ontario Medical Association 2008

The absolute number of past quit attempts does not predict future success in quitting smoking; rather, the length of the longest quit attempt and length of the most recent quit attempts may be the most relevant predictors (Abrams et al. 2003). In general, people who have quit for longer periods of time have more practice abstaining from smoking, and also have more experience in adapting to being a non-smoker. People who have less experience attempting to quit in the past may be better candidates for intensive cessation counselling.

The social and contextual circumstances in a person's life that promote or maintain smoking are also key areas for consideration. For example, do other family members or close friends smoke? Does the person smoke indoors? What are the financial, social, and other costs associated with smoking? Other environmental factors include social/cultural norms, government tobacco control activities, and social support (West and Shiffman 2007). Addressing environmental factors, especially those over which a smoker has direct influence, is key to preparing to quit.

In general, a combination of counselling plus medication has been shown to be most effective in helping people to quit smoking (Fiore et al. 2008; West and Shiffman 2007). Counselling can take the form of group or individual sessions with a health professional or therapist, and are generally time limited (e.g., four to eight sessions). Cognitive behavioural approaches, emphasizing coping skills development, stress management, and relapse prevention strategies, are most commonly used. A number of evidence-based clinical tools and guidelines have been developed for professionals to help plan and maintain quit attempts (see, for example, Fiore et al. 2008; Perkins, Conklin, and Levine 2008; Britton 2004; Abrams et al. 2003).

Pharmacological Approaches to Cessation

There are a number of effective medications that have been shown to increase the success of quit attempts. The most commonly used are nicotine replacement therapies (NRT), bupropion (Canadian trade name Zyban), and varenicline (Canadian trade name Champix). Taking medication to stop smoking approximately doubles a person's chances of successfully quitting (Nides 2008), and can help to ease the nicotine withdrawal symptoms and cravings that lead to a high risk for relapse.

Nicotine replacement therapies available in Canada include the nicotine patch, gum, lozenge, and inhaler. These act by replacing some, though not all, of the nicotine that a smoker would otherwise obtain through cigarettes. Nicotine in the patch is absorbed through the skin into the venous system, and maintains a steady release of nicotine into the body. The lozenge, gum, and inhaler act more rapidly than the patch, as they are absorbed buccally (through mucus membranes in the mouth). Because of their slow absorption NRT medications have extremely limited addictive liability. In contrast, the nicotine in cigarette smoke is absorbed through the arterial system, resulting in intense "peaks and valleys" of nicotine levels in the brain. Nicotine replacement therapies can be used in combination with one another. For example, the patch can provide a steady dose of nicotine, while the gum or inhaler can be used occasionally as "breakthrough" medication in situations that are especially high risk for smoking (such as being in a bar or social gathering with people who smoke).

Bupropion, marketed under the trade name Zyban, was originally researched as an antidepressant drug (trade name: Wellbutrin). Both Zyban and Wellbutrin are identical medications; the names differ depending upon the purpose for which they are prescribed. The neurobiological mechanisms by which bupropion acts to reduce cravings to smoke are not well understood. Studies have found that it doubles a person's chances of quitting (compared with placebo), and also suppresses weight gain associated with quitting smoking (Nides 2008). Bupropion is contraindicated for people with seizure disorders, patients taking monoamine oxidase inhibitors (MAOIs, a class of antidepressant drugs), and pregnant women. Bupropion can be used in combination with nicotine replacement therapy.

Varenicline, marketed under the trade name Champix in Canada and Chantix in the US, is a relatively new cessation medication. It acts by binding to nicotinic acetylcholine receptors in the brain, and stimulates dopamine to 32–45 percent of the levels elicited by cigarettes. This results in reduced cravings and withdrawal, and people who smoke while taking varenicline experience only minimally reinforcing effects from cigarettes. Common side effects include nausea, vivid dreams, and headache, but there have also been a few anecdotal case reports of more serious psychiatric side effects. Clinical trials have not substantiated these anecdotal reports of psychiatric risk, and varenicline appears to be even more effective than bupropion as a cessation medication (Nides 2008).

A series of decision rules was recently developed to help guide clinicians in matching specific medications or combinations of medications to diverse clients (Bader, McDonald, and Selby 2009). This algorithm used a Delphi method with a panel of international experts in cessation to make specific recommendations for on- and off-label prescribing of NRT, bupropion, and varenicline.

Other medications less commonly used in cessation are nortriptyline, an antidepressant, and clonidine, an antihypertensive. Although both of these drugs have been shown to be effective for tobacco cessation, their risks or side effects make them less desirable than the first-line medications discussed above.

Treatments still being researched for cessation include rimonabant, a drug that was recently approved as an anti-obesity medication in Europe, as well as the nicotine vaccine (now undergoing human trials; Cornuz et al. 2008). The vaccine acts by inducing the body to manufacture nicotine antibodies; these antibodies bind to nicotine in the blood and prevent the nicotine from reaching the brain. Although preliminary results are not overly promising (at six-month follow-up the vaccine did not appear to increase continuous abstinence rates in the study sample), these findings may have been due to insufficient antibody levels induced by the vaccine. Research is continuing, but a clinically effective vaccine is likely years away.

Non-pharmacological Strategies in Quitting Smoking

Cognitive, behavioural, and environmental strategies can provide a pragmatic and powerful counterpoint to the dilemma of "not enough willpower to quit." For example, just writing down the time and place of every cigarette smoked each day raises people's awareness of when and why they smoke. Like any repetitive behaviour, many people smoke without really thinking about it—self-monitoring in and of itself can affect behaviour and motivation for change.

Other effective strategies include the following:

> identifying the good things and "less good" things about smoking
> telling friends, colleagues, and family members how they can be of support
> substituting a less-preferred brand for your favourite brand of cigarettes and delaying the time between cigarettes

> managing withdrawal symptoms through medication and/or self-care strategies (taking a warm bath, distracting yourself with another activity)
> setting a concrete quit date, or gradually cutting down on the number of cigarettes smoked
> noting times and places that will be challenging to not smoke, and either avoiding them or writing down a concrete action plan
> reading self-help books, joining online support groups, or attending a cessation counselling program
> keeping track of the money saved by not smoking, and committing to using some of that money for a reward or incentive

In addition, it is advisable to cut down on coffee or other caffeinated beverages when quitting smoking. This is because tobacco use speeds up the liver's metabolism of caffeine, while cessation results in a decrease in caffeine metabolism. Maintaining or increasing caffeine consumption after quitting can result in caffeine toxicity, characterized by feeling anxious and "jittery." Some people mistake these aversive symptoms for nicotine withdrawal and return to smoking, but simply cutting back or eliminating caffeine will resolve them to a considerable extent.

Finally, there are number of useful environmental strategies for preparing to quit smoking:

> identify people who can provide positive support in cessation attempts, as well as who will not be supportive
> while preparing to quit, smoke outside and impose a "no smoking" rule in the home
> take note of environmental "triggers" to smoke, such as talking on the phone, after finishing a meal, being in social settings, and so on
> seek out or create new smoke-free environments

Attending to environmental factors can reduce tobacco-related harm even if cessation is not a goal. For example,

Are Acupuncture and Hypnosis Effective in Smoking Cessation?

A meta-analysis of research studies evaluating the efficacy of acupuncture in cessation was carried out in 2000, and found no evidence that this approach is effective in cessation (Fiore et al. 2008). Results of the research suggest that individual positive effects may be due to positive expectancies. The same holds true for electrostimulation and laser acupuncture. The effectiveness of hypnosis is harder to assess on scientific grounds, as the overall rigour and quality of research studies is weak. At this time hypnosis is not recommended as an evidence-based approach to cessation (Fiore et al. 2008; West and Shiffman 2007). Given that there are many other well-established and well-supported medical and psychosocial approaches to cessation, acupuncture and hypnosis are not recommended treatment modalities, at least on scientific grounds.

making homes or cars smoke-free protects other family members, pets, and friends from the effects of second-hand smoke.

Subpopulations with High Tobacco Prevalence

Nigel is 37 years old and receives government disability support due to his mental illness (schizophrenia). Although his psychiatric medication is effective in controlling his symptoms (delusions and hallucinations), he often stops taking the medication because of the side effects (mainly weight gain and drowsiness). Nigel smokes approximately 50 cigarettes per day and has been smoking since his early teens. He says that smoking helps him relax and socialize with others, and gives him something to occupy his time. Although he buys the cheapest brand, Nigel is concerned about the money he is spending on cigarettes. He was recently rehospitalized for a recurrence of mental illness symptoms, and while in the hospital he was alarmed to find out that the smoking room on the inpatient unit was closed, and that the hospital implemented a smoke-free policy. Although he was given a 21-milligram nicotine patch, he found that he still had very strong cravings to smoke and was irritable and upset almost all of the time. He concluded that the patch doesn't work and that quitting is just not possible for someone like him.

Although national smoking prevalence is at 18 percent, rates of smoking among specific subpopulations are much higher (Health Canada 2008). In particular, people who are dependent on alcohol, cocaine, or opioids, and people with mental illness have much higher rates of prevalence. For example, up to 90 percent of people with opioid dependence are smokers, as are 90 percent of people with schizophrenia (Kalman, Morisette, and George 2005; NIDA 2008). Other populations with high tobacco prevalence include youth, Aboriginal peoples, people who are or identify as lesbian, gay, bisexual, transgendered, transsexual, two-spirited, intersex, or queer, people who are involved with the criminal justice system, people with low incomes, and people who are under-housed or homeless.

It has been hypothesized that as overall tobacco use prevalence declines, there is a "hardening" of the population that continues to smoke. This theory posits that people who have an easier time quitting are more likely to respond to such broad, population-based approaches as increased taxes on cigarettes, smoke-free policies, denormalization of tobacco use and health information and warning messages (such as those found on cigarette packages), while the "shrinking, residual population of smokers" may be more highly addicted (Ontario Medical Association 2008, 3) or are experiencing other interacting psychological, social and/or structural factors that make it difficult to quit. These factors include marginalization, internalized and external oppression, racism, discrimination, and poverty. In addition, the high rate of smoking among people with schizophrenia is thought to be due in part to how nicotine acts on the brain to mitigate some of the cognitive deficits and other symptoms associated with schizophrenia (NIDA 2008).

The above case of Nigel illustrates that people with complex needs who want to quit smoking may not be given adequate information, medication or support to do so. Tobacco use by people with severe mental illness is often regarded by health care professionals as "their only pleasure," yet research shows that a large proportion of clients with addictions and mental health problems want to quit smoking (Selby and Els 2004). Nigel's subjective experience using the 21-milligram nicotine patch suggests that it was probably inadequate in addressing his nicotine withdrawal. In addition, training of health providers in how to provide cessation interventions is uneven, as demonstrated by the lack of counselling support or follow-up provided to Nigel.

Ideally, people like Nigel who are hospitalized and cannot smoke should be offered cessation counselling, a combination of nicotine replacement options, and encouragement and support. Even if Nigel did not want to quit smoking, his withdrawal symptoms while in hospital need to be addressed along with his other co-occurring mental health issues. This would also be true for people with co-occurring medical conditions or people who are incarcerated.

Creation—A Relationship with Tobacco Begins to Emerge: An Interview with Ernie Benedict

Ernie Benedict is an Elder of the Iroquois Nation and has been extensively involved in the Native community all his life. Here he recounts the story of tobacco and its traditions:

Sky Woman began to fall to earth, and as she fell she brought with her two main plants of Tobacco and Strawberry. The water animals watched her descend. In preparation for her, the muskrat took bits of dirt and carried them to the surface of the water. The dirt was placed on the back of the sea turtle, and it is here where Sky Woman landed. The plants she was carrying took seed and continued to grow as Strawberry and Tobacco on what is now known as Turtle Island.

Tobacco was symbolic of the initiation of life, while strawberries symbolized the afterlife. Tobacco was given honour as a plant of a heavenly nature.

When Tobacco is burned the smoke rises, which provides the link to all the spirits beyond the sky. Tobacco was a gift that was given to Aboriginal people, and it had a spiritual place within our community. This carried with it a great honour.

Pipes are also tools that assisted with communicating with the spiritual world. Therefore, smoking Tobacco in pipes was held in a high regard, as symbols of communication with higher powers and great symbols of peace. The pipe was a communicator—a strong symbol of peace when oral language and speech became barriers to communicating.

Is the Traditional Tobacco in this story the same as the tobacco they sell in stores? If not, how is it different?

Tobacco in its original form had both honour and purpose. As well, Traditional Tobacco did not contain all the chemicals that are now put into tobacco. Its purpose is to communicate with the spiritual world, beyond the skies. What is sold today has been tampered with for business and profit, taking away from its original purpose.

There is a belief held by some Native people that commercial tobacco and Traditional Tobacco can be used interchangeably. What do we say to people who believe this?

When Tobacco is used in a spiritual way, it serves a purpose to aspire to good things. However, when commercial tobacco is used for ceremonial purposes, it loses something. It loses the ideal of sacredness in the ceremony. Tobacco is meant to be used in a sacred manner and not to satisfy an addictive need built up within you.

Source: adapted from Ontario Cancer Care

Aboriginal Peoples and Tobacco Use

Tobacco as a spiritual and ceremonial plant has been used among many of Canada's Aboriginal peoples for thousands of years, long before contact with European colonists and the subsequent widespread use of commercial tobacco. The cultural and geographical diversity among Aboriginal populations makes generalizing about the sacred use of tobacco problematic—many Aboriginal peoples have no history of traditional tobacco use. However, the addiction and disease associated with the use of commercial tobacco represents a post-colonial legacy that has affected virtually all Aboriginal populations (Health Canada 2003).

Traditional tobacco (*Nicotiana rustica*) is a different variety than tobacco grown for commercial purposes (*Nicotiana tabacum*). The ceremonial uses of traditional tobacco vary depending on a Nation's culture and customs. Communicating with the spirit world through sacred smoke, thanking the Creator, praying for a good harvest or fish catch, marking a rite of passage as in birth, marriage, or death, and committing to peace with enemies are some of the many ways tobacco is used ceremonially. Moreover, traditional tobacco is not only smoked—it may be burnt over a fire, thrown on water, or chewed. As medicine, tobacco has been used to treat earaches and snakebites and to purify the mind and heal the body (Health Canada 2003).[2]

In contrast to the traditional ceremonial and medicinal uses of tobacco, commercial tobacco use by Aboriginal peoples has resulted in devastating health and social consequences (First Nations and Inuit Health Committee 2006). Recent data indicate that 59 percent of Aboriginal peoples in Canada smoke, roughly three times the overall Canadian prevalence. Smoking initiation among Aboriginal youth can occur as early as seven or eight years old. Among Inuit peoples, who have little or no history of traditional tobacco use, over 70 percent now smoke, and Inuit women have among the highest rates of lung cancer worldwide.

Although smoking cessation medications, including nicotine replacement therapies, are available as a prescription subsidy to Canadian Status Indians living on- or off-reserve, Aboriginal peoples are less likely than non-Aboriginals to access cessation medications and counselling support from mainstream health practitioners (Wardman et al. 2007). Wardman and colleagues suggest that this may be due to lack of physical access to physician services, the need for a prescription to access subsidized NRT, and systemic issues such as racism, lack of culturally appropriate health care services, and underutilization of mainstream health care services. Integrating traditional healing approaches within mainstream cessation interventions is suggested as a possible way to honour Aboriginal beliefs about healing and wellness within Western medical approaches.

Aboriginal organizations and community groups have worked to address high rates of prevalence and loss of traditions through culturally adapted community-based and national initiatives (Health Canada 2003). However, these initiatives have been hampered due to other multiple and pressing social and health issues faced by Aboriginal communities. Like alcohol and other drug use among Aboriginal peoples, the historical and continuing structural inequities and oppression make tobacco use a symptom of broader, intersecting social injustices. The economic incentives of cigarette manufacturing, smuggling, and organized crime on some First Nations reservations further complicate tobacco control efforts.

Conclusion

This chapter has outlined the many dimensions of the complex problem of tobacco use and dependence. Tobacco control efforts at the population level are challenged by the vested interests of tobacco companies in increasing profits; at the individual level, cessation efforts must overcome the addicting nature of the drug nicotine and the effectiveness of cigarettes as a drug delivery mechanism for inducing and maintaining dependence.

As attitudes toward smoking change at a societal level, and as prevalence continues to decline, smoking is becoming systematically "denormalized." Evidence-based and effective population-level and treatment interventions are widely available, although still not as widely accessed as would be ideal. There is also a need to engage and intervene appropriately with populations that continue to experience high rates of smoking. As one of the most pressing global public health problems, and the single leading preventable cause of death in Canada, tobacco use needs to remain at the forefront of our policy and treatment agendas.

In summary, the following quotation from Sante's book *No Smoking* (2004) illustrates both the appeal of smoking and the long-term impact of dependence:

> Now that you have chosen the path of righteousness, can it be that the decision is fixed and irrevocable?... Is it possible that you will never again be able to enjoy the comfort of knowing that you have traded five minutes of life for five minutes of serenity? We may all have stopped smoking, but we continue to burn.

Chapter 4

Opiates and Opioids

"Everything one does in life, even love, occurs in an express train racing towards death. To smoke opium is to get out of the train while it is still moving. It is to concern oneself with something other than life or death."

Jean Cocteau, artist, writer, and filmmaker,
Opium: The Diary of a Cure (1958)

Introduction

Human beings have always been concerned about pain—how to avoid it, how to manage it, and, on the darker side, how to inflict it. But mostly, humans have been driven to do as much as possible to prevent the occurrence of pain, and when pain occurs, to find solutions and give relief to the sufferer. The project of preventing and treating pain goes far back in the historical record, even into the archaeological record. Ancient artifacts from earliest civilizations show evidence of medicines and substances that would have been used to treat and control pain. Of all psychoactive substances ever discovered by humankind, those in the drug class called opioids have been the most important to pain management for thousands of years.

Opioids are still the most commonly prescribed and powerful pain relieving drugs available. They are superb at treating even the most severe and chronic pain associated with illness, disease, and disability. However, these drugs also possess extremely pleasurable psychoactive effects, and their reinforcing properties make them liable to abuse and dependence, both physical and psychological. The drug class of opioids includes a variety of substances, such as opium, heroin, and morphine, as well as many prescription and non-prescription medications.

Though classically shaped by images of poppy fields and syringes, the profile of this drug class is changing, as are the issues faced by clinicians, policy makers, law enforcement, and the public. The chapter begins with a brief look at the important historical role that opium has played in the West and describes some of the ways that opiates (drugs made from opium) and opioids (synthetic opiates) continue to play a major role—in medical pain management, in the illicit drug scene, and in the problems of abuse and dependence. As in earlier chapters, a set of narratives accompany the discussion, bringing a human face to this topic. The stories and accompanying analysis offer a deeper understanding of abuse and addiction, and address Canadian rates of use and evidence-based treatment approaches.

A note about terminology

The word "opioids" describes the entire class of drugs whose chemistry and action are similar to those of the master drug in this class, opium; however, the terms *opioid* and *opiate* are often used interchangeably. The term "opiates" properly refers only to drugs derived from the naturally occurring substances (for example, morphine) in a particular type of poppy, while "opioids" refer to drugs (like OxyContin) with similar molecular structures that are artificially synthesized in a laboratory. To make things even more confusing, a number of drugs are called "semi-synthetic opioids" because they are formulated with both naturally-occurring and synthetic components (heroin falls into this category).

George Chuvalo's Story

George Chuvalo's name will be recognized by anyone familiar with the history of heavyweight boxing. A Canadian champion as an amateur and then as a professional, he fought every major heavyweight boxer of his era, including Floyd Patterson, George Foreman, Joe Frazier, and—most famously—Muhammad Ali. Chuvalo's legend is that he was never knocked out in the ring. Muhammad Ali called him the toughest fighter he ever saw. They fought twice, Ali winning both times, but he never did knock out Chuvalo, even though (especially in the second fight) George took a pounding.

But the biggest challenge in Chuvalo's life took place outside of the ring. The father of four sons and a daughter, he saw three of his sons become addicted to heroin in the 1980s. They became involved in drug-related crime, and each spent time in jail. In 1985, his son Jesse shot himself, desperate because he couldn't handle his addiction. Then in 1993, another son, Georgie Lee, overdosed in a Toronto hotel only a few days after being released from prison. Two days following the funeral, Chuvalo's wife took an overdose after writing a suicide note, and lay down on the bed of her dead son. Three years later, a third son, Steven, was found in his apartment, dead from heroin with a syringe still in his arm.

After his first son's death, Chuvalo said in a television interview, "It's like everything you breathe in is grief ... [and] you just can't believe your son is dead" (Canadian Broadcasting Corporation 1995). Amazingly, Chuvalo has been very public about his extreme personal grief. He has dedicated much of his life since to talking about the perils of drug use, especially to children.[1]

A Brief History of Opiates
"The poppy that brings sleep"

For the past 3,000 years, humans have been harvesting a particular plant in more or less the same way, and its uses have remained more or less the same. The plant is called *Papaver somniferum*—the opium poppy. Its Latin name means "the poppy that brings sleep." While there are many other

A Short Glossary of Terms

analgesics. Substances that block the experience of pain.

codeine. An active ingredient in opium that is less powerful than morphine.

heroin. A semi-synthetic derivative of morphine.

morphine. The major active ingredient in opium.

narcotics. All substances that belong to the opiate or opioid families, though sometimes used (incorrectly) to refer to all illicit drugs.

opiate derivatives. See *semi-synthetic opioids*.

opiates. Ingredients and derivatives of opium, such as morphine, codeine, and thebaine.

opioids. Synthetic substances that produce opiate-like effects; also the term for the drug class that includes opiates as well as synthetic and semi-synthetic opioids.

opium. The resin that is extracted from the seed pod of a particular species of poppy (*Papaver somniferum*).

semi-synthetic opioids. Drugs composed of both synthetic and naturally occurring opioids; examples include heroin, hydromorphone (trade name Dilaudid), oxymorphone (Numorphan, Opana), oxycodone (Percodan, Percoset), and hydrocodone (Hycodan, Vicodin).

synthetic opioids. Drugs with similar properties to opiates, synthesized in laboratories; examples include methadone, meperidine (Demerol), propoxyphene (Darvon), and buprenorphine.

thebaine. An active ingredient in opium.

variations of the poppy plant, only this one type yields opium. Opium poppies grow to a height of three to four feet and produce flowers that are four to five inches in diameter. Below those flowers, a seed pod develops; after the petals have fallen off, if small incisions are made in the sides of the seed pod, a white discharge oozes. If left overnight to dry, the liquid discharge will partially evaporate into a syrup and change to a brownish colour. That product is called opium.

Evidence of peoples' harvesting of opium goes back to the late Bronze Age. The Egyptians, the Greeks, and the Arabs all knew about its medicinal powers. The Arabs introduced opium to Western Europe during the Crusades in the eleventh and twelfth centuries, and if there was a substance that served as a panacea in many of these early societies, it was opium. The interest in obtaining access to opium and finding new supplies was considerable. For example, before Christopher Columbus sailed west from Europe in the fifteenth century on his voyage of discovery, King Ferdinand and Queen Isabella of Spain instructed him to seek out and bring back opium, among other goods (Booth 1996).

In the sixteenth century, Paracelsus, a physician who pioneered the use of minerals and chemicals in medicine, used tincture of opium as the core ingredient in a concoction he called laudanum (a Latin word meaning "deserving praise"). Laudanum, a liquid preparation containing wine and spices to disguise opium's bitter taste, endured as one of the most accessible forms of pain medication for over 300 years, until modern pharmacology developed new ways of manufacturing opiates and other medicines. In addition to pain relief, laudanum was used in the treatment of a variety of physical afflictions, as well as for mental illness (Brands, Sproule, and Brands 1998).

Opium wars of the 1800s

The story of opiate use can be likened to a war, one that breaks out within the person who falls into addiction. Yet this is not the only battleground on which control over opium has been fought. In the 1830s and 1840s the "opium wars" between Britain and China were declared when Britain's mercantile interests came into conflict with the Chinese government. At that time China wanted to put strong limits on the sale and use of opium, but this posed a threat to the enormous profits reaped by the British, who were importing opium from India into China. This "trade dispute" led to two wars: one lasting from 1839 to 1842, the other from 1856 to 1860. China lost on both occasions, and that country's attempts to assert its rights by restricting trade with the West and constructing its own laws limiting drug use failed. Defeated militarily, China

Samuel's Story

Booth (1996) describes a case of opiate dependence in a man who lived over 200 years ago. Born in England in 1772, Samuel had health problems in childhood, including fever and jaundice. Before the age of 10, he was given laudanum on several occasions. As a university student, he was diagnosed with rheumatism, and over the next several years used laudanum for relief from neuralgia, dysentery, and toothache. Before the age of 30, Samuel was taking laudanum and brandy regularly for relief from acute back pain.

Samuel realized that he was addicted and wanted to break his habit, so he left England and sailed to Malta. However, the change of geography did little to help him overcome his dependence. Although the stereotype is that people addicted to opiates attempt to conceal and deny their dependency, Samuel talked about it openly with friends. He referred to his addiction as an affliction about which he was ashamed, but he needed the drug to manage his chronic health problems. The extent of his physical dependence was such that where 1,000 drops of laudanum would be fatal to a first time user, Samuel's tolerance allowed him to use 20,000 drops per day (Booth 1996).

Samuel earned much of his living by giving public lectures. The mix of ill health and opiate addiction meant that he performed poorly or had to cancel scheduled lectures, ultimately wrecking his career as a public speaker. Samuel sought medical assistance on a number of occasions, usually leading to reduced consumption but never complete abstinence.

However, there was another side to Samuel's laudanum use. He told his brother that from the very beginning, "Laudanum gave me repose, not sleep ... [and] how divine that repose is, what a spot of enchantment, a green spot of fountains and flowers and trees in the very heart of a waste of sands" (Booth 1996, 42). Drug use shaped, for better and for worse, Samuel Taylor Coleridge's life as an artist, a writer, and a poet.

The remarkable talent of Samuel Taylor Coleridge drew on both the painful and the sublime aspects of his substance use, communicating vividly, in the most sensual and potent language, human experiences set in fantastical landscapes:

> In Xanadu did Kubla Khan
> A stately pleasure-dome decree:
> Where Alph, the sacred river, ran
> Through caverns measureless to man
> Down to a sunless sea.
> So twice five miles of fertile ground
> With walls and towers were girdled round:
> And there were gardens bright with sinuous rills,
> Where blossomed many an incense-bearing tree;
> And here were forests ancient as the hills,
> Enfolding sunny spots of greenery.
> (Coleridge, "Kubla Khan")

While it is important not to attribute Coleridge's art solely to his drug use, the evidence is clear that laudanum was an inspiration for much of his writing. However, Coleridge himself viewed his addiction as a scourge, and near death wrote a plea that "a full and unqualified narrative of my wretchedness, and of its guilty cause, may be made public, that at least some little good may be effected by the direful example" (Booth 1996, 45). Samuel's story characterizes the ironic drama of addiction that has been played out over and over in different variations. On one hand, there is the need to deal with pain and distress. On the other, there is the ecstatic relief that the user feels, as he or she discovers the transporting powers of opiates, from abject torment to sublime satiation.

Coleridge's is one story in a larger narrative about drugs and artistic creativity that has created a mythology about opiates that informs popular perception, imagination, and attitudes today. The list of nineteenth-century authors who used opium includes Elizabeth Barrett Browning, Wilkie Collins, Sir Walter Scott, Thomas De Quincey, Baudelaire, Berlioz, Rimbaud, and Edgar Allan Poe.

was forced to sign treaties that opened its ports to British trade.

Opium was important to the British because it was the primary commodity traded with the Chinese in exchange for that most desired product, on which the good humour of the British Empire rested—tea (Booth 1996). Now, 150 years later, circumstances are reversed: Britain and other Western countries are preoccupied with their ineffective control and prohibition of global trafficking in illegal drugs, mainly heroin and cocaine, exported from Asia and Latin America.

As is the case with the histories of many drugs (both legal and illegal), the story of opium's role across many societies over thousands of years is as much about political, military, and economic factors as it is about medicinal applications. The power of this substance to produce effects that human beings find so desirable has entangled it in politics, conflict, trade, and commerce.

From opiates to opioids

Today, it is hard to believe there once was a time—and not so long ago—when opium, morphine, heroin, and cocaine were legal drugs, widely available as a variety of "patent medicines." Up until the early twentieth century, many of these patent medicines were variations on Paracelsus's laudanum, advertised to soothe a variety of complaints including babies' teething pains, menstrual cramps, diarrhea, yellow fever, meningitis, colds, and cardiac disease. Until as recently as the 1930s it was fairly common in North America to treat ailments of the body and mind with these drugs. But if drinking opium-based elixirs was actively marketed, one form of use had become demonized: smoking opium.

The earliest Chinese immigrants to Canada came in the mid-to-late 1800s to find employment as labourers on the construction of the Canadian Pacific Railway, working in some of the most adverse conditions of the time. At that time opium was legal in Canada; however, the "opium den" soon emerged in the popular imagination as a degenerate and ruinous world, even as opium-based patent medicines were commonly used in the social mainstream.

The themes of racism, prejudice, and stereotypes are crucial ingredients in the formation of social attitudes towards particular substances and particular ways of consuming drugs (Giffen, Endicott, and Lambert 1991; Booth 1996; Heyman 2009). Before long, racial stereotyping had given opium smoking a stigma that was never applied to other forms of opium consumption by Canadians of European extraction. These issues are not restricted to opium, but nowhere is the importance of these social phenomena more evident than in the history of opium and its pharmaceutical derivatives.

The reliance on tincture of opium—Paracelsus's laudanum—lasted until the early nineteenth century, when a new stage of pharmacological progress was ushered in: a German technician isolated a substance in raw opium that he called morphine, named after Morpheus, the Greek god of sleep and dreams. Morphine turned out to be the active ingredient in opium. It is ten times more potent but only a tenth the weight of raw opium. Subsequent research led to the identification of codeine and over 20 more products contained in opium. When morphine went into commercial pharmaceutical production, the modern age of opioids had begun. The growth of pharmacology (the scientific study of drugs) and of the pharmaceutical industry have been essential in the development of opioid drugs up to the present day.

The modern scene

A major technological advance in 1856 set the stage for the aggressive use of opioids in humanity's quest to remediate pain and suffering: the invention of the hypodermic needle. As a result, a whole new realm of possibilities opened to medical science. Drugs could now be directly injected into tissue, muscle, and blood, dramatically accelerating the delivery and action of various medications. Many advances in medicine, anesthesia, disease control, diagnostics, treatment of both acute and chronic illness, and pain control have been the direct result of this remarkably recent medical technology that we now take for granted. It is hard to imagine where medicine would be today without the hypodermic needle.

The combination of the pharmaceutical production of powerful drugs and the discovery of how to deliver them in a dramatic fashion (injection into tissue and vein) made it possible for the modern era of pharmacology to develop, and develop it did. This growth also spurred a parallel rise in rates of abuse and dependence. The first significant sign of these new troubles with drugs occurred on the military battlegrounds of the nineteenth century. The pain of battlefield injuries could now be treated by injections of morphine, carried by soldiers (along with a syringe) in their battlefield kits. Although morphine was important in providing immediate relief for acute pain, injectable morphine led to high rates of addiction among returning soldiers. In fact, in the years following the American Civil War, morphine addiction came to be referred to as "the soldiers' disease" (Booth 1996).

One theme that appears over and over in the history of pharmaceutical innovation is the search for new drugs that will match or exceed the benefits of previous drugs—but with fewer side effects. In the nineteenth century, pharmaceutical companies, with increasing public and medical awareness of the addictive liabilities of morphine, realized the commercial potential if they could create a product that had the analgesic power of morphine without the downside. That pursuit led German pharmaceutical company Bayer (the maker of Aspirin) to market a new medication they claimed would fulfill that promise.

The new opioid—diacetylmorphine, a semi-synthetic opium derivative—was actually three times more potent than morphine, but, Bayer claimed, free of its dependence-producing qualities. Bayer introduced its new drug in 1895, and marketed diacetylmorphine under the trade name "heroin." Whatever initial research had led to Bayer's confident assertion that here was a powerful painkilling medication without addictive risk, it quickly became clear that heroin's appetitive powers—and consequently its addictive potential—actually exceeded that of morphine. By the 1920s, most governments throughout the world had passed laws making heroin, except in extreme circumstances, an illegal drug—illegal to produce, to trade, and to use. That has remained heroin's fate today, but it has not caused heroin to disappear.

As a desired intoxicant, heroin has perhaps come to represent in Western culture the archetypal substance of addiction. Many of the attitudes, values, and beliefs that inform social perceptions of addiction today are based on the lore associated with heroin, with notions of the "rush," the "high," and "the junkie" that accompany them.

Perversely, heroin's status as a forbidden fruit with remarkable psychoactive effects made it the perfect product for illegal trade. This combination—an appealing "fruit" that is legally forbidden—forms an irresistible logic for illegal activity. The low costs to produce heroin and the high price it yields when sold on the streets of cities around the world combine to ensure that there are people who will take the risk to produce it, smuggle it, and sell it. Heroin's compact size and the knowledge that on the street it yields a price as high as fifty times the production costs have continued to motivate people to find users who will pay what it takes to obtain the drug.

If heroin is the archetypal illicit drug forming the imagery that has shaped social perceptions and drug laws for over a hundred years, it is worth noting that the percentage of people in Canada reporting heroin use even once in their lifetimes is very low—around 0.9 percent (Adlaf, Begin, and Sawka 2005). As an issue, heroin is outside the orbit of most people's direct experience. However, close to one in three people who use heroin becomes dependent, at least for a period of time. That is over three times the rate of dependency among alcohol users, and about the same "capture" rate as cocaine. (As was mentioned in Chapter 3, tobacco produces the highest rates of dependency among users, reaching 80 percent—so that four in five smokers meet dependence criteria, as defined by the *DSM*.)

Today there is a wide variety of drugs that are derived from opium (opiates), or that have opiate-like properties and are synthesized in pharmaceutical laboratories (opioids). Like heroin, many opioids have been marketed for their superior capacity to relieve pain and their lower addictive liability. And, like heroin, these promises have not been uniformly borne out.

Canada's "Wild West" Drug Scene
An Interview with Donald MacPherson

Few people have as grounded an understanding of the drug scene in Vancouver and the lower mainland of British Columbia than Donald MacPherson, who is the drug policy coordinator for the Community Services Department of the City of Vancouver. We had the opportunity to interview him in June 2009.

MacPherson points out that there were legal opium factories in BC into the early 1900s. He sees a line of persistent and serious heroin use in the population of Vancouver and other communities on the coast that continues today:

> In 1952 a special Senate Committee was set up to investigate why Vancouver had at that time a larger "drug problem" than other Canadian cities. Of course the committee really didn't come up with any conclusions on this. Bruce Alexander's theory is that Vancouver is "Terminal City" and is inhabited by those who are dislocated from the places they originally came from (2001). The Le Dain Commission also noted the inordinate number of injection drug users in Vancouver, I think stating that in 1972 there were 6,000 injection drug users in the country and 4,000 of them were on the west coast. So you have a historical relationship to opioids and a market that has been in existence for many years.
>
> In 2000, global markets changed, heroin prices plummeted, and purity went up. One of the unique aspects of the Vancouver scene is that there was a crisis—not just a drug scare as has been used for many years to mobilize communities and authorities—but a real crisis. People were dropping dead in great numbers, and the Chief Coroner of the province responded with an inquiry that led to some very good recommendations that were basically ignored for many years. On top of that, the drug market expanded into the downtown eastside, an area of that was being abandoned by the business community. The combination of public health problems and increased drug-related criminality drove the urgency of developing a response. Another unique issue was the HIV epidemic among injection drug users, which became another crisis. Also unique was that we had a poet by the name of Bud Osborn who came on the Vancouver Richmond Health Board in 1997, and he had a great deal to do with the public health emergency being declared.

We asked MacPherson about the relationship between heroin and prescription opioids, and he had a very clear answer:

> Heroin is clearly the drug of choice among people who use Vancouver's supervised injection facility, with cocaine being a close second. From my perspective it appears that heroin, cocaine, crack cocaine, and methamphetamine continue to be more popular than the prescription drugs. This probably has to do with supply routes, who is in the business (for example, methamphetamine is manufactured here in BC), and perhaps no one has yet cultivated the market for prescription drugs.

Vancouver has taken unique steps to deal with its inner city drug problems, including electing a city government on a harm reduction drug policy platform, and the creation of innovations that are unique in the Canadian context, including a safe injection site and a heroin substitution trial. Vancouver was also the first city in Canada to develop its own drug policy. MacPherson notes that the city's current focus is on drug addiction and social disadvantage:

> Because of the increase in homelessness between 2001 and now, the overarching theme that is top of mind is supportive housing. So, all of the discussion about harm reduction and treatment ends up being framed as connected to supportive housing. Therefore the specific discussion about how many injection sites do we need, or how many more treatment beds, etc., is couched within the framework of "where will people live?" The danger with this is that we may be focusing too much on the homeless population and not considering the many more individuals at risk of homelessness who are not well-served by health and social services. Of course, the advantage of this focus is that we acknowledge the primacy of housing as a basis for self-determination. Without stable housing, all other interventions are limited to a great extent.

A strong public-health sensibility informs these observations. In addition to addressing drug use in marginalized neighbourhoods like the downtown eastside of Vancouver, there needs to be parallel attention to the less dramatic but equally serious effects of substance abuse in mainstream Canadian society.

Becoming Addicted

Opioids and the body

Opioid intoxication produces a state of euphoria that is powerfully reinforcing. A brief, euphoric "rush" is followed by a tranquil and drowsy state ("being on the nod") that typically lasts for three to four hours. Opioids possess appetitive powers that have been immortalized in poetry, prose, music, fashion, and film. Their allure is revealed in the language that people use to describe their intense and pleasurable psychoactive effects:

The "rush"
"I'll die young, but it's like kissing God."(Lenny Bruce, died in 1966 of a morphine overdose)

"People think it's all about misery and desperation and death and all that shite, which is not to be ignored, but what they forget is the pleasure of it. Otherwise we wouldn't do it. After all, we're not fucking stupid. At least, we're not that fucking stupid. Take the best orgasm you ever had, multiply it by a thousand and you're still nowhere near it." (Renton, a character in the film *Trainspotting* [2004. DVD directed by Danny Boyle. New York: Miramax.])

The "high"
"Using heroin becomes the shortest, most efficient route from pain to numbness and then back again. (It's not called 'a fix' for nothing.) Addiction manages to translate big insoluble problems into one that can be cured—for a while." (Jackson 2002, 298)

"The nearest I can come to explaining to someone who doesn't really take illegal drugs the unrecapturable specialness of your first heroin high is to invoke the deep satisfaction of your first cup of coffee in the morning. Your subsequent coffees may be pleasant enough, but they're all marred by not being the first. And heroin use is one of the indisputable cases where the good old days really were the good old day." (Marlowe 1999, 9)

Feeling "straight"

"Heroin can promote concentration; an artist friend brags he can draw for six hours straight on dope, and I found myself able to sit still and work on my writing much more easily." (Marlowe 1999, 184)

"So cozy is heroin's aura of enlightenment, so heated the drug's initial passage through your bloodstream, that you think of it as vaguely warm." (Marlowe 1999, 286)

Feeling "sick"

"Life on heroin doesn't lend itself to lots of animated facial expressions. Your lows are higher and—because of the physical annoyances of addiction—your highs are lower. There are not a lot of surprises, which is often the point; your rhythms are defined by the familiar and predictable arc of the drug's breakdown in your body, rather than the hazards of time. It is absence of pain that you are looking for, but absence of living that you get. Your last few years of use are like suspended time, and this absence of living tells on your face, and, alas, on your heart." (Marlowe 1999, 10–11)

"The downside of coming off junk was that I knew I would need to mix with my friends again in a state of full consciousness. It was awful: they reminded me so much of myself I could hardly bear to look at them." (Renton in *Trainspotting* [2004. DVD direced by Danny Boyle. New York: Miramax.])

Each person's response to taking opioids is affected by a number of factors. The purity and quantity (dose) of the drug is obviously important, as is the degree of tolerance the person has (tolerance is determined by the amount of opioids the person has been using on a regular basis). Individual variation in the effects of opioids is also a product of variability in metabolization (breakdown) of the drug by specific enzymes in the liver. The activity of these enzymes is genetically determined.

Another important factor in the subjective effects of opioids is the route of administration. Intravenous injection will lead to a "rush" or euphoric surge, as the drug reaches the brain almost immediately. Heroin users often compare the initial rush of injecting the drug to sexual orgasm, but stronger and longer-lasting. Smoking heroin can produce the same dramatic effect; however, much of the drug is wasted in combustion, so smoking is a less efficient and more expensive way to administer a dose. Snorting or injecting opioids into muscle results in a slower onset of drug effects and a less intense "high." Taking the drug orally means the slowest onset of drug effects and is the least reinforcing mode of administration.

Opioids cause pupil constriction in the eyes, making "pinpoint pupils" a common diagnostic sign. Other effects of opioid use include dry mouth, runny nose, flushed skin, and constipation (the latter because these drugs slow down activity in the digestive tract). People who have low tolerance to heroin or other opioids, or who take a higher than usual dose, tend to experience nausea, and many users report itchy skin and a heavy feeling in their arms and legs (Kahan and Wilson 2002). More worrisome is the way that high doses can depress breathing. Respiratory failure is the most frequent cause of death in opioid overdoses (Brands, Sproule, and Brands 1998).

Using enough opioids to become intoxicated is referred to as getting high or going "on the nod." Prolonged use may lead to weight loss, frequent "nodding off," drowsiness, lethargy, and slurred speech. Injection drug users are at risk of collapsed and scarred veins, abscesses, bacterial infections, pulmonary difficulties, liver and kidney disease, and subacute endocarditis (inflammation of the lining of the heart). Sharing needles can lead to HIV infection, and, even more common among intravenous drug users, hepatitis B and C, as well as other blood borne diseases. Risky sexual behaviour while under the influence of opioids or other drugs is another factor in disease transmission (Kahan and Wilson 2002). Although opioids tend to mute sexual appetite, especially in men, women who have had traumatic experiences with sexual intimacy may find intoxication disinhibiting, so that they can allow, tolerate, or even enjoy sex.

Withdrawal is the negative side of opioid dependence, with dramatic implications for the body and the subjective experience of the user. Withdrawal symptoms are generally rebound processes, where the opposite effects of intoxication manifest themselves as the body attempts to find a new balance or homeostasis. For example, since opioids slow down the digestive process to the point of constipation, withdrawal leads to digestive upset and diarrhea. Other symptoms of opioid withdrawal include vomiting, sweats, chills, cramps, muscle and bone pain, loss of appetite, insomnia, and depressed mood. Cravings are part of the process, and the one solution to the torments of drug withdrawal that will bring immediate relief is a return to drug use. This means that resumption of use is a compelling option for anyone who is not prepared for the challenges of withdrawal, particularly if it involves going "cold turkey"—abruptly ceasing use (Brands, Spoule, and Brands 1998; Dziegielewski 2005).

The time of onset for withdrawal symptoms relates to the half-life of the particular drug, with heroin having the shortest half-life and most pharmaceuticals the longest. In heroin, withdrawal symptoms start within hours of the last dose, peak within 24 to 72 hours, and take about one week for physical withdrawal symptoms to resolve.

Opioids and the brain

Recent advances in neurobiology have led to a more sophisticated understanding of how opioids work in the brain

Where Does the Expression "Cold Turkey" Come From?

"Quitting cold turkey" is a common expression for a person's decision to abruptly stop using a particular drug or quitting several drugs at the same time. A possible origin for this term is the *cutis anserina* (the medical term for "goose flesh" or "goose bumps" on the skin) experienced by people in opioid withdrawal: goose flesh looks similar to the plucked skin of an uncooked (cold) turkey.

than was ever available before. It appears that all of the rewarding experiences that humans have originate in a central brain pathway involving the prefrontal cortex, the nucleus accumbens, the ventral tegmental area, and the amygdala, collectively known as the brain's reward system. The motor memory circuit involves different parts of this central brain pathway, and associates certain stimuli ("triggers") with past rewards.

Scientists continue to develop more comprehensive models of the neurobehavioural basis of compulsive drug taking (WHO 2004b; Kalivas and Volkow 2005). Initial drug use produces a powerfully rewarding experience, which creates "incentive sensitization," making the drug more attractive to the user. The repeated pairing of pleasurable effects with the drug and the setting in which it is administered leads to drug-associated stimuli gaining control over behaviour. This learning is posited as the basis of ongoing drug cravings and the increased likelihood of further drug use despite negative consequences.

The repeated administration of dependence-forming drugs alters the circuitry of the brain so that other positive experiences or natural rewards (such as food or sex) no longer have the same potency, and the brain itself becomes biased towards, preferential to, and finally dependent on the rush and the high of drug use (Kalivas and Volkow 2005). These internal processes occur within the context of social and environmental factors that condition and trigger drug urges and substance use behaviour. Even when the focus is on neurobiology, the psychosocial context is essential in developing an effective understanding of the ways that drug addiction develops.

Thus, addiction is not solely a brain disease. The mapping of the geography of the brain and the processes that occur under varying conditions are helping us to understand not just the brain itself, but the ways that environment, experience, genetics, and biology interactively shape human behaviour and subjectivity.

Advances in neurobiology have brought parallel advances in pharmaceutical interventions to prevent, interrupt, or resolve processes of addiction in the brain. Certain medications have been shown to dampen or even eliminate the rewarding aspects of drug use, while others can, conversely, increase the likelihood that drug use will occur. There are already interventions in the treatment of opioid dependence that bear witness to these "brave new world" possibilities.

Opioids inside and out

The human brain is structured to reinforce and reward behaviours associated with survival of the human species, such as attention, motivation, learning, eating, drinking, and procreation. Pleasurable and rewarding experiences activate neurotransmitters in a common brain pathway (the mesolimbic pathway), stimulating the release of naturally occurring, or *endogenous*, chemicals into our brains. Among these neurochemicals associated with subjective feelings of reward and pleasure are endogenous opioids. There are three specific types of endogenous opioids in the brain—endorphins, enkephalins, and dynorphin—but all do essentially the same thing. Endogenous opioids work by binding to specific opioid receptor sites in the brain, activating systems of reward and reinforcement.

The brain, however, does not differentiate between *endogenous* opioids (those naturally occurring in the brain) and *exogenous* opioids (opioid drugs such as heroin, morphine, and codeine). Ingesting opioid drugs stimulates the same opioid receptors sites as endogenous opioids, and produces the analgesic (painkilling) effects so important in pain management, as well as the euphoric effects that come with drug abuse. Therapeutic doses provide just the right dose to blunt or remove pain, while intoxication involves using more of the drug to achieve a psychoactive effect.

Overdose happens when so much of the drug is actively present in the bloodstream and the brain that it overwhelms the brain's opioid receptors. Because these drugs also act on sites in the brain that control respiration, too high a dose results in a signal to the body to stop breathing. Without intervention, the person will die. Understanding these processes has allowed medical science to develop ways of interrupting overdose situations and save lives. Researchers have developed medications, such as *naloxone*, that push the exogenous opioids off the brain's opioid receptor sites and replace them with the new drug, but with no psychoactive effects.

To explain further, opioids are called *agonist* drugs because of their ability to bind to opioid receptors in the brain. There is another class of drugs called opioid *antagonists* that also bind to opioid receptors, but have no psychoactive effects. Antagonists override the pain-killing and intoxicating potential of agonist opioids by displacing the heroin (or morphine, codeine, etc.) from the receptor sites. In other words, antagonist drugs have a high *affinity* (preference) for the opioid receptors in the brain, but they have no subjectively rewarding effects. Brain receptor sites "prefer" some of these antagonist drugs over agonist opioids.

For example, in a heroin overdose, when the person is administered the commonly used opioid antagonist naloxone, the naloxone displaces the heroin on the opioid receptors in the brain. This allows the receptors to start doing their job again, sending the messages telling the lungs to breathe. Note that the opioid agonist, heroin, is still in the body; it is just that naloxone prevents heroin from being able to access the opioid receptors. Gradually, if the person maintains a steady dose of naloxone, the heroin circulating in the bloodstream will be metabolized by the liver and the overdose risk will subside. It is important to note that opioid antagonists like naloxone do not eliminate opioid agonists such as heroin, morphine or codeine; they just block their ability to act on the brain by occupying the opiate receptor sites.

Marco's story

Marco is the son of Portuguese immigrants who settled in Vancouver shortly before he was born. Marco and his younger brother Jake had a troubled childhood, with a father who was verbally abusive and persistently negative. Marco's dad ridiculed his interest in art and music, and was convinced that Marco would never do anything productive with his life. In their late teens, Marco and Jake started smoking, drinking, and occasionally using cannabis. The year that Marco turned 22 and his brother turned 20, they were introduced to heroin, and Marco said afterwards that he was "instantly hooked."

On heroin, Marco felt content, centred, and strangely able to focus, particularly on his music. He was becoming a very proficient guitar player and was often invited to play in bars with established musicians. Jake also became addicted to heroin, and he and Marco used the drug together. However, Marco's growing dependency on heroin began to take a toll, particularly because of the variable quality, unpredictable supply, and high cost to buy the drug for what quickly became a daily habit. Marco had several arrests by the time he was 30.

In his mid-30s, Marco agreed to enter methadone treatment, which he found to be a humiliating experience and a sign that he had really lost control of his life. Jake also tried to stay in treatment, but neither brother ever settled into a stable pattern of care. The lure of heroin caused them to be terminated from their methadone program, or they just never bothered to stick with it.

Marco is now nearly 50, and has experienced considerable misfortune and tragedy in his life. Three years ago, Marco discovered Jake's body in the garage. He had hanged himself. Since then, Marco has had flashbacks and invasive thoughts related to Jake's suicide. He has become even more disorganized in his drug use and has great difficulty engaging in care even when it is offered.

Marco is currently living with his aging mother, who is unwell. Marco dreams of a day when heroin is legal and he can feel truly well again. In the meantime, he is an opportunistic user of opiates. He is dependent on social assistance. He is demoralized, and is showing symptoms of post-traumatic stress related to discovering his dead brother.

Marco's story is not uncommon in its trajectory of addiction and the accompanying constellation of problems and impacts. His history demonstrates some of the complexities of treatment and recovery: a difficult childhood, past trauma, problems with money and housing, legal problems, limited social and family support, lost dreams, and a marginalized and stigmatized lifestyle. For Marco, getting help must involve more than just treatment for heroin dependence, yet few programs and resources are equipped to deal with a host of issues in an integrated and holistic way.

Sometimes, however, change can occur opportunistically and as a result of a sudden life crisis. Marco was using heroin with some friends in a back alley when he miscalculated the amount he was injecting and lost consciousness. Marco's friends saw what was happening, and one of them actually started to give him CPR. Another called "911," and then both friends left the scene when they heard the ambulance approaching. (Marco's friends wanted to make sure Marco was going to be okay, but they also wanted to stay out of trouble with the law.) Paramedics answering the call gave Marco an injection of naloxone which immediately resuscitated him and also induced active opioid withdrawal. Naloxone ended up saving Marco's life.

Marco was taken to the emergency department and observed for the rest of the night until his body was clear of heroin and he was stabilized. The ER doctor connected Marco with a social worker from the hospital's addiction program and Marco agreed to come back for an outpatient appointment a day later. Marco was fortunate that his friends called for help before leaving the scene—many times other drug users are too concerned about legal consequences to call for medical help. The social worker also helped save Marco's life: a former drug user himself, he refused to give up on Marco. The social worker's support and advocacy became the key to Marco accessing—and sticking with—the care and treatment he needed.

Prevalence of Opioid Use in Canada

Jill is a 32-year-old woman who suffers from severe migraine headaches. Over the years, her family doctor has prescribed a variety of codeine-based drugs. Migraines are a frightening, disabling, and overpowering experience that has disrupted Jill's life. She often spends whole days in the dark because her eyes are so sensitive to light. Although the pain medication is effective, it takes time to work and the whole experience leaves Jill exhausted and fearing the next episode. In the past few months, Jill has begun taking medication even before she has a migraine in an attempt to prevent an attack. Gradually she has became tolerant to the drugs, and has been seeing a second doctor who is prescribing the same medications as her first doctor, without either physician knowing Jill is "double-doctoring."

Jill's story illustrates the less-recognized side of opioid abuse and dependence. As primary as heroin has become in shaping social attitudes and beliefs about drug abuse, less than 1 percent of Canadians will use the drug even once during their lifetimes (Adlaf, Begin, and Sawka 2005). If heroin is the drug that has shaped our knowledge and perception of opioid abuse in the past, the present and future require at least as informed an understanding of pharmaceutical opioids, which are almost exclusively prescribed for their pain-relieving abilities.

In their 2007 annual report, the Royal Canadian Mounted Police suggest that heroin has become an increasingly marginal form of illicit drug use in Canada (RCMP 2008). Police and research data suggest that heroin, a mainstay of the illegal drug scene in many cities in Canada, is now a major issue in only two Canadian cities, Vancouver and Montreal. In other communities heroin has been replaced by pharmaceutical opioids as the primary drug problem in the opioid group (RCMP 2008; Fischer et al. 2008).

For example, in 2007 police seized over $2.6 billion in illicit drugs (estimated street value), of which $20 million was heroin and $4.4 million was opium. Those figures represent less than 1 percent of all illegal drugs seized during that year in Canada. Indeed, cannabis accounts for over 90 percent of all illegal drugs taken by police: this in spite of the fact that the unit value of a gram of heroin was estimated to be $180, while cannabis is estimated at $10 per gram. In the interdiction of illegal drugs, heroin and opium are hardly on the radar (RCMP 2008).

It is estimated that there are 125,000 injection drug users in Canada, primarily using heroin and cocaine (Fischer, Rehm, et al. 2006). A recent report by Popova and colleagues (2009) estimates the number of heroin users in Canada at 37,000, with slightly more than half of them using only heroin, and the rest using heroin plus pharmaceutical opioids. Yet within this small segment of the population, the health impacts are severe: high crime, morbidity, and mortality. The death rate among illicit opioid users ranges from 1 to 3 percent yearly (Fischer, Firestone Cruz, and Rehm 2006). In 2003, there were 958 overdose deaths in Canada, 225 of which were women (Popova et al. 2009).

As difficult as it is to estimate heroin's prevalence, determining the numbers who abuse pharmaceutical opioids is even harder, as researchers and law enforcement are only beginning to become aware of the severity of pharmaceutical opioid abuse. Recently, Popova and colleagues (2009) looked at this question using data estimation methods from other jurisdictions. The ratio of non-medical prescription opioid users to heroin users is estimated to be about 14:1 at the lower limit, and about 40:1 at the upper limit. That means that for every heroin user, there are from 14 to 40 people abusing pharmaceutical opioids in Canada. In terms of actual numbers, anywhere from 914,000 to roughly 3.3 million Canadians abuse prescription opioids (Popova et al. 2009).

Canada: An opioid-rich environment

Canadians are among the highest consumers of opioids in the world. Canada has been termed an "opioid-rich environment," "the world's top per capita consumer of a number of opioids" (Fischer, Rehm, et al. 2006, 1387). The high numbers of Canadians abusing pharmaceutical opioids can be partly accounted for by the relative ease by which these drugs can be acquired. Codeine, for example, is available over the counter in compounds such as 222 or Tylenol with codeine. In contrast, drugs containing codeine require a prescription in the US and many other Western countries. Also, opioids are the most widely prescribed pain medications. Any time that a psychoactive drug is easily accessible, it is more liable to recreational use and abuse.

There are other reasons besides easier access that account for why prescription opioid abuse has surpassed heroin use in Canada. Pharmaceutical opioids have consistent and rigorous quality controls as would be expected of any pharmaceutical product. Taking a prescription opioid means there is good reliability in the dose amount. Illicit drugs such as heroin are variable in quality, and the correct dose can be hard to determine. Also, these drugs are restricted, not illegal, and the legal penalties for improper use of prescription opioids tend not to be as severe as those attached to illegal street drugs.

The vocabulary of opioid abuse has gone well beyond opium, morphine, and heroin to include Demerol, Dilaudid, OxyContin, Percoset, Percodan, Tylenol 3 and 4, and MS Contin, among others. Today we know more about how to use opioids, how they work in the body and the brain, and how to produce new and more targeted drug compounds, with more choices available to address the problems of acute and chronic pain. A comprehensive description of every pharmaceutical opioid available in Canada would fill this book on its own; however, the following summary covers some of the main medications that are prescribed and abused in Canada.

Demerol is a trade name containing pethidine, a short-acting analgesic. This drug is less commonly prescribed nowadays due to its short half-life and more serious side effect profile compared with other opioid medications. Dilaudid is a trade name for hydromorphone (also called Hydromorph Contin in Canada), a semi-synthetic opioid derived from morphine. It is prescribed for acute and chronic pain.

OxyContin is a trade name for a time-release version of the generic drug *oxycodone*. Oxycodone is a semi-synthetic opioid that is chemically similar to morphine and codeine, and is the main active drug in many opioid medications, including Percoset (oxycodone and acetaminophen) and Percodan (oxycodone and aspirin). OxyContin tablets are coated so that the drug is absorbed slowly and steadily over 12 hours. It is indicated for moderate to severe pain, but crushing and snorting or injecting the tablets produces a rush and a high similar to heroin. Note that OxyContin is often confused with MS Contin, an analgesic with a similar time release formulation but containing morphine sulphate as the primary active ingredient.

Tylenol No. 3 is a combination of acetaminophen, codeine sulphate, and caffeine, and is prescribed for mild to moderate pain or cough. Tylenol No. 4, prescribed less often, contains acetaminophen and a higher dose of codeine. Codeine is the common name for methylmorphine and is synthesized from morphine (but codeine is much less potent, has fewer and less severe withdrawal symptoms, and a lower abuse liability than other opioids like oxycodone and hydromorphone). In Canada, medications containing codeine can be sold without a prescription in pharmacies, but only in preparations with at least two other active ingredients—for example, codeine plus acetaminophen (an analgesic) and caffeine (a stimulant used to offset the drowsiness that can accompany codeine).

Over-the-counter medications containing codeine are sometimes used by people who are dependent on stronger opioids to stave off withdrawal. Because opioid-dependent people generally have quite high tolerance, large amounts of these low-dose codeine medications are typically needed (for example, 10 to 20 Tylenol No. 1 tablets or even more). Aside from possible opioid overdose, such high doses of acetaminophen (one of the other active ingredients in Tylenol No. 1) can cause severe liver damage. Some people crush and inject the pills; however, this also causes serious problems like endocarditis (infection in the lining of the heart valve), phlebitis (inflammation of the vein), blocked or collapsed veins, abscesses at the injection site, and sepsis (whole-body inflammation), among other risks. These problems are also associated with injection drug abuse more generally.

Despite the many opioid medications on the market, an "addiction-proof" drug that will effectively treat pain remains elusive. Some pharmaceutical companies have been criticized for minimizing evidence of the addictive liability of new drugs.

Cottonland: A Community Overdoses on Oxycodone

Photojournalist Nance Ackerman was sent by the *Toronto Star* on assignment to Glace Bay, NS, where 18 people had recently died of drug overdose. The culprit was a prescription medication called OxyContin, which makes its manufacturer, Purdue Pharmaceutical, over a billion dollars every year.

Ackerman interviewed a number of people who were actively abusing OxyContin. One man, Eddie, was prescribed the drug for migraine headaches. He quickly became addicted and introduced his girlfriend, Mary, to the drug. With both parents now dependent, child protection services became involved, apprehended their children, and placed them in foster care. Ackerman decided that the situation in Glace Bay was so serious and little known that it needed to be documented. She decided to make a film about what he saw and heard, called *Cottonland*.

Eddie agreed to narrate Ackerman's documentary film, providing an entry point into the lives affected by opioid dependence in this modest city on Cape Breton Island. Glace Bay has high unemployment due to the collapse of coal mining, fishing, and steel industries over the past decade. Many people who worked in these areas developed a host of health problems, including black lung, various cancers, and chronic pain due to back and limb injuries. Medical treatment for these problems included prescription opioids, and in the context of unemployment, financial stress, and other risk factors, resulted in high rates of dependence.

When Eddie made the decision to get treatment, he found that the closest withdrawal management program was five hours away, in the city of Dartmouth. He ended up moving there, overcame his addiction and regained custody of his children. Mary also recovered from her addiction, and the family is now together again.

The juxtaposition of the personal stories that fill the foreground in this film and their social context (and its overbearing presence in the background) underlines the reality that each person has to find his or her own way out of the dilemma of addiction. The film also vividly conveys the conditions in which addiction can emerge and grow. It is a stirring demonstration of the possibility of change and renewal, even in compromised circumstances.[2]

Recently, Purdue Pharma was found guilty for understating the addictive liability and "misbranding" its long-acting pain medication MS Contin. The drug is based on a pure form of an old substance, oxycodone, formulated in a time-release tablet. Purdue Pharma encouraged the view that its new formulation rendered the drug less vulnerable to abuse. However, they were aware that crushing the tablets and snorting or injecting the powder would provide psychoactive effects on par with heroin.

The consequences of Purdue Pharma's enthusiastic promotion and marketing of MS Contin has resulted in considerable harm, including addiction and death. In a US court in 2007 the company pleaded guilty to misbranding the drug and was fined over $660 million. However, from 1995 to 2001, Purdue Pharma earned $2.8 billion in revenue from MS Contin, accounting for 90 percent of its profits at one point (*New York Times* 2007).

The promiscuous use of opioids by Canadians represents a crisis in the making. This drug class remains a fundamental strategy in the medical pain-management arsenal, yet if the primary approach continues to be prescription opioids (or "pain-killers" to the general public), the current problems we have will become entrenched and expand. These drugs are taking a toll in communities as diverse as Glace Bay, NS, Constance Lake, ON, St John's, NL, and Nanaimo, BC.

Assessing Opioid Dependence

Determining whether and to what extent a person is dependent on opioids is an important precursor to treatment planning. The results of a full clinical assessment can help to determine what types of treatments are appropriate, including which medications would be recommended to alleviate withdrawal and prevent relapse. In addition, assessment is an opportunity to actively engage a person in treatment and enhance motivation for change. Assessment is an ongoing process as opposed to a single event, given that clients' needs and goals can change over time.

In the initial assessment it is important to avoid immediately jumping in with a series of detailed, highly personal questions. Instead, it is critical to take time to connect with the person, and to convey a spirit of welcome, interest, and respect. Only within a framework of trust and understanding is it possible to proceed with the work of assessing the person's drug use and overall situation. Key assessment goals include identifying crises needing immediate attention, understanding the nature and extent of the problems the person wants to address, exploring the goals the person has in seeking help, and presenting a menu of options and resources.

The naloxone challenge

A collaborative and client-centred approach to assessing opioid dependence has not always characterized clinical approaches. In the past, opioid-dependent people were subjected to often-painful tests and procedures before they could access treatment. For example, a widely used assessment protocol in the 1980s and 1990s was the Clinical Institute Narcotic Assessment procedure, or CINA, developed in the 1980s in Toronto (Peachey and Lei 1988). The objective is to identify the severity of withdrawal symptoms that are induced by injecting the patient with the drug naloxone, an opioid antagonist. Withdrawal symptoms are measured by a trained nurse at three five-minute intervals using an 11-item questionnaire. A physician or nurse evaluates observable signs of opioid withdrawal such as sweating, tremor, restlessness, tearing (lacrimation), yawning, and piloerection (raised hairs on the skin), as well as subjective symptoms such as chills, abdominal discomfort, nausea, and pain.

Given that opioid withdrawal is so powerfully aversive, why would anyone voluntarily submit to *induced* withdrawal? In the past, methadone maintenance treatment programs for opioid dependence required the administration of the CINA in order to confirm that a patient was actually physically dependent as well as to assess the level of dependence. While the CINA is a valid tool for assessing opioid withdrawal, clinicians no longer intentionally induce a state of withdrawal in order to prove that some people get sick enough to qualify for treatment. Instead, a cluster of factors and measures are now considered in determining whether someone meets diagnostic criteria for opioid dependence. Access to treatments now has a less aversive logic than subjecting opioid users to the "naloxone challenge" as a condition for getting help.

Assessing opioid dependence: The *DSM* way

Today the assessment of problems related to opioid use is very much governed by the fourth edition of the *Diagnostic and Statistical Manual* (*DSM*) of the American Psychiatric Association (2000). The *DSM* is a called a "multiaxial" diagnostic assessment tool because various disorders are broadly grouped into five general categories, or *axes*. The *Axis I* grouping contains the major mental illnesses, including addictive disorders. *Axis II* diagnoses refer to the various personality disorders, such as borderline personality disorder and antisocial personality disorder. The other three axes are less commonly used by mental health and addiction professionals, but are important to a full understanding of *DSM*'s ambition to be a comprehensive tool encompassing mental health, medical, and psychosocial functioning. *Axis III* identifies general medical conditions, *Axis IV* focuses on psychosocial and environmental problems, and Axis V is the global assessment of a person's overall functioning.

Opioid use disorders are a subcategory of substance use disorders, which fall under Axis I in the *DSM*. Substance use disorders are classified into two levels, *abuse* (continued use despite harm) and *dependence* (progressive increases in dose taken to achieve the same effects, failed attempts to quit using, and negative psychosocial consequences). There are two states—or disorders—that are substance-induced: *intoxication* (acute, due to recent use of a psychoactive substance; or chronic, resulting from persistent use) and *withdrawal* (behavioural, cognitive, and biological destabilization due to stopping or reducing the use of a substance on which the person has become dependent). The four central concepts of abuse, dependence, intoxication, and withdrawal are strongly evident in the clinical presentation of people experiencing problems with opioid use.

It is noteworthy that in the *DSM* system of diagnostic classification, drug dependence is seen to be a syndrome that is multi-dimensional in its scope, including physical, behavioural, cognitive, and psychological dimensions (APA 2000; Dziegielewski 2005). Although the scientific literature often suggests that addiction can be reduced to a neurobiological problem, the DSM considers biological criteria alone to be insufficient in diagnosing dependence. In the DSM, tolerance and withdrawal are listed among a number of other possible diagnostic criteria for dependence, but are not themselves sufficient to make a positive diagnosis.

In addition to exhibiting signs of tolerance or withdrawal, an opioid user has to meet one or more of four other criteria in order to be diagnosed with *opioid dependence*. These criteria are (1) inability to control use, characterized by persistent desire to use, or at least one failed attempt to limit or stop use; (2) important occupational, social, or recreational activities abandoned or reduced because of drug use, or use of higher amounts or for longer periods than intended; (3) a great deal of time spent in activities related to, using, or recovering from drug effects; and (4) continued use despite psychological or physical problems that come from drug use or are aggravated by it.

The diagnosis of *opioid abuse* in the DSM reflects less severe problems than those related to opioid dependence. Having only one diagnostic criterion present qualifies a person for a diagnosis of opioid abuse. However, any previous diagnosis of substance dependence means that even one current symptom returns the person to a diagnosis of substance dependence.

A person's diagnosis determines his or her eligibility and entitlement for particular types of treatment. In the domain of opioid problems the diagnostic formulation attends to two key domains: the level of severity and the existence of other co-occurring conditions. Mild severity will generally point to a diagnosis of opioid abuse, while moderate to high severity will lead to a diagnosis of opioid dependence. Other diagnoses may also be made, including other substance use problems or other mental health, physical health, or psychosocial problems. These determinations are crucial to treatment planning and access to particular types of psychosocial and pharmacological treatments.

Too often people with opioid dependence do not access care even if they meet diagnostic criteria because of the larger and more complex set of problems with which they present. The use of multiple substances, co-occurring mental health problems, physical health issues, and social instability often make finding appropriate treatment a formidable challenge. Treatment engagement, retention, and holistic care are therefore major issues in successful interventions with opioid users.

Beyond the *DSM*: A holistic approach to assessment

Ken is a 25-year-old Cree living on a First Nations reserve in Northern Ontario. His father drank and smoked heavily, leading to his premature death at age 49 from esophageal cancer. As a teenager, Ken drifted into substance use with his peers—alcohol, gas sniffing—but had gotten away from that in the past few years. He was employed as a logger, cutting trees, when a disabling work accident occurred: a tree limb fell on him, causing a concussion and an upper back and shoulder injury that left him with chronic pain, for which he was prescribed opioids.

Over the past two years, Ken's tolerance to his medication has increased, and his pain problems have persisted. Recently Ken has been taking more than his prescribed dose so that for periods of time he can feel high and without pain. He has been crushing and snorting his pills as that gives him more of a "high," but it also means that he frequently reports to his doctor that he has lost his medication and needs a new prescription. His doctor is becoming suspicious, and Ken is finding it harder and harder to get the drugs that he needs.

Ken's mother suggested that he receive teachings from a Cree Elder, but Ken has felt disconnected from his culture and uncomfortable with traditional healing approaches. In desperation, Ken decides to go for an assessment at an addiction treatment centre. He isn't sure what they can do for him, but he figures that almost anything is better than the pain and anxiety he is feeling. He is determined to follow a better path than his father and some of his friends.

Ken's case illustrates both the challenges and the opportunities of the assessment process. He came to his first appointment at the addiction treatment centre feeling hopeful, but also anxious and ambivalent. Ken knows that he needs help, but he isn't sure that any treatments will work for him. At its best, the assessment process marks the beginning of a positive relationship that instills optimism for change, commitment to work towards recovery, and willingness to trust. In turn, Ken needs to feel heard, respected, and understood such that his history, goals and values are considered as the context in which his drug problems are occurring.

Assessment requires a comprehensive approach that includes biological, psychological, and social factors. The initial appointment should address the following key areas:

> the need for emergency care
> the presence and severity of opioid use
> other drug use, including alcohol and tobacco
> screening for medical and mental health problems
> living situation
> family and social supports and problems
> financial issues
> legal issues, if any

Source: Kaufman and Woody 1995; Martin, Brands, and Marsh 2003; Dziegielewski 2005

Opioids are one of only two areas in addictions where a diagnosis of dependence makes the person eligible for drug substitution therapy (the other is tobacco). People who are opioid dependent can be offered one of two possible medications (methadone or buprenorphine) that substitute for the opioid drugs they have been using. Determining eligibility for opioid substitution medication is a core task in assessment, particularly with people who are moderately to severely dependent.

Exploring a person's current level of opioid use is a common starting point. Questions typically focus on the type(s) of opioid drugs used, the typical dose, how often the drugs are used, when they last used the drugs, and the route of administration (oral, nasal, smoking, injecting). Treatment professionals also need to know how much a person uses in one day, and the date and duration of the last period of abstinence. Questions about the person's drug use history, including questions about the age of first use, the duration of periods of use, the extent of periods of abstinence, the types of opioids used in the past, and past treatment experiences are also explored. It is also important to document overdoses or other drug-related negative events.

In addition to finding out about current and past opioid use, the counsellor will want to know about other types of substances used. Acting on the assumption that clients are likely to have experimented with (and may be currently using) a number of drugs, it is important to investigate past and current use of all substances. Usual questions about other drugs include the age at which they first drank alcohol, had their first cigarette, their history of prescription drug use (including minor tranquillizers and other psychotropic medications) and their use of other illicit substances, including stimulants (cocaine, amphetamines, coffee, tobacco), hallucinogens (cannabis, LSD, ecstasy), and depressants (alcohol, benzodiazepines).

It is important to assess other biopsychosocial domains as well: co-occurring health or medical concerns (for example, infectious diseases such as hepatitis and HIV), psychological functioning (including current suicide risk, history of violence and self-harm behaviours), education, employment, housing, family and social supports, and financial or legal issues. If the assessment reveals that there are urgent issues besides substance use (for example, acute health concerns or lack of shelter), these should take precedence. The substance use and other issues would become the focus only after more pressing concerns are addressed. A comprehensive psychosocial history can be complemented by a medical assessment and physical examination by a nurse practitioner or physician. The presence of acute mental health concerns could involve a psychiatric consultation. Finally, urine samples may be required to assess for the presence of opioids and other substances including alcohol, stimulants, cannabis, barbiturates, and minor tranquillizers, particularly benzodiazepines.

Just talking about drugs and drug use can be triggers for someone with a substance abuse problem. Some recommended safeguards during an assessment appointment include checking in with the person throughout and at the conclusion of the assessment, exploring what parts of the conversation were triggering, and developing a safety plan with the person should the urge to use become too strong. Letting people know that they are in charge of the pace of the assessment and that they can decline to answer any of the questions can, paradoxically, makes clients feel safer, allowing for more self-disclosure.

In Ken's case, going through an assessment was an enlightening and motivating experience. Ken was pleasantly surprised by how non-judgmental the counsellor was and how easy she was to talk to. He liked that she didn't just focus on his drug use but was also concerned about how he was surviving financially, how his drug use might affect his disability support, his determination to not end up like his father, and his feelings of disconnection from his culture. Ken left the assessment feeling like he had control over making the treatment decisions that would be right for him. He also decided to meet with the Elder as his mother suggested; speaking to the counsellor about what it meant to him to be a Cree made Ken appreciate his First Nations heritage as a core part of who he is—something worthy of his own and others' respect.

Treatment planning

Based on the emerging picture and clients' treatment preferences and readiness, specific options can be explored. Treatments available in most Canadian communities include the following:

> detoxification and withdrawal management, particularly if abstinence is a goal and medical or social support and stabilization are needed

> treatment for co-occurring medical issues given the high risk of infectious disease, particularly if the client is an intravenous drug user, as well as the likelihood of other concerns and compromised health

> treatment for mental health problems if there are signs that consultation and treatment is required

> outpatient counselling, especially if clients have good social support and low to moderate levels of dependence

> residential treatment, especially for clients with more severe levels of dependence and low levels of social support and stability

> therapeutic communities, which can be a helpful option for people who are willing to commit to abstinence from all drugs, and to step out of regular social living into an intense supportive environment for at least three months or longer

> substitution therapies (methadone or buprenorphine) for clients who meet criteria for taper-oriented or maintenance therapies

Kaufman and Woody (1995) suggest five guiding questions to help determine the most suitable treatment options for a particular person:

> What is available?
> What are the treatment admission criteria?
> What is realistic for the client?
> What does the client want?
> What will the client accept?

These questions recognize that not all treatment options are available in all communities, particularly those outside of major cities. In addition, referral to treatment is itself a process, and requires negotiating waiting times, admission criteria, client motivation and preferences, cultural appropriateness, and past treatment experiences. The answers to the above questions set the stage for how the treatment referral and preparation process will proceed.

Missing the link versus making the connection: Case management and beyond

Case management refers to more than referral to appropriate services, reminding clients to keep treatment appointments, and ensuring that assessment and treatment data are shared with the helping professionals who are involved in the clients' care. Case management also needs to be about active and intentional efforts to keep connected with clients, especially when—as is commonly the case—various service components are not well integrated. In addition, many clients who need and would benefit from treatment get lost in bureaucratic roadblocks and often unrealistic treatment compliance expectations.

It is very easy to disqualify clients because of their problematic behaviours and inability to live structured lives. Treatment engagement, better retention in care, and better outcomes are achieved when programs appreciate and accommodate these issues as part of their overall approach. The core to successful case management means advocating on clients' behalf when needed and communicating a sense of welcome, respect, openness, and support.

Ken's case described above illustrates how a constellation of factors can lead towards opioid abuse and dependence. A number of warning signs in his use of opioids began to emerge: Ken was using more medication than prescribed, using more often than he intended, and most recently, was crushing and snorting his pills for the psychoactive effect. Ken's assessment was a positive beginning, and when he began seeing a community addiction counsellor Ken started thinking that maybe things could change. Ken was struck by the counsellor's belief that it wasn't right for someone like him to just be left with his problems and that Ken had a bigger contribution to make in life. He realized that he didn't want to be written off as another hopeless case, and felt encouraged knowing that there was someone who was concerned enough about him to want to help him find a way out.

Medications to Treat Opioid Withdrawal and Dependence

Clonidine is a medication used to treat a variety of medical concerns and problems, including hypertension, menopausal symptoms (hot flashes), and Attention Deficit Hyperactivity Disorder (ADHD). It is also used to ease withdrawal symptoms from opioids, nicotine, and alcohol.

Methadone was developed in Germany in the late 1930s as a substitute for the medical analgesic morphine, which was anticipated to be in short supply during World War II due to enemy blockades. Under the German trade name, Dolophine, it was introduced to the United States after the war, as a result of the requisitioning of German patents and research by allied forces. Dolophine was given the generic name methadone in the US in the 1940s. Methadone is a synthetic opioid that is taken orally in a liquid suspension, usually flavoured with orange juice to make its bitter taste more palatable. It is absorbed in the body through the gastrointestinal tract, taking effect in about 30 minutes. It is a long-acting drug, taken only once a day, and its effects wear off in about 24 to 36 hours. Methadone has important advantages over shorter-acting opioids such as heroin or morphine. On a stable dose, people can go about their lives free from the constant drug-seeking behaviour that characterizes heroin use (where a dose is needed every 3–4 hours to avoid withdrawal). At the correct dose methadone has minimal psychoactive effects, meaning that people taking this medication can drive, work, study, and so on. Also, because methadone is taken orally, the risks of infection and disease from injection drug use are avoided, as are the criminal or other high risk activities that often accompany illicit opioid use. Finally, research shows that methadone can safely be taken for long periods (two years or even much longer), and can safely be taken by pregnant women who are opioid-dependent.

Buprenorphine is a newer treatment option for opioid-dependent clients and received Health Canada approval in 2006. It has some advantages over both clonidine (for withdrawal management) and methadone (for maintenance). Research suggests that buprenorphine tapering may be more effective in managing opioid withdrawal, as there is evidence of fewer withdrawal symptoms when it is discontinued. With respect to maintenance options, although both methadone and buprenorphine have long half-lives (that is, they are similarly long-acting), buprenorphine carries a lower risk of overdose because it has a "ceiling effect" on opiate activity in the brain (Srivastera and Kahan 2006). (A ceiling effect is the maximum dose beyond which effects do not increase.) Buprenorphine is formulated in sublingual tablets (dissolved under the tongue).

Before Canadian physicians are allowed to prescribe methadone or buprenorphine, they are required to attend training, pass an examination, and complete a practicum. Upon completion of these requirements, they receive a special licence allowing them to prescribe these medications to patients. Common side effects for both methadone and buprenorphine include sweating, constipation, reduced sex drive, and weight gain (although increased weight may be a function of healthier eating and more regular meal times). Some people stay on these medications for years, while others prefer to taper off as soon as possible. To avoid relapse back to illicit opioid use after stopping methadone or buprenorphine, patients are recommended to first be stable on their medication, maintain positive lifestyle changes, develop supportive networks and coping skills, and not be using other illicit drugs.

Psychosocial Treatments for Opioid Abuse

Many people with problems related to opioid use, including very serious problems, recover without ever engaging in the formal addiction treatment system. There is evidence that even seriously addicted people recover from problems without formal treatment (Sobell, Ellingstad, and Sobell

2002). Research on "natural recovery" (as it is called) suggests that people's ability to draw on social support is a key factor in successfully resolving substance abuse problems (Granfield and Cloud 1999). However, many people with substance abuse problems lack the social and family supports to help facilitate recovery. Others may get better on their own, but do so only after experiencing major negative consequences— perhaps avoidable, had they accessed treatment and support sooner. Still others experience such complex and major co-occurring issues that recovery from substance abuse becomes their last priority in a chaotic existence marked by the sheer struggle to survive.

Mutual aid fellowships such as Narcotics Anonymous (NA) are also an important path to recovery for many people. These invite people to join and participate in a culture of recovery based on a desire to be abstinent. Spirituality is often seen as an essential ingredient in mutual aid fellowships based on the 12-step model. The interpersonal and group context is the foundation of mutual aid fellowships, giving members positive social alternatives and an around-the-clock buddy system of members further along in their recovery, called sponsors. Research supports the effectiveness of 12-step-based mutual aid fellowships for people who actively involve themselves and commit to their own recovery (Humphreys 2004). Being able to access such readily available, community-based peer support can be a valuable option or a life-saving necessity for a wide range of men and women whose lives have been derailed by opioid abuse.

One of the threshold requirements for mutual aid participation is the way a person answers the question, "Would I call myself an addict?" For many whose lives have been marked by chronic, severe use of opioids and serious negative consequences, this description fits their experiences and self-perception well. Making the statement "I am an addict" can be, for many, an empowering step away from denial and towards recovery. Accepting that recovery means abstaining from all drugs can provide a clear and unequivocal goal to move towards, one day at a time.

Other individuals, especially those with lower levels of drug use severity, may not accept the term "addict" as a valid self-description. However, accepting the label of "addict" is not an essential precondition to recovery for all people with substance use problems. Even people who want to just cut down on their use of some or all substances can be motivated to seek help and make positive changes. The evidence strongly suggests that outpatient treatments, even brief ones of four to six weekly sessions, can help or resolve substance use problems. Outpatient treatment approaches such as cognitive-behaviour therapy (CBT), motivational interviewing (MI), and drug counselling are all recommended "best practice" treatments for opioid abuse and dependence, especially in conjunction with pharmacological substitution therapies for more chronic and severe opioid users (Health Canada 1999).

Residential treatment programs, typically lasting 3 to 4 weeks, are suitable for people with high levels of severity, other co-occurring problems, and lower social stability and support. Such programs usually require the person to be abstinent from all drugs, although some programs allow clients who are on methadone or buprenorphine therapy to participate. Even more intensive are therapeutic communities, which have a strong peer culture, often use confrontational therapy processes, and attempt to re-socialize the person to anti-drug values and develop positive coping skills and lifestyles. Therapeutic communities would generally not be accepting of people using methadone or buprenorphine, and may be inclined to regard pharmacotherapy as "substituting one addiction for another."

A very well validated approach to opioid treatment is contingency management. This treatment model assumes that there is a learned system of rewards and punishments built into all human behaviours, including drug taking. Contingency management uses principles of cognitive behavioural psychology to intentionally and explicitly shape the rewards and consequences that are linked to substance abuse.

In this approach, rewards are contingent with the clients' performance of desired target behaviours, such abstaining from illicit drug use, keeping treatment appointments, and attending adjunct programs (parenting, job training, etc.). Clients can accumulate rewards in the form of vouchers (for an exercise class, restaurant meal, or other enjoyable activity), goods (toys or clothing for a new parent's baby), or (less often) money. Methadone itself can be a focus of contingency management, allowing the client increased choice over dosage, dosage schedules, and carry-home medication. Urine screens, a necessary requirement in methadone programs, can also be the focus of contingency management—for example, rewarding every "clean" urine sample (that is, one that is free of illicit drugs).

The intentional use of a system to reward positive behaviours can be a powerful tool in developing new lifestyles and habits. There is strong evidence that clients in contingency management programs have better all around outcomes than psychosocial counselling alone. These arrangements work best when the clients feel that they are choosing their goals and participating in the process of developing a contingency contract as active partners in a plan of care (Martin, Brands, and Marsh 2003; Stitzer, Petry, and Silverman 2005).

Beyond the cognitive and behavioural strategies with a psychological focus, there is strong support for socially oriented treatment components oriented to couples and family education and therapy, as well as vocational and employment supports, all based on the assumption that basic housing and income needs of the clients and their families need to be addressed. Holistic treatment programs that also include pharmacotherapy show the best outcomes in treating severe opioid dependence (Martin, Brands, and Marsh 2003).

Special consideration needs to be given to working with adolescents, especially about not hurrying them into maintenance therapies without offering them opportunities to be drug-free and to receive help for what are usually complex problems that need time to heal. In addition, working with women raises other considerations, such as using substitution as the safest option for opioid-dependence during pregnancy, and addressing the social contexts that create disadvantages to treatment success (Naylor 2008). A broad diversity orientation with strong cultural competencies is also key to providing appropriate and effective treatment.

Clients are sometimes vulnerable to the belief that they do not need continuing care and support, especially if they have made significant progress in treatment and are feeling that they have moved beyond the drug problems that have preoccupied them in the past. It is important to offer clients options that keep the door open for continuing treatment and aftercare support. This should include proactive strategies that reach out to make follow-up contact with clients, whether they have left treatment prematurely or successfully completed a cycle of care.

An Addiction Therapist's Perspective on Opioid Dependence and Treatment

An Interview with Kate Tschakovsky

Kate Tschakovsky is a clinical social worker with many years of experience working with opioid-dependent clients. Recently, she authored a book on best practices in case management for people in methadone treatment (Tschakovsky 2009). In June 2009, she shared some of her insights with us.

What do you think are the most important factors in dealing with opioid dependence?

I just finished interviewing methadone clients (for the *Best Practice Guide* research project) from all over Ontario, in large cities and small towns, in comprehensive care clinics, methadone-only clinics, and clients who were getting methadone from family doctors in office-based practices. We had a range of things that we asked them to rate in terms of what was most important for them in the provision of methadone treatment. Overwhelmingly, they talked about being treated with dignity and respect, and developing a trusting relationship with the care provider(s)—more important than help with housing or filling out forms, or advocacy, or any of the "hands-on" types of services. I think this is really telling. We sometimes try to address opioid dependence by providing more services and programming, but we miss what clients tell us makes the biggest difference in addition to having medications like methadone to stop withdrawal symptoms: connection with another person. Positive regard. Acceptance of the person and belief in the ability to change, even when they can't believe it for themselves.

What could be done better to address the problem of opioid dependence?

With the rise of prescription medication as a significant type of opioid of abuse, it begs the question: Why don't we monitor our prescribing practices better? Why don't we train and support doctors to deal compassionately and holistically with patients? Why don't we emphasize whole-person health care rather than symptom management? Why don't we have more social supports, integrated healthcare, treatment programs, and community resources available for people so that they have options other than (or in addition to) prescriptions for dealing with their stress, pain, anxiety, or mental health issues? Why don't we have more widespread harm reduction programs and supports in place so that people who are not ready to make changes in their use can stay well, reduce the costs to society in terms of health care costs and criminal justice costs? It's actually economically cheaper to provide these things to deal with the harms caused by opioid use. But I think it's stigma and moral judgments about substance use that still drive those social and political agendas, as well as the over-medicalization of complex human problems.

Pharmacotherapies for Opioid Dependence: Evidence-Based Tools for Withdrawal and Maintenance

The use of pharmacotherapies is one of the oldest—and most contentious—interventions in the treatment of opioid addiction. A series of studies with a clinical population of heroin users in the early 1960s by Dole and Nyswander (1967) provided science-based evidence and a theory about opioid addiction that created a strong logic for including methadone maintenance as a valid treatment for heroin dependence. Dole and Nyswander found that, compared to the poor treatment results they were obtaining using other medical and psychosocial interventions, patients with a history of severe opioid dependence showed dramatic improvements when offered methadone treatment. First of all, they found that high rates (90 percent) of people entering their program stayed in treatment. About 70 percent of those who were retained obtained employment. Just about all had stopped heroin use and the lifestyle related to it.

Dole and Nyswander were surprised that their "simple medical program" had produced such impressive results among a population of stigmatized and ostracized clients, most from the most marginal neighbourhoods in the city of New York. They proposed that heroin addiction is not based on a weakness of character, but instead needs to be understood as a metabolic disorder. The antisocial behaviours (such as stealing and lying) among people addicted to heroin disappeared when they were enrolled in methadone therapy. These surprising findings led Dole and Nyswander to propose that the characterological deficits attributed to people addicted to opioids may instead be consequences—rather than causes—of drug addiction.

Dole and Nyswander's groundbreaking work in the 1960s demonstrated how a pragmatic response to drug addiction can be effective, despite being counter to the values and beliefs of the general population, public officials, and others in the addiction treatment field (most of whom were categorically committed to total abstinence as the only acceptable goal). Nonetheless, if policy and treatment professionals are committed to following research evidence, they have to come to grips with methadone (and, more recently, buprenorphine) maintenance therapy (Health Canada 2002; Martin, Brands, and Marsh 2003).

Before the 1980s most Canadian methadone programs operated under stringent admission guidelines, had long waiting lists (two years or more), required abstinence from all drugs of abuse, and discharged patients who did not comply with program rules. Then, in the late 1980s, there arose something worse than being a person with an addiction: being HIV-positive. Because injection drug use carries a high risk of infection (notably HIV and hepatitis B and C), it became more important to retain people in treatment than to set tough standards that weed people out.

HIV also made health professionals become concerned about shared needles, a common practice when syringes were difficult to obtain. This led to needle exchange programs and education about safer injecting practices for drug users. Gradually a philosophy grew that has come to be known as harm reduction, which values abstinence if it can be achieved, but also acknowledges the pragmatic reality that many people are not willing or able to achieve abstinence from drugs. The philosophy of harm reduction recognizes the need to reduce harms to non-treatment-seekers by reaching out, and providing information and support in order to prevent or minimize the negative consequences that such individuals might experience.

Pharmacotherapies such as methadone and buprenorphine are more than drug substitutes for addictive opioids; they are active treatments that help compensate for neuronal changes in the brain's reward system resulting from chronic opioid administration (Kosten and George 2002). In this view, opioid addiction is a chronic relapsing condition requiring long-term treatment. An analogous example is the treatment of type 2 diabetes—another chronic, relapsing condition often caused by unhealthy lifestyle "choices" and biological predisposing factors. Insulin is not a cure for diabetes; it only treats the chronic medical condition and allows the person with the problem an improved chance at a normal life.

There are, however, some significant differences in treating opioid dependence over other chronic diseases. Doctors must get a special licence to prescribe methadone or buprenorphine, which is provided by Health Canada upon approval by the doctor's provincial regulating body. Patients are subjected to strict conditions and continuing monitoring via regular, supervised urine screening ("supervised" means that the patient is observed by an attendant when providing the urine sample). Patients have to attend the clinic or community pharmacy every day to drink their methadone under visual supervision by the pharmacist. In time, patients may be allowed to take home the medication (called "carries"), but even in the most favourable situation that would only be for up to six consecutive days.

However, as Stitzer, Petry, and Silverman (2005) point out, methadone maintenance treatment is an "effective but incomplete" treatment for opioid addiction. Why incomplete? Because it does not treat other forms of substance abuse or behavioural addictions the person might have, or provide necessary psychosocial, medical, or mental health supports in domains other than opioid dependence. Research shows that rates of mental health problems and other forms of substance abuse are alarmingly high among opioid users, particularly depression and anxiety (Westphal et al. 2005; King and Brooner 1999). The ability to screen for and respond to concurrent mental health issues in people in opioid treatment is a key function in providing effective health care to this population (Martin, Brands, and Marsh 2003; Health Canada 2002).

The value of pharmacotherapies for opioid dependence can be seen poignantly in how highly clients value being able to pass as "normal" and to participate in everyday pleasures. Feeling part of a family again, getting back custody of one's children, and having a home, a job, friends, and the stability of predictable routines become possible. Luty and Lawrence (2009) describe how the values and priorities of opioid users seeking treatment are much the same as those in the general population: children, friends, intimate relationships, and food are rated as more important than heroin, which, while very pleasurable, is recognized as extremely disruptive and damaging.

The growth of methadone maintenance and other substitution therapies such as buprenorphine (and in some jurisdictions, even heroin substitution) has been accompanied

A Physician's Perspective on Opioid Dependence and Treatment: An Interview with Dr Michael Lester

Dr Michael Lester is a physician who specializes in addiction medicine. He has a special licence to prescribe methadone, which is required of doctors in Canada who want to offer this option to individuals with opioid dependence. Dr Lester works in the Addiction Medicine Clinic at the Centre for Addiction and Mental Health, and also in a community clinic in Toronto. He has taken an active role in training doctors and consulting with health care workers about the treatment of addiction. We interviewed Dr Lester in June 2009: his comments here are clearly based on his personal experience working with people with problems related to opioid dependence, and are supported by his strong understanding of the scientific and professional literature.

What do you think it is about opioids and opioid users that gives rise to the risk for addiction?

Individuals commonly experiment with multiple drugs before taking on a "drug of choice." Choosing opioids is a very personal decision that is influenced greatly by a person's personality and biology. Most people who try opioids don't like how it makes them feel. For those people with the right disposition and risk factors, their initial reaction is "ahh—this is what I've been looking for...."

Partly this difference in people's reactions is due to genetics— some people's brains will just have a different experience from opioids than others, and partly it is that some individuals suffer from some kind discomfort that is relieved by opioids. That discomfort may be physical—under- or untreated chronic pain—but it can also be emotional or reflect under- or untreated psychiatric problems, like social phobias, significant self-esteem issues, painful family problems, etc.

What begins as a "little treat" once in a while may slowly expand to daily use, and with daily use comes physical dependence. After several months of daily use, brain changes occur that make it harder and harder to stay permanently off opioids, even after long periods of abstinence.

What do you think are the most important factors in dealing with opiate/opioid dependence?

The treatment of opioid dependence is similar to the treatment of other drugs of abuse, with some special differences. For milder degrees of opioid dependence, some people respond to detoxification (either in- or outpatient) followed by ongoing counselling. Detoxification without counselling has a very poor success rate.

Opioid dependence is one of the few drug dependencies that are helped greatly by substitution therapy. If people are unable or unwilling to stop taking opioids, then prescribing methadone or buprenorphine (which are also opioids) works very well. Unlike the short-acting opioids people are dependent on, methadone or buprenorphine are long-acting, allowing people to be free of withdrawal symptoms, while not getting "high" from the drug. For most people this results in a dramatic improvement in their quality of life. Some people stay on substitution therapy until they feel they are ready to taper off opioids and remain abstinent. Others find they require substitution therapy indefinitely.

Whether detoxification or substitution therapy is chosen, counselling is an essential part of getting better. People benefit from coaching on how to remain drug-free. People frequently need assistance in dealing with immediate concerns like housing, medical, or financial problems. As opioid dependence is a chronic, relapsing illness, long-term follow up is commonly needed.

People have misconceptions about how success is defined in treating opioid dependency. Success in treating opioid dependency is helping an individual enjoy a life that is worth living. Success is not defined by stopping drug use. Abstinence is wonderful, but not a realistic goal for all people. Relapses are symptoms of an illness, and not a sign of moral or personal weakness. No one is critical of people who can have difficulty getting their high blood pressure under control. Success is not defined as being able to leave treatment: opioid dependence is a chronic illness, and no one criticizes diabetics for not being able to stop taking their medication.

Here are some indicators for assessing success in treating opioid dependency:

> Stopping drug use is success.
> Reducing drug use is success.
> Reducing harm to the individual and the community is an achievement to be proud of.
> Not reducing drug use is success.

If an individual stays connected with treatment to receive encouragement, is instructed on how to use drugs in a safer way, or just feels cared for during a painful time of his or her life, then continued treatment is valuable.

by research clearly supporting their effectiveness (Mattick et al. 2003; Mattick et al. 2009). Evidence shows that pharmacotherapies on their own are reasonably effective treatments for opioid dependence, and work even better when psychosocial counselling is also included. Unfortunately, there are formidable gaps in addiction services in many communities. In some cases, there are no doctors who are willing to prescribe methadone. In others, there are doctors with patients on methadone who cannot access the psychosocial services they need, either because they do not exist or because the addiction treatment service does not work with people on methadone or other psychoactive medications.

Conclusion

Why does an addict get a new habit so much quicker than a junk virgin, even after the addict has been clean for years? I do not accept the theory that junk is lurking in the body all that time ... and I disagree with all psychological answers. I think the use of junk causes permanent cellular alteration. Once a junky, always a junky. (William S. Burroughs, in Grauerholz and Silverberg 1998, 66)

Two key concepts inform contemporary health perspectives on opioid problems. One is that abuse and addiction occur along a continuum, from low to high severity, and appropriate treatment options will vary according to severity

Michele's Story

"Michele" (like others who share their stories in this book) requested that her real name not be used. When asked how she came to use drugs, Michele linked her personal vulnerability to drug use to the painful events in her childhood: "I probably became an injection drug user and addicted to opiates because of my own history with very traumatic life experiences, many of which were not addressed. I did not get counselling around these experiences—sexual abuse at age 5 and again at ages 11 to 12, and physical and emotional abuse repeatedly throughout my early life up until 14."

In her mid-teens Michele became pregnant, "and I then was forced to relinquish a child to adoption and told to go on with my life and forget about that experience. I made poor choices in my life based on so many of these experiences, which led me to continuous negative consequences."

Michele sees herself as having struggled with low mood for much of her life: "I believe that I have been depressed most of my life and that my choosing opiates as opposed to stimulants is not by accident. I totally believe that it's because I was missing the ability to produce enough endorphins." Michele also points out that as she became more and more seriously involved in drugs, the addiction itself became a factor in making it hard to escape: "Also, there is the issue of having a serious physical dependence, which makes it very difficult to get off opiates."

From Michele's personal experiences and observations of others people's struggles, she states that the most important factors in treating addictions are a *range of options* (including longer-term treatment for those who need it), and *integrated care* that addresses the other problems a person might be having. In Michele's view, methadone treatment should also be available to those who need and want it in the "long term, medium term, or short term." She would like to see other drug substitution therapies available too, including heroin substitution (available in some European countries).

Michele's comments reflect the need to provide a menu of pragmatic and holistic supports to users, including harm reduction approaches: "I believe that supervised injection sites and supervised inhalation sites need to be available for opiate-addicted people. I also believe that opiate addiction is somewhat different than other addictions." This is because of the strength of the physical dependence (and the severe discomfort of withdrawal) that frequent, heavy opiate use produces.

Michele is active today in consumer advocacy for addiction problems, especially for people who use opiates. She is employed and has reconnected with the daughter she lost contact with as a troubled teenager. As our conversation was wrapping up, Michele added: "The only thing I would like to emphasize is that people who become addicted to opiates don't end up there by mistake! There are many reasons and those reasons need to be looked at for success to happen." Circumstances create injuries to the spirit—the core of who we are as human beings—and opiate drugs, with their strong intoxicating potential, offer a powerful, if temporary, respite.

and complexity. The second key concept is that opioid addiction—especially where problematic use is severe—is a chronic, relapsing condition. The strategies for managing any chronic health problem apply, including educating patients about potential risks and harms, enhancing motivation for change, ensuring continuity of care, integrating psychosocial and pharmacological treatments, working to prevent relapse, and using harm reduction approaches (Martin, Brands, Marsh 2003; Van den Brink and Haasen 2006).

For people with severe levels of dependence, maintenance strategies (methadone or buprenorphine) are indicated. Because most people with opioid dependence are also experiencing physical or mental health problems, treatment programs need to be able to identify these and respond. The risk of arrest and imprisonment is also high because of the illegal activities commonly related to obtaining money to support daily drug habits.

Stigma and discrimination toward opioid users are persisting problems in the general population and among many health care providers. Yet adopting a moralistic perspective towards drug use discounts the biological, psychological, and social factors leading to addiction. Drug abuse and addiction should be regarded as health problems, requiring appropriate evidence-based treatment and compassionate and respectful care. To work effectively with people affected by these problems requires an ability to address the immediate issues that affect the person's daily functioning and to have a long-term view of service and support that recognizes the potential for change, growth, and recovery.

Chapter 5

Canadian Alochol and Drug Policy

Travels in Disputed Territory

Introduction

There is comfort in being able to reduce a problem to a single dimension, its understanding to a single viewpoint, and its solution to a single action. Drug policy, however, is anything but simple. There will always be drugs in society, and there will always be drug abuse—the questions are, how much (if any) should we as a society tolerate, and what can we do to prevent and minimize drug-related harms? These are complex questions because of the diverse ways in which drug abuse and addiction are understood by government, law enforcement, health practitioners, researchers, and the general public.

History illustrates the ways in which drug policies have changed radically over time. Even a glancing review of Canadian drug laws over the past 100 years reveals that substances that are anathema today, unequivocally demonized and subjected to the most unrelenting policing and criminal sanctions—cocaine and heroin—were initially heralded as important advances for treating a range of health problems. Today, controversies over appropriate sentencing for drug-related crimes (and whether the use of drugs like marijuana should even be considered a crime) illustrate the contested terrain on which policies are formed and applied.

The development and widespread adoption of new drug delivery technologies have informed the scope and breadth of substance abuse problems at the population level, creating new targets for policy and legislation. For example, the invention of machines to mass-produce cigarettes paved the way for a tobacco epidemic in Canada and around the world. Less than 200 years ago, the invention of the hypodermic needle created the potential to introduce psychoactive drugs directly into the bloodstream. With the advances in pharmaceutical science that resulted in the extraction of the key psychoactive agents in opium (morphine and codeine) and in coca (cocaine), the modern world has numerous addictive possibilities, allowing intoxicants to be delivered to the brain through the lungs in smoke, or through the blood via intravenous injection.

Ronald Siegel, a psychopharmacologist, argues that the pursuit of intoxicants is natural to almost all animal species, and has "so much force and persistence that it functions like a drive, just like our drives of hunger, thirst and sex" (Siegel 2005, vii). He calls intoxication the "fourth drive," based on his years of researching the effects of psychoactive drugs on a variety of animal species, including humans. For Siegel, the issue is not *whether* society should tolerate psychoactive drugs, but *how* we manage to do so, suggesting that a war against drugs is a war against ourselves, a "denial of our very nature." However, for Siegel, unfettered legalization is not a solution either; instead, he leads us into a grey zone, somewhere in between prohibition and legalization, where wise and informed policies are shaped by an educated and engaged public.

The problem is that Canadian drug policy is not uniformly wise and informed. The scientific understanding of addiction has shifted away from earlier perspectives where alcohol or other drug problems were regarded as a sign of moral weakness and degeneracy, but addiction and morality remain firmly linked in the popular imagination. To use an archeological analogy, this deep "moral substrate" is always active and circulating, contesting the other value frames that have emerged to shape how we see substance use and abuse, addictive behaviour, and healthy human functioning. The circulating moral substrate is often at the heart of drug policy debate, as we will see in this chapter.

Is Addiction a Personal Choice?

Biopsychosocial and public health models argue that drug problems stem from diverse and interacting causes and involve multiple systems. These perspectives challenge traditional thinking about dependence as a dispositional disease or a moral weakness. The disease perspective regards "addicts" as qualitatively different from "normal" drinkers or "recreational" drug users. Orthodox disease concepts tend to focus on biology—the interaction of a person with a drug. This ignores the fact that drug problems exist as much in social situations and processes as in people. For example, cultural norms influence attitudes toward drinking, the availability of drugs influences patterns of consumption, and low prices tend to increase overall use. Nevertheless, proponents of the disease model would argue that even in communities that favour drug use, only people with the underlying and pre-existing disease will become addicted.

The disease concept has, nevertheless, been useful to combat moralistic views; and many people with substance abuse problems would remain untreated if the moral view on addiction still held sway. At the same time, this narrow biological view on addiction is limiting: while severely dependent individuals may be regarded as ill, the problem may be as much—or more—the social environment as the person.

A recent book by Harvard psychologist Gene Heyman, *Addiction: A Disorder of Choice* (2009), enters this debate through the lens of psychology flavoured with economic theory. Heyman outlines the research evidence against the disease model of addiction, especially when disease is expressed as an involuntary condition that is unrelated to behaviour and personal choice. Heyman notes that most of what mammals do, including drug self-administration, is voluntary. But— and it is an important "but"—voluntary behaviour is mostly shaped by incentives. The way a person subjectively appraises different options (including drug-taking), and the proximity of positive or negative consequences that follow the behavior are the key influencers of personal choice.

Heyman points out that we live in world of appetites and temptations. Since drug-taking is generally followed by immediate and extreme pleasure, why aren't there more addicts? When the logic of immediate reward would seem to incline people to substance abuse, why don't more people default to the impulse-driven option? Heyman replies that choice depends on context. Society provides the countervailing context that keeps so many people away from the addictive option. For most people the immediate rewards associated with drug-taking are just not that compelling and the risks are clearly evident—physical health, psychological bondage to a drug or behaviour, loss of close relationships with family and friends, or social embarrassment. In the end, Heyman argues that neither explanation alone (that is, disease versus personal choice) is sufficient to explain addiction.

Unfortunately, the nuances of Heyman's argument are not reflected in much of the media attention that his book has garnered. For example, a Canadian television network (CTV) ran an online poll on their website, asking people if they thought addiction was governed by free choice. The response, "Yes, it is a matter of free will," was selected by 72 percent of respondents. The other response, "No, it's a disease," was endorsed by 28 percent of those who replied. Forcing a choice between two dichotomous options illustrates the reductive logic that shapes addiction as a popular concept: on one hand, substance abuse is a disease which (unfortunately) happens to some people; on the other hand, people are responsible for becoming addicted because they make too many bad choices.

Heyman's "disorder of choice" model does not imply a moral view of addiction; instead, substance abuse is said to occur in relation to biological and social reinforcers. He points to evidence that most people start using drugs in adolescence and early adulthood, and most have abandoned substance abuse by the time they are thirty (usually on their own without formal help). Those who remain stuck, Heyman observes, commonly have co-occurring problems or multiple disadvantages that keep them in a cycle of addiction. Even then, Heyman shows that a combination of factors, particularly those that change the contingencies related to substance use, increase the likelihood that individuals with addictions and co-occurring problems will make positive changes.

So, the answer to the question, "Is addiction a personal choice?" is yes ... and no. While it is true that people's decisions to use substances in the first place are volitional, these decisions occur in the context of community, peer group and family norms, drug availability, occupational, educational, or social opportunities, psychological factors, genetic predisposition, and so on. In addition, the majority of drug experimentation occurs in adolescence or young adulthood, when rebellion and risk-taking are normal characteristics of that developmental stage. In previous chapters we discussed the powerfully reinforcing effects of drugs in the brain, and that long-term use can lead to possibly permanent changes in the brain's reward system. Therefore, although personal choice is an important part of the initiation, maintenance, and cessation of drug use, it would be a gross oversimplification to argue that this is the sole—or even the most important—driving force behind addiction.

Nonetheless, when the social consensus (or at least the majority) votes for "personal choice" on issues as fundamental as the nature of addiction, public opinion often trumps research. Perceptions about people with drug problems have a strong influence on the range of policy options are considered and enacted.

"The Conservative Government will clean up drug crime"

During the 2008 federal election, the Conservative Party mailed a pamphlet to voters across the country. The first line of the pamphlet read, "Junkies and drug pushers don't belong near children and families," followed by the statement, "They should be in rehab or behind bars" (*Edmonton Journal*). There is considerable meaning in the few words of this campaign message, starting with "junky"—a term that conjures up every stereotype of the "depraved addict." In fact, using this word to describe people with substance dependence is on par with calling people with developmental delays "retards," or describing people with schizophrenia as "mental."

Equally offensive is the suggestion that people with substance use problems do not belong around children and families. It ignores the fact that families are where people come from, and many individuals who experience drug use problems are adolescents and young adults—people in need of parental and family support and guidance. If older, they are most likely to have started their drug use when they were young. They are children of parents, sometimes parents themselves, and always members of families.

The pamphlet also takes aim at "drug pushers" as the criminals behind the scourge of addiction. Yet the vast majority of substance abuse and dependence in Canada occurs in relation to legal drugs—alcohol, tobacco, and pharmaceuticals. One could argue that the government itself is the major "drug pusher" in this country by permitting the sale and consumption of these substances. This is not to trivialize the very real problems of the illicit drug trade, but rather to contextualize the message in a broader landscape populated with both licit and illicit drugs. Perhaps most troubling, the intent behind this campaign literature is not to get people thinking about the prejudice and illogic in its commentary. It is to appeal to perceptions and beliefs that already exist in the popular imagination.

Resorting to emotional arousal tactics in response to drug problems may be morally and ethically objectionable, but the Conservative Party's approach shows a certain strategic brilliance. Political writers need to stir people emotionally with a compelling point of view. In this case, stigmatizing and demonizing a vulnerable part of the population was intended to encourage the electorate to see the Conservatives as the party that "gets" this issue. The implicit promise is that they alone are committed to protecting the public against an evil presence that has invaded the social body. People with drug problems, based on this description, don't belong in the human community. Instead they should be ferreted out and put away, in rehab or behind bars.

Morality and drug policy

Skewed or biased political communication is a powerful tool to direct public discourse about drug policy. These types of messages short-circuit the rational discussion of drug use problems in society by appealing directly to the parts of the brain that govern emotional arousal. Evoking fear, apprehension, and intolerance makes it difficult to consider reasoned approaches to address the issues effectively. Instead, moral panic and outrage provoke a sense of urgency to do the "right" thing: support the political party that will keep your family safe.

The moral model sees addiction as a result of an underlying characterological weakness or as moral depravity, and this perspective persists as an active part of the drug discourse in Canada and around the world. Fairly primitive emotions can be sparked and ignited by politicians and moral crusaders, which helps explain why even in an age of science, drug policies and practices do not always follow the evidence.

This is not to suggest that morals and values have no role in policy and in how we give meaning to knowledge and factual information. Quite the opposite: our frames of mind are moral frames that shape personal and social values, expectations, and goals. In Canada, a country characterized by cultural, religious, social, and economic diversity, these frames of mind will be multiple. However, at the same time there is a need to come together on some basic level to find a social consensus.

George Lakoff is is a professor of linguistics at the University of California, Berkeley, where he studies language and cognition. In his recent work, he has explored the use of language in politics and its influence on public opinion and policy. For Lakoff, politics are not just about power but about morality. The moral struggle Lakoff sees in Western democracies, especially the US, is between the conservative politics of obedience to authority and the progressive politics of empathy and care.

Lakoff (2008) argues that recent developments in neuroscience are integral to understanding social policy in the twenty-first century. Research in this area is beginning to challenge the traditional idea that reason and emotion are diametrically opposed. Instead, neuroscientific evidence suggests that rationality and emotion are intertwined in "a vast landscape of unconscious thought—the 98 percent of thinking your brain does that you're not aware of" (Lakoff 2008, 3). In other words, much of human cognition is reflexive rather than reflective—it comes about before we are aware of it. Lakoff notes that political conservatives seem to be instinctively in tune with this new science of the mind in the ways their messages appeal to fundamental drives and feelings (like love for one's children and fear of harm).

In contrast, Lakoff suggests that politically progressive perspectives originated in an eighteenth century Enlightenment mindset, where reason was viewed as superior to emotion: "Progressives have accepted an old view ... that reason is conscious, literal, logical, universal, unemotional, disembodied, and serves self-interest. As the cognitive and brain sciences have been showing, this is a false view of reason" (Lakoff 2008, 1–2). For example, social progressives argue for more liberal drug laws, citing research and the logic of compassion, while social conservatives use rhetoric, stressing the urgency of "getting tough on crime." Lakoff suggests that in order for a socially progressive agenda to really take hold, the Enlightenment paradigm needs to give way to a new model of mind that understands reason as embodied and intertwined with emotion.

Lakoff's views tend to polarize two extremes, and the truth is likely somewhere in the middle. On the one hand, not all socially conservative drug policies are shaped by strategic messaging that appeals to people's precognitive instincts. On the other hand, progressive drug policies do not uniformly represent a reasoned approach based on evidence and rational debate. Nonetheless, Lakoff's work provides a helpful lens through which to critique the messaging, dialogue, and language around drug policy. Where drug abuse is seen as a health issue, where policy is more pragmatically inclined than ideologically aligned, and where objective evidence is a test by which practices are measured, then very different approaches to these human problems emerge.

Framing Canadian drug policy

Canada's Drug Strategy was developed just over a decade ago by an interdepartmental working group with representation from across federal government ministries (Health Canada 1998). The *Drug Strategy*, a document meant to inform all drug policy in Canada, calls for a balance between supply reduction (enforcement) and demand reduction (prevention and treatment), and states that drug use needs to be addressed within the context of social determinants of health. In addition, the *Drug Strategy* frames substance abuse as primarily a health problem (4), and states that "the fundamental objective of harm reduction remains constant" (16). This progressive stance on drug abuse and policy is now changing—in recent years, the Conservative federal government has begun to radically reconstruct Canada's drug strategy.

The 1998 *Drug Strategy* addressed all drugs (including alcohol, pharmaceutical drugs, and illicit substances) in one unified strategy, whereas the current federal government has shifted the focus to illicit drugs almost exclusively, more in line with US drug policy approaches. For example, in the US the scientific funding and research bodies focused on alcohol and on other drugs are completely separate. Among the various US National Institutes of Health, there is the National Institute on Alcohol Abuse and Alcoholism (NIAAA) and the National Institute on Drug Abuse (NIDA), representing an institutionalization of a great, unnecessary, and unhelpful divide.

Meanwhile, in Canada the government lead on drug policy has now been moved from Health Canada to the Ministry of Justice, a clear indicator of shifting the policy frame from health to enforcement. Harmful substance use in a broad sense has been replaced by illegal drug use and drug-related crime as the new focus.

Reframing drug policy manifests in fairly direct ways. If we believe that the national priority should be targeting drug-related crime, stiffer legal penalties and more active policing are logical developments. In line with this approach, programs that are "soft" on substance abuse need to be challenged, contained, and defunded. Viewing substance abuse and addiction as criminal behaviours, versus seeing them as health or social problems, makes public safety the paramount concern. Spending public money on treatment for people who may not get better becomes less important than enhancing law enforcement capacity.

Today, the federal paradigm is swinging back toward a view of drug abuse as a manifestation of delinquency and deviance. It is important to respect that these developments require the always implicit, and sometimes active, support of a considerable segment of the population, not just on election day but through whole terms of office. And much of the discourse is at the not-quite-conscious level of emotionality that creates the frames from which our mostly reflexive thinking comes.

Prohibition or Moderation?

Prohibition is based on the view that a certain substance or product is so disproportionately harmful that it should not be allowed in the social body because of the high risk it poses in corrupting the lives of individuals, families, and communities. It is most immediately associated with alcohol, especially during the 1920s and 1930s throughout North America, when the use of beverage alcohol was outlawed. Now, prohibition applies to any drugs that are classified as illegal. The moral frame that this perspective requires is that a certain drug is so harmful that it should not be allowed for use under any (or at least most) circumstances.

Alcohol

By the 1940s alcohol prohibition was repealed in nearly every jurisdiction in North America.[1] This does not mean that the harms of alcohol have diminished; in fact, alcohol causes more problems in Canadian society than all illegal drugs combined. Rather, the framing of the "alcohol problem" has shifted: unlike during the prohibition era, alcohol itself is not seen as the problem—certain forms and patterns of use are.

The first iteration of a shift away from prohibition as a response to alcohol-related problems can be seen in the recovery philosophy of Alcoholics Anonymous (Alcoholics Anonymous 1984). AA does not demonize alcohol or advocate that it be banned; its members take the view that they have a personal vulnerability to alcohol. They see themselves as "alcoholics" who must remain abstinent if they are to remain healthy, but do not make recommendations about alcohol policy in general. For AA, people who do not have the disease of alcoholism are able to drink in moderation without problems, so prohibiting alcohol for all people is not essential. AA members work in fellowship, take personal responsibility, and acknowledge their vulnerability to addiction by committing to abstinence one day at a time and following the 12 steps (Alcoholics Anonymous 1976; Kurtz 1979)

Moderation is the latest articulation of post-prohibitionist thinking on alcohol. At a policy level, Canada mostly aspires to a culture of moderation, as the current alcohol strategy document declares in its very title—*Reducing Alcohol-Related Harm in Canada: Toward a Culture of Moderation* (National Alcohol Strategy Working Group 2007). A post-prohibitionist policy perspective accepts alcohol as situated within the basic context of social life. It also generates questions about how to regulate alcohol sales and alcohol consumption. Over time, policy and legislation have been influenced by research evidence about a range of topics, from legal drinking age, to hours and conditions of operation of drinking establishments, to taxation and price.

Detailed and comprehensive regulations govern the sale and consumption of alcohol products across Canada. Although there is some variation among provinces in minimum drinking age, hours of sale, municipal policies, and so on, there is a strong common core of agreement that regulations should act to reduce alcohol-related harms to individuals and communities. There are also legitimate economic and entrepreneurial interests in alcohol as a product, for both the public and private sector. A considerable body of scientific information has informed these policies, recognizing that

> alcohol is no ordinary commodity. It is a legal psychoactive drug that enjoys enormous popularity and special social and cultural significance in Canada. Evidence also suggests that alcohol consumed at low to moderate levels can benefit the health of some individuals. Alcohol also plays an important role in the Canadian economy, generating jobs and tax revenue for governments. (National Alcohol Strategy Working Group 2007, 1)

Regulatory laws governing the production of beverage alcohol ensures quality and consistency for consumers. Legislation governing alcohol sales and licensing of drinking establishments addresses issues of individual and community safety and protection.

How Old Should a Person Be to Buy Alcohol?

Legal purchase ages for alcohol vary throughout North America and around the world. In Canada, the minimum age to buy alcohol is 18 in Alberta, Manitoba, and Quebec, and 19 in the rest of the country. The US and Chile have the highest minimum purchase age in the world (age 21), though in Chile this is not much enforced. There is no minimum purchase age in Brazil, Columbia, or Peru, though 18 is set as the minimum drinking age. In Britain, youth aged 16 and over can purchase beer or cider with a meal in a restaurant but must be 18 or over to buy alcohol in a bar. The minimum purchase age ranges from 16 to 18 in other European countries, and is 18 in Australia and New Zealand. (Blocker 2003)

There is evidence that cost has a direct relation on consumption, as does the density of alcohol points of sale in a given community (Giesbrecht, Patra, and Popova 2008). This research shows that alcohol policies can have a significant impact on harm at the population level—limiting the number of alcohol outlets, their hours of operation, and the cost are powerful policy tools. Therefore, regulations concerning alcohol sales limit vendors' hours of operation, the number of liquor licences granted, the density of outlets in a community, as well as their location. The range of policies is variable: beverage alcohol can be sold in corner stores in some provinces, and its availability is much more limited in others. Taxation is used to keep the cost of alcohol at levels that discourage overconsumption while providing needed government revenues.

Policies regulating alcohol prices and sales are essential because alcohol-related harms at the population level can be severe. Research shows that alcohol is a factor in up to 70 percent of violent injuries, and up to one-third of accidental injuries (National Alcohol Strategy Working Group 2007). Young Canadians between ages 10–24 are the highest risk group for alcohol-related trauma. These data support restricting access to alcohol by youth, although having minimum purchase age legislation is only effective to the degree to which it is enforced.

Impaired driving is another key area in alcohol policy. Although the vast majority of Canadians report not consuming alcohol before driving, roughly 3.2 million (or 15 percent) do drink and drive. People aged 16–19 have four times the fatality risk of drivers aged 25–34, and nine times the risk of drivers aged 45–54, as reflected in higher automobile insurance rates for younger drivers. Males make up 87 percent of fatalities related to impaired driving and 89 percent of serious injuries (National Alcohol Strategy Working Group 2007). Death and injuries are also most likely to occur on the weekend and in winter, and a large minority of fatal traffic collisions are alcohol-related. For example, a 2008 report from Alberta found that 22.5 percent of drivers involved in fatal collisions had consumed alcohol prior to the crash (Alberta Transportation 2008).

In North America .08 blood alcohol concentration (BAC) is the common standard for legal definitions of impairment, but the adoption of graduated licensing systems in some Canadian provinces effectively sets a zero blood alcohol level for new drivers (who are statistically more likely to be involved in traffic fatalities). Some European countries, like Norway, Poland, and Sweden, set the legal limit at .02 for all drivers, while .05 is the limit in most other European countries as well as in Australia. Many countries set the legal limit at zero, meaning that *any* alcohol in the bloodstream would qualify a person as impaired.

There is an ongoing policy debate in Canada about whether the legal limit for impairment should be lowered from .08 to .05. A number of private member's bills have been introduced in Parliament over the years, most recently in 2006 (Bill C-376). The arguments against lowering the legal limit are well summarized in this excerpt from a briefing note from the Canadian Criminal Justice Association (CCJA):

> Impaired driving is already the most oft prosecuted offence in the *Criminal Code*. Lowering the BAC level to .05 is guaranteed to increase the number of criminal prosecutions and further clog an already overcrowded system. Given the fact that impaired driving is on the decline, and that provincial legislation removes drivers with BAC levels over .05 from the road this legislative proposal seems highly costly and unnecessary.
>
> Finally, the CCJA is not convinced that lowering the BAC will achieve its intended objective. Most Canadians are not aware of the specific correlation between consumption and BAC levels. Responsible Canadians will choose not to drive if they believe their ability to do so is impaired by alcohol. Those who choose to drive while impaired will do so whether the allowable BAC is .05 or .08.
>
> The CCJA believes that the money required to increase criminal sanctions could be better spent on educational programs intended to increase awareness of the consequences of drinking and driving while discouraging that behavior. (CCJA 2006)

In this view, impaired driving is already on the decline, those who drink and drive will disobey the law regardless, and public money could be better spent on prevention.

On the other side of the debate, there have been numerous international research studies assessing the impact of lowering the legal limit from .08 to .05. Evidence consistently shows that single-car fatal crashes and serious injuries (those most associated with impaired driving) decline substantially when BAC limits are lowered. It is estimated that motor vehicle crash fatalities in Canada would be reduced by 6–18 percent if the law was changed (Fell and Voas 2006). Nonetheless, research evidence alone is not enough to influence policy; political will and public opinion are equally, if not more, important.

The existence of laws against impaired driving will not, in itself, stop the problem. Ensuring public compliance with legislated BAC levels for impaired driving has been shown to be the most effective when combined with enforcement, usually in the form of random roadside breath testing of drivers. Although North America has a higher BAC threshold than many other countries, the frequency of random breath testing in Canada and the US ensures that people are more likely to comply. For example, Equatorial Guinea, Malawi, Nigeria, and Panama all have laws mandating zero BAC, but police in these countries rarely or never conduct spot checks on drivers (WHO 2004a). There also needs to high public awareness of the legislation as well as fairly serious consequences to breaking the law. All in all, effective legislation is a fine balancing act between research, public opinion, and costs and consequences (both intended and unintended).

Illicit drugs

If, in the last century, Canada has moved from alcohol prohibition to a culture of moderation, we have actually moved in the opposite direction with regard to other drugs. At the beginning of the twentieth century, drugs like opium and cocaine were widely available as commercial products promising relief from pain and enhanced well-being. Today, and for most of the past century, there are serious consequences for producing, selling, and using these and other substances under Canada's drug laws. The sheer number of illegal drugs in Canada has increased over the years, and will likely continue to do so as the technology to invent and produce new intoxicants advances.

A common expectation among much of the health profession, judiciary, and general public is that recovery from substance abuse problems equals abstinence—quit using altogether and never use again. This goal is part of the process of self-recognition that is the core of the 12-step approach to recovery. The 12-step approach, born when Alcoholics Anonymous was formed by a small group of self-admitted alcoholics in 1935, has been foundational to the development of the modern addiction treatment system in North America. Although different ways of treating addictions have also developed, most have been oriented to helping substance abusers achieve and maintain sobriety.

However, an alternative perspective started to gain ground in the 1960s and 1970s. Evidence began to emerge that people with mild to moderate alcohol or other drug problems might be able to return to low-risk drinking or other drug use without needing to become or to stay abstinent (Sanchez-Craig 1995; Sobell and Sobell 1993; Miller and Munoz 2005). Based on these empirical data, the concept of addiction began to be framed as less a binary problem and more as a continuum from low to high severity. This was accompanied by research showing that people tended to do better in treatment when they felt that they had choices over their substance use goals (Sobell and Sobell 1999). Some treatment programs began to offer services based on these new research findings, and some of these programs (and the scientists who ran them) became the object of intense criticism from proponents of abstinence-only approaches, who even went as far as to question researchers' integrity and professional conduct (Saladin and Santa Ana 2004). A number of impartial scientific panels were convened, and in the end exonerated the scientists.

"Harm Reduction 101"

Harm reduction is a controversial approach to dealing with substance abuse because it seems diametrically opposed to traditional treatment services and philosophies. Some people believe that harm reduction encourages and enables drug abuse and endangers the health and well-being of individuals and communities. However, the wealth of research evidence supporting harm reduction programs and interventions is so compelling that Ontario's Centre for Addiction and Mental Health (CAMH) is one of many Canadian research and treatment facilities that have made an organizational decision in support of harm reduction. The following are some highlights from the policy paper on harm reduction produced by CAMH in 2002:

> Harm reduction is any program or policy designed to reduce drug-related harm without requiring the cessation of drug use. Interventions may be targeted at the individual, the family, community or society.... The primary focus of harm reduction is on people who are already experiencing some harm due to their substance use. Interventions are geared to movement from more to less harm. Examples of proven harm reduction programs are: server intervention programs which decrease public drunkenness; needle and syringe exchange programs which prevent the transmission of HIV among injection drug users; and, environmental controls on tobacco smoking which limit the exposure to second hand smoke. (CAMH 2002)

Harm reduction is organized around a number of core principles:

> Pragmatism—while some level of drug use in society is inevitable and normal, though varying widely due to culture and cultural values, it is important to act to reduce the more immediate and tangible harms rather than just embracing vague goals of a future drug-free society.
> Focus on harms—reducing negative consequences of drug abuse does not always require reduced use, especially when the harms are related to health, social, or economic factors that affect the individual, community, and society as a whole.

> Prioritizing goals—priority is given to the most immediate and realistic goals of each client, and working to reconcile conflicts that may exist between the community and the individual.
> Flexibility and maximizing intervention options—flexible planning and resetting goals keep options open for clients, and include drug substitution, drug maintenance, and interventions that adopt safer methods of use.
> Respecting clients' autonomy—using or not using drugs is up to each person, meaning the individual plays a primary role in determining what to do about his or her addiction; the emphasis is on community reintegration rather than social exclusion or marginalization.
> Evaluating effectiveness of policies and programs—evaluation is as important as responsiveness and innovation; goals must be clearly stated and harms being addressed clearly identified; individual and community indicators need to be measured to determine success.

An Aboriginal perspective on harm reduction nicely captures the essence of this approach: "The philosophy of harm reduction encourages us to reach those outside of the circle and welcome them back in.... [We] recognize that everyone in the circle is affected and thus has a responsibility to make this circle whole" (CAMH 2002)

Today, a large proportion of Canadian addiction treatment programs have incorporated goal choice as a key component of evidence-based services. Addiction counsellors in these settings practice with a pragmatic awareness that treatment is not about insisting that people to do the "right thing," but is instead focused on working effectively towards sustained behaviour change, including moderate or low consumption as well as abstinence.

As philosophies and approaches have evolved in the addiction treatment system, parallel changes in the legal system have begun to emerge. There is a large body of evidence showing that putting people in jail or exposing them to criminal sanctions for illegal drug use often does more harm than good (Dackis and O'Brien 2005; Lenton 2003). This research has fuelled the establishment of special treatment options within the criminal justice system for people with serious addictions. "Drug treatment courts" are alternative justice settings where people who are charged with drug-related crimes (indicative of chronic, severe cycles of addiction) have the option of attending ongoing, intensive treatment instead of jail or other legal sanctions. Clients who are successful in drug court programs can receive an absolute discharge when they "graduate" (usually at the end of one year). The goal of such programs is to actively involve people, through close supervision and treatment support, in a helping process aimed at drug-free lifestyles (Miller and Carroll 2006).

HIV, AIDS, and the Rise of Harm Reduction

Users of illegal drugs are exposed to risks beyond those experienced by people who abuse licit drugs, and many of these risks are the direct result of drug policies and legislation. Unreliable quality and high prices are characteristics of products that can only be obtained illegally, creating a dynamic that leads to economic crimes or sex trade work. Criminal subcultures that have a predatory interest in people who are drug dependent bring another set of hazards and risks as well.

Perhaps the most dramatic developments in policies aimed at illicit drug use arose in response to a health problem that did not directly result from substance abuse. In the 1980s, health practitioners and health epidemiologists began to identify an outbreak of infectious disease that they called *acquired immune deficiency syndrome* (AIDS), and further research led to the identification of the *human immunodeficiency virus* (HIV). HIV is not transmitted through drugs, but it can, it was soon realized, be transmitted through the behaviours related to drug use.

The two most important vectors for HIV are (1) sharing injection equipment, especially (but not only) hypodermic needles; and (2) unprotected sex. The risk of the former is amplified when users are engaged in clandestine drug use without access to safe equipment, including syringes, alcohol swabs, clean spoons, and filters. The second vector of transmission, unprotected sex, is more likely when people have sex when they are intoxicated and therefore compromised in their capacity to avoid risk. The two together create pathways of infection that intersect and magnify the risk of HIV infection in drug users, particularly among intravenous drug users. For example, a person may contract HIV through shared needle use but then pass the infection to his or her partner, even when in a monogamous relationship with a partner who does not inject drugs.

This constellation of factors added to the stigma of drug abuse during a period when contracting HIV was tantamount to a death sentence. Already stereotyped as the "gay plague" but increasingly manifesting in the heterosexual population, the added colour of drug addiction and sexual promiscuity led to increased negativity and moral opprobrium towards people with substance abuse problems. As time went on, it became clear in the popular imagination that HIV could not be isolated and contained within discrete populations. Instead, anyone with a new sexual partner or with multiple sexual partners was at risk for HIV infection. This included some people, particularly women, who contracted the virus from their spouses who had other undisclosed sexual partners.

What to do with the risk of infection among drug users and those who are intimate with them became a compelling public health question, and because of that, a public policy issue. The past 25 years could be considered an "in vivo experiment" where different jurisdictions across Canada and around the world have gone different ways in response to these issues. It was on the horns of this dilemma that the harm reduction movement was born.

Over 20 years ago, Bateson and Goldsby (1988) observed that "all the documented modes of the transmission of AIDS, except through the placenta, are based on voluntary behavior, shaped by learning and influenced by culture" (35). The authors were speaking particularly about sexual behaviour and intravenous drug use when they made this comment, and emphasized that the niche in which disease and illness occur is important to understand. In order to get infected, people must be in contact one way or another. HIV and AIDS require blood-to-blood contact, and in that regard, biological, social, and psychological factors are all in play. Biopsychosocial factors "co-construct" the niches in which the potential for transmitting infectious diseases occurs, and also—and perhaps even more importantly—how they are addressed.

HIV prevalence rates among injection drug users led public health officials in some jurisdictions to decide that, since the ideal lifetime of a hypodermic needle should be one use, it was important to see whether drug users could be encouraged to use a syringe only once and then dispose of it safely. Needle exchange programs are now considered a best practice in public health approaches to intravenous drug use, and policies to encourage pharmacies to sell syringes "no questions asked" complement needle exchange programs. Providing safe disposal options for used syringes is also recognized as important, and a crucial advance occurred when law enforcement changed their policing practices from arrest and detention to acceptance and support for public health alternatives.

A third tradition of care

> It should be possible to adjust the social patterns of drug use to reduce the real dangers presented by these different kinds of drugs.... A puritanical condemnation of drug use as a search for pleasure is not the best place to start. (Bateson and Goldsby 1988, 40)

Many of the problems faced by people who use illicit drugs are primarily due to the circumstances in which they live and in which the drug use takes place, as opposed to problems resulting from how drugs themselves affect the body. For example, legal drugs like tobacco and alcohol are directly associated with a variety of serious physical health issues, while opioids—including heroin—are not in and of themselves harmful to the body (unless too high a dose is taken). Instead, the greatest harms associated with illegal drug use often result from

> the circumstances in which people tend to use these drugs (in unsafe settings, in public, under non-sterile conditions, in a hurry, with strangers);
> the legal consequences that come from using illegal substances;
> committing crimes to get money to buy drugs;
> lack of access to clean injection equipment;
> limited knowledge about low-risk injection practices (as in which parts of the body to avoid injecting into, like the neck, groin, or wrists);
> unsafe additives or adulterants in the drugs themselves.

Harm reduction policies and initiatives generally focus on mitigating the risk factors surrounding drug use, and are less concerned with persuading users to quit. This pragmatic and nonjudgmental approach recognizes that drugs will always exist in society, that people will always abuse them, and that not all people are willing or able to quit. Given these realities, minimizing the harms associated with drug use is seen as the most humane way to address the needs of vulnerable populations.

Abstinence-only responses to people with substance use problems represent the first tradition of care and treatment, goal choice or moderation approaches represent the second, and harm reduction can be framed as a third tradition of care. If the first two traditions of abstinence and moderation serve their clients by offering them outpatient or residential services where they come to participate in assessment and treatment, the primary locus for harm reduction services is outreach—towards the environments where high-risk substance users live. All three traditions claim to offer an open door for people with substance use problems; however, the first two require clients to find and come through the door themselves. Harm reduction is more about helpers moving out of these doors to

The Unusual Journey of Larry Campbell

Larry Campbell was trained as an RCMP officer and worked as a member of its drug squad in Vancouver. In 1981, he joined the coroner's office, and between 1996 and 2000 served as chief coroner of British Columbia. His work there inspired the TV series *Da Vinci's Inquest*, which ran on CBC Television from 1998 to 2005. The show was filmed in Vancouver and revolved around the character of Dominic Da Vinci, an undercover RCMP officer who became a justice-seeking coroner.

Like his television alter ego, Campbell was concerned about the social conditions and human tragedy behind the downtown eastside drug scene, which at one point averaged one overdose death per day. During his years as coroner, Campbell helped champion Vancouver's "four pillars" approach to drug policy (prevention, treatment, law enforcement, and harm reduction). In 2002, as a member of the Coalition of Progressive Electors (COPE), he was elected mayor of Vancouver. The main platform of the COPE campaign was addressing Vancouver's drug problems, including a commitment to set up a safe injection site. Insite, the name of Vancouver's safe injection site, has been operating in the downtown eastside area since 2003.

In 2005, Campbell was called to the Senate of Canada, and has become a champion for cannabis legalization. He sees the less radical solution of decriminalization as "a simpler form of prohibition" that sends the wrong message. Decriminalization means making a drug illegal to produce and sell, but not prosecuting the people who use it. Campbell argues that Canada should

> legalize it, control it and tax the livin' hell out of it and put it all into health care, straight in.... If you want to reduce the use of marijuana, you reduce it exactly the same way as we do with cigarettes—you raise the taxes and educate the people on any harms that there may be, and there are harms. (*Vancouver Province* 2007)

where the risk is greatest, rather than waiting for those who are ready and looking for help.

High-need, high-risk individuals are often people who have been in treatment multiple times but who have not had good outcomes. They might also be people who feel marginalized and have opted out of mainstream society. Even more likely, they are people who have complex and multiple co-occurring problems. They are particularly at risk of being labelled as either not ready or not appropriate for most mainstream treatment services.

In addition to being a diverse set of pragmatic practices aimed at minimizing risk and harm (regardless of whether the person is still actively using drugs), harm reduction has taken shape as a broadly integrative philosophy with a particular value set. Its inclusive outlook provides an overarching framework that draws together public health, treatment services, social services, and law enforcement. Harm reduction also represents a new way of locating moderation and abstinence-oriented treatment approaches as vital options on a continuum that extends from prevention, early intervention, tertiary care, and palliative interventions for people with chronic injuries and problems due to severe drug use. It provides a humanizing lens that can inform law enforcement and criminal justice systems.

Drug policy as a local issue

Canadian policy debates on harm reduction occur not only at the national level but at the provincial and local levels as well. Cities have taken an especially active and at times provocative role in addressing issues related to drug use problems, especially when these problems affect whole neighbourhoods and communities. This has been most noticeable (some would say most notorious) in Vancouver, BC. The downtown eastside neighbourhood in Vancouver has seen highly visible and public drug use for many years. In 2002 the issues related to drug abuse were so serious that the mayor, Larry Campbell, and his civic government were elected on a platform to address Vancouver's drug problems in a new and innovative way. One of the most significant products that emerged during those years was the city's drug policy, the first of its kind in Canada, which articulated a "four pillar" approach to drug problems: prevention, law enforcement, treatment, and harm reduction (MacPherson 2001).

This new policy approach places traditional prohibitionist and abstinence perspectives within a broader framework that accepts substance use and related problems as persisting realities. The four pillars of drug stategy—prevenion, treatment, harm reduction, and law enforcement—are not meant to function as isolated silos; instead, policies and practice approaches are meant to be integrative across the four pillars. For example, law enforcement officers collaborate with treatment and harm reduction clinics by not arresting drug users who want to obtain clean needles or access other services.

Consistent with the values of the harm reduction approach, there have been deliberate and active attempts to bring the people with substance use problems into the dialogue, giving them a say in how substance use issues should be addressed and what services and supports are best suited to provide effective responses to their problems (Canadian HIV/AIDS Legal Network 2006). All of this is a marked shift away from responding to drug abuse through a moral-legal lens of deviance and correction. More recently the City of Toronto has developed its own drug policy, modelled on Vancouver's (City of Toronto 2007). Here again, harm reduction appears as one of the four pillars and as the overarching philosophical framework guiding the policy as a whole.

Vancouver's efforts to address substance use problems from a harm reduction perspective led to the radical (for Canada) decision to open a safe injection site, called Insite. With cooperation from the federal government, the site was set up on a pilot basis in 2003 under a constitutional exception to the Controlled Drugs and Substances Act, and is run by the Vancouver Coastal Health Authority in partnership with Portland Hotel Community Services. People with chronic and severe addictions can access Insite to inject their own drugs in a safe and medically supervised setting, putting them in contact with health providers and social services. The service is open from 10 a.m. to 4 p.m., seven days a week.

When clients enter the facility, they are assessed and led to a 12-seat injection room, and provided with sterile injection equipment (spoons, tourniquets, and water); however, Insite does not provide drugs to clients and staff members do not assist with injecting. After injecting, clients go to a post-injection room where they can receive primary medical treatment for wounds or abscesses (common among injection drug users), or access addiction counselling, peer support, or other treatment services. The intent is to prevent overdose deaths, get treatment referrals for health or other problems, and generally provide care to a population that does not access mainstream service systems.

Rigorous evaluation of Insite's services and impacts on drug users and the wider community has supported the effectiveness of this approach (Kerr et al. 2007; Wood et al. 2004). Over 8,000 clients have been seen at Insite since 2003, with roughly 600 visits per day. The facility has been successful in attracting clients with chronic and severe levels of dependence: clients report injecting drugs for an average of 15 years, 87 percent are infected with the hepatitis C virus, 17 percent are HIV-positive, 20 percent are homeless, 80 percent have been in jail, and 38 percent work in the sex trade (Insite Expert Advisory Committee 2008). Approximately half the clients inject heroin and roughly a third inject cocaine; although there have been hundreds of overdose episodes at Insite, there have been no overdose deaths.

Research shows that clients visiting Insite are more likely to access withdrawal management and addiction treatment services (Wood, Tyndall, Zhang, et al. 2006); the facility has not led to increased drug-related crime, and vehicle break-ins and theft have significantly declined (Wood, Tyndall, Lai, et al, 2006); and the downtown eastside neighbourhood has seen decreased public injecting and injection-related litter (Wood et al. 2004). Despite these encouraging outcomes, the continued support of Insite by the federal government is far from assured.

A Shift in Canada's National Drug Policy

I find the ethical considerations of supervised injections to be profoundly disturbing.... Is it ethical for healthcare professionals to support the distribution of drugs that are of unknown substance, or purity, or potency—drugs that cannot otherwise be legally prescribed? (Federal Health Minister Tony Clement, in *Canadian Medicine* 2008)

Canada's *National Drug Policy* (1998)—which integrated both licit and illicit drugs and promoted understanding drug abuse as primarily a health problem—was replaced in 2007. The Conservative government developed a new policy document, the *National Anti-Drug Strategy*, which focuses exclusively on illicit drugs. Like its predecessor, the Anti-Drug Strategy lists prevention, treatment, and law enforcement as key components, but in the new iteration, harm reduction is glaringly absent. Criticism of this change has been pointed among the scientific community, as in this excerpt from a 2007 editorial in the *National Review of Medicine*:

> The exclusion of harm reduction initiatives from the new Anti-Drug Strategy is a dangerous step backwards in the fight against HIV/ AIDS. Its increased emphasis on law enforcement has potential to further increase HIV and other [blood-borne] infections among IDU [injection drug users]. Through sexual transmission, the partners of infected IDU can then be expected to spread the virus among a wider population. The focus on law enforcement will also likely prompt a rise in the incarceration rates of IDUs, with marginalized populations, particularly Aboriginal peoples, being hardest hit. Imprisonment may further fuel the rate of disease transmission as incarceration has been independently associated with HIV infection among Canadian IDU.
>
> Canada's new "Anti-Drug Strategy" appears ill conceived. Furthermore, the new Anti-Drug Strategy is not anti-HIV.... This strategy may in fact be better described as "anti-health" and "anti-science." It has been over four years since former US president Bill Clinton publicly acknowledged that he was wrong to withhold federal funds for needle exchange programs in the United States. How long will [it] take before the Government of Canada expresses the same regret? (DeBeck et al. 2007)

The current government's steps to return drug policy to a more punitive orientation echoes US federal drug policy approaches. In the US there has been a virtual interdiction on the phrase "harm reduction" and an unwillingness to provide funding for harm reduction services and research. The federal policy direction in Canada brings a similarly one-sided approach to addressing and responding to drug problems.

Following the money is one way of seeing how governments frame drug problems and how they propose to address them. In the new *National Anti-Drug Strategy* the government has promised funding in the next five years in the amounts of $30 million for the Prevention Action Plan, $100 million for the Treatment Action Plan (with one focus being money for the RCMP to set up court diversion programs, or "drug courts"), and $169 million in the Enforcement Action Plan (Department of Justice Canada 2008). Among this trio, it is clear that law enforcement receives the lion's share of federal funding related to drug problems.

An important feature of government in Canada is that health is a provincial responsibility, while justice and the criminal code are federal responsibilities. This means that the criminal code applies everywhere in Canada, but the laws that govern health care are set by the ten provincial and three territorial governments. The philosophical basis behind the current federal policy approach to drug problems is in open conflict with the harm reduction approach that has been taken up by just about every provincial jurisdiction, as well as by most treatment systems across the country.

The federal government's open opposition to Vancouver's safe injection site emerges in this broader context. Speaking at the XVIII International AIDS Conference in Mexico City, federal Health Minister Tony Clement had this to say about programs (like Insite) that help users to inject drugs more safely: "Allowing and/or encouraging people to inject heroin into their veins is not harm reduction, it is the opposite.... We believe it is a form of harm addition" (Picard 2008). Critics were immediate in their reaction, both across Canada and around the world. They redirected the ethical challenge back to the Canadian government, questioning the ethics of abandoning the most vulnerable. A Malaysian scientist pointed out that there are 49 safe injection sites around the world, mostly in Europe and Australia, adding that harm

A Sociologist's View on Harm Reduction and Canadian Policy: An Interview with Dr Pat Erickson

Dr Pat Erickson has been a champion of knowledge-informed approaches to drug policy in Canada and around the world. She is a senior scientist at the Centre for Addiction and Mental Health (CAMH) and formerly at the Addiction Research Foundation (which merged with other institutions in 1998 to create CAMH), and she has played a lead role in drug policy research and advice. We spoke with Dr Erickson in July of 2009 about her experience and views on harm reduction policies in Canada.

Dr Erickson comments that when she started working at the Addiction Research Foundation in 1973, "I thought I'd have a three-year job, and then cannabis would be legalized and I'd move on. Apparently, I am not much on prophecies." Her groundbreaking and influential studies of "cannabis criminals" in the late 1970s and 1980s were among the first to make a science-based case for non-criminal approaches to cannabis use. Dr Erickson then turned her attention to cocaine users, and by the 1990s harm reduction had become her primary research focus. She was involved in the first harm reduction conference in North America, held in Toronto in 1994 with the Addiction Research Foundation as a sponsor. This conference made harm reduction a common currency in the public forum. The research and writing of Dr Erickson and other leaders in the harm reduction arena led to a number of advances. For example, the body of scientific evidence flowing from her and her colleagues' work formed the basis for contesting the former Ontario provincial government's 1997 decision to disallow people from receiving disability benefits if their "sole condition" was addiction. After a legal battle lasting over a decade, the Ontario Divisional Court ruled in 2009 against the government, a ruling that has enormous implications for people with substance abuse problems in Ontario and elsewhere in Canada.

Despite research evidence and advice from a number of credible sources (including the Canadian Senate), government and policy-makers have been reluctant to adopt progressive approaches like cannabis decriminalization or legalization:

For some time, evidence seemed to be getting through to policy makers. We seem to be entering a backlash period, obviously in Canada, but also in the UK and Australia where cannabis has been subject to more punitive approaches again. I am not optimistic that science will hold sway anytime soon. Even if we see progress in treatment modalities for the most marginalized users, I think the continued or even more punitive response ... will flood the prisons.

Dr Erickson is also concerned that harm reduction has become "much too focused on the street users, and serious problems, and lost sight of the vast majority who use without problems, yet are still subject to arrest, stigma, and punishment."

As Dr Erickson's original three-year project for science-based drug reform has stretched into a 30-year mission, she has become cautiously realistic about the prospect of significant policy shifts: "Ahead, in Canada, I can believe that things will not have changed at all. I'm not sure they can get worse. There will be new drugs, new scares, and no new responses."

However, Dr Erickson does see some positive signs:

I am encouraged that a new organization, the Canadian Drug Policy Consortium, seems to be taking shape, aiming for a "civil society voice on drug policy." The old CFDP (Canadian Foundation for Drug Policy), thanks to Eugene Oscapella, did what it could with virtually no funds or organization, so perhaps this new group will be better able to get things moving. Also, Students for Sensible Drug Policy are active.

The work of Dr Pat Erickson and others committed to building the knowledge base for drug abuse and drug policy has given Canada an impressive archive that can be accessed as public policy develops and matures—even as unpredictable political processes continue to produce drag and inertia in the face of scientific evidence.

reduction initiatives including safe injection sites have a measureable impact in reducing the spread of HIV. Peter Piot, the executive director of UNAIDS, stated that "it is high time every country in the world resolutely embraced the full spectrum of harm reduction among injecting drug users. Not doing so will only perpetuate the spread of HIV" (Picard 2008).

In Canada, it is estimated that there are 58,000 people who have been infected by HIV, with about 15 percent of these being intravenous drug users. Although these figures are worrisome, Canada's HIV rates compare quite favourably with other countries. This is attributed to our comparatively more progressive and active harm reduction policies and initiatives (Boulos et al. 2006). Because health care policy is primarily shaped and governed by provincial and territorial governments where this approach has a strong footing, in the end the Conservatives' stance marginalizes the federal government rather than putting it in a position of leadership, both nationally and internationally.

The federal government's attempts to shut down Insite have led to court challenges and a round of appeals. The most recent was a decision by the Supreme Court of British Columbia that Insite is a health centre, and therefore under the authority of the provincial government (which supports its continued operation). The federal government has appealed this decision to the Supreme Court of Canada which will have the final say on this matter.

The Curious Case of Cannabis

Another drug policy domain which has been the subject of high-profile legal challenges has been the medical use of cannabis. There is evidence that cannabis can be helpful in managing the severe pain, nausea, or weight loss that accompanies serious illness (Joy, Watson, and Benson 1999). In the 1990s "medical marijuana" became a rallying point for advocacy groups in favour of cannabis legalization, as well as some health practitioners and progressive policy advocates. Various groups deliberately flouted the law and in some cases set up "compassion clubs" to make the drug accessible to those in need of it for medical reasons (although the rigour with which access was restricted only to people with valid medical need was likely variable). Inevitably, these clubs came under police surveillance and were subject to police raids and charges for possessing, and more importantly, trafficking an illegal drug.

These charges made their way gradually through the courts, with the losing sides, crown or accused, appealing verdicts that went against them. Finally, the Supreme Court of Canada ruled that on the basis of the medical evidence, it offended the human rights of people with specific illnesses and health conditions to be denied the option of using cannabis as part of their treatment. The Supreme Court directed the federal government to provide and make cannabis available and to desist from prosecuting people with valid medical need from possessing and using cannabis. People were also not to be prosecuted for growing cannabis for their own use if the drug was not being provided by the government. Thus, in 2001 medical marijuana officially came to Canada.

The regulations for the legal use of medical cannabis outline two categories of people who can make an application to Health Canada:

Category 1: This category is [composed] of any symptoms treated within the context of providing compassionate end-of-life care; or the symptoms associated with the specified medical conditions listed in the schedule to the Regulations, namely:

> Severe pain and/or persistent muscle spasms from **multiple sclerosis**;
> Severe pain and/or persistent muscle spasms from a **spinal cord injury**;
> Severe pain and/or persistent muscle spasms from **spinal cord disease**;
> Severe pain, cachexia, anorexia, weight loss, and/or severe nausea from **cancer**;
> Severe pain, cachexia, anorexia, weight loss, and/or severe nausea from **HIV/AIDS infection**;
> Severe pain from **severe forms of arthritis**; or
> Seizures from **epilepsy**.

Applicants must provide a declaration from a medical practitioner to support their application.

Category 2: This category is for applicants who have debilitating symptom(s) of medical condition(s), other than those described in

Category 1. Under Category 2, persons with debilitating symptoms can apply to obtain an *Authorization to Possess* dried [marijuana] for medical purposes, if a specialist confirms the diagnosis and that conventional treatments have failed or judged inappropriate to relieve symptoms of the medical condition. While an assessment of the applicant's case by a specialist is required, the treating physician, whether or not a specialist, can sign the medical declaration. (Health Canada 2005)

People who receive Health Canada approval to use medical marijuana can obtain the drug in a couple of different ways. Health Canada has a contract with a company (Prairie Plant Systems) to cultivate cannabis that is standardized and homogenous, and can supply the drug to authorized individuals. Alternatively, individuals who are authorized to use medical cannabis can apply to Health Canada for a Personal Use Production Licence, or can apply to have someone else grow cannabis for their use (a Designated Person Production Licence) if unable to grow their own.

Policy debates about cannabis extend well beyond the legality and appropriateness of medical marijuana. The question of the legal status of cannabis more generally has been contentious for decades. Cannabis is the most commonly used illicit drug in the world (Tan et al. 2009), and its use among Canadians is on the increase. According to the most recent Canadian Addiction Survey (Adlaf, Begin, and Sawka 2005), 14 percent of Canadians use cannabis, although 46 percent of people reporting past-year use did so very infrequently (that is, only once or twice in the three months preceding the survey). Cannabis use is now double the rate reported in 1994 (7.4 percent), and is highest among youth and young adults: 30 percent of Canadians aged 15–17 and 47 percent of those aged 18–19 report past-year use.

Decades of sociological studies have shown that the current laws are ineffective and capable of doing more harm than good, specifically in terms of stigmatizing people convicted under the criminal code of Canada for cannabis possession for personal use (Cussen and Block 2000; Erickson and Murray 1986). Decriminalization is suggested as the preferred policy direction by a number of key agencies that are considered to be international centres of excellence, including Ontario's Centre for Addiction and Mental Health (CAMH 2007c). Even with this growing consensus among the expert community (and increasingly among the Canadian public), it was surprising to many that the Canadian Senate recommended that Canada not only decriminalize, but legalize the production, sale, possession, and use of cannabis.

Decriminalization moves cannabis possession outside the Criminal Code, but can be seen as a compromise between prohibition and complete legalization. Legalization, on the other hand, would allow the drug to be produced, taxed, sold, and consumed under government regulation, similar to alcohol and tobacco. Although the Senate's recommendation represents one of the most progressive expressions of Canadian drug policy, it is counterbalanced by the current view of the federal Conservatives—that penalties for all illegal drugs, including cannabis, should be more strictly enforced and even increased. Hence, it is unlikely that cannabis legislation and policy will become more lenient any time soon.

However, even if Canadian policy eventually moves towards cannabis decriminalization or legalization, it is important to note that the use of this drug has a number of accompanying health risks (Kalant et al. 1999). Both tobacco and cannabis smoke contain a similar range of harmful chemicals, and short-term cannabis use by young adults has been shown to adversely affect lung function. Furthermore, the concurrent use of both cannabis and tobacco can have a synergistic effect on lung function and the risk of chronic obstructive pulmonary disease (COPD; Tan et al. 2009).

Cannabis use among youth is also a risk factor for experiencing first-episode psychosis, and is associated with poorer prognosis and higher relapse of psychotic symptoms (Rosenbaum et al. 2005). Research shows that adolescents who use cannabis on a weekly basis have a greater risk of developing acute psychosis three or more years later, compared with youth who do not use cannabis (Veen et al. 2004). In addition, the main psychoactive ingredient in cannabis (THC, or tetrahydrocannabinol) has increased substantially in the past three decades (Hardwick and King 2008; National Drug Intelligence Center 2008), likely due to advances in indoor cultivation methods. This higher potency results in more rapid intoxication—akin to the difference in effect of drinking vodka versus a similar volume of beer.

The Evolution of Drug Policy

A political reality is that governments come and go, accompanied by oscillations and shifts in belief systems, frames of mind, and approaches to legislation. These swings show that policy change around drug reform is a slow-moving, nonlinear process, subject to interruptions, detours, and reversals.

The emergence of a base of evidence to guide and shape policy does not guarantee an impact on governments that are more oriented to moralistic and punitive approaches. However, the federal government is one of many influential bodies that set drug policy. Collaborative action towards a national approach to drug problems continues to be led by the provinces, national lead agencies—such as the Canadian Centre on Substance Abuse (CCSA), the Canadian Executive Council on Addictions (CECA), and the Mental Health Commission of Canada (MHCC)—and science-based organizations—such as Centre for Addiction and Mental Health (CAMH) and the Centre for Addiction Research of British Columbia (CARBC), among others.

A basic feature of policy in Canada has been gradualism—an incremental tendency to follow the unfolding evidence, supported by a spirit of pragmatism and tolerance. This has allowed for practical responses to contentious issues, and local action that is responsive even when formal laws and regulations are no longer apt but still remain in force. This leads to unevenness of implementation, and contradictions; but, policy has gradually moved along, and practices that attend to the disadvantages of marginalized and victimized groups have become incrementally improved. This gradualism satisfies neither those opposed to change and accommodation, nor those who insist that more fundamental structural change is necessary. But it does ensure that policy debates will continue, unabated.

Finding Colour in the Grey Zone

Drug policy in Canada is, as we have seen, characterized by inconsistent approaches and divergent priorities. In an effort to introduce greater cohesion and collaboration into policy and legislation, a group of over 100 representatives—from governments, non-government organizations (NGOs), research, health care, law enforcement, and Aboriginal service providers—came together in June 2005 in a national forum to collaboratively develop a comprehensive policy document. The result was the *National Framework for Action to Reduce the Harms Associated with Alcohol and Other Drugs and Substances in Canada*. That document was the product of two years of nationwide consultations under the leadership of Health Canada, its federal partners (Public Safety and Emergency Preparedness, and the Department of Justice), and the Canadian Centre on Substance Abuse (CCSA; see Figure 5-1).

The National Treatment Strategy Working Group is one of the components of the *National Framework*, and in 2008 released its report, *A Systems Approach to Substance Use and Substance Use Problems in Canada: Recommendations for a National Treatment Strategy*. The report recommends developing a continuum of services for people from low to high risk of substance use problems. The continuum is based on a tiered model, where each tier represents logical groupings of services according to the acuity, complexity, and chronicity of the populations they serve. In other words, each tier (or service group) should offer a continuum of care for people at all levels of risk, from prevention through to tertiary care.

The document developed by the National Treatment Strategy Working Group recognizes that people with substance use problems are not only seen in the specialized addiction treatment system. This approach enshrines the principle

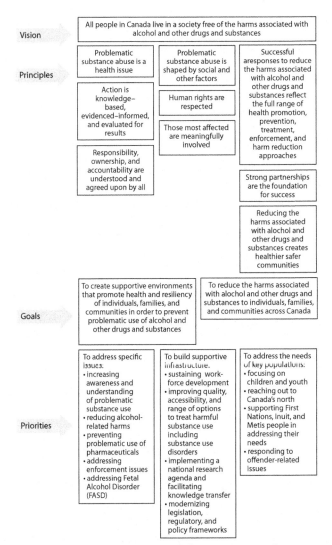

Figure 5-1 National Framework for Action to Reduce the Harms Associated with Alcohol and Other Drugs and Substances in Canada

Source: Canadian Centre on Substance Abuse 2005

of broadening the base of addiction services, where there is no "wrong door" to addiction treatment. The core principles informing a national treatment system include

> recognizing the full range of risks and harms associated with substance use and focusing services and supports on both risk and readiness;
> adopting a coordinated multi-sectoral approach in addressing the risks and harms of substance use;
> informing practice with research evidence and being accountable for providing effective service and supports;
> organizing service systems around people's needs and ensuring that services and supports are person-centred;
> integrating gender- and diversity-based components into services and supports, and recognizing families and other loved ones as integral.

Source: National Treatment Strategy Working Group 2008

In addition, services and supports identifying and addressing substance use problems need to be accessible, flexible, responsive, and coordinated. Collaboration among health and allied health providers and attention to appropriate client-treatment matching are also recognized as being fundamental to an effective treatment system.

An important advance in the document is its broader vision of ways of responding to substance use problems in Canada. Substance abuse and addiction are not isolated issues; they are linked with a variety of other health and social problems. Substance abuse co-occurs with cardiovascular disease, diabetes, cancer, and mental disorders. It is also related to family violence and child welfare, workplace productivity and criminal justice involvement.

The National Treatment Strategy acknowledges the need for a range of services, from brief, early interventions to ongoing continuing care. Access to primary care is seen as a vital component underpinning the strategy, as are the informal sources of support that are the ultimate indicators of community health. These sources include nurturing and supportive families, safe and inviting neighbourhoods, and recreational and cultural options that engage people across their lifespans. In this vision of a positive society, education and productive employment are respected as entitlements, and people with special needs and disabilities receive the inclusive supports that empower them to live lives of value and accomplishment.

As of 2009, 44 partners from across Canada have endorsed the *National Framework*, ranging from hospitals, teachers' associations, addiction service agencies, law enforcement, municipal and provincial governments, researchers, and NGOs. Change is slow and incremental, but the National Framework is an important step in a positive direction.

Conclusion

The drug policy arena reflects our most fundamental issues and assumptions about substance abuse. Viewing addiction as a personal choice unfettered by social determinants of health leads to policy focused on criminalization and enforcement. Using a broader health and social justice lens leads in other policy directions pointed more toward care and treatment. This discourse includes human rights, personal responsibility, community values, and the laws that govern us.

Gabor Maté is an author and staff physician at a medical clinic in Vancouver's downtown eastside neighbourhood. His experiences led him to write *In the Realm of the Hungry Ghosts: Close Encounters with Addiction* (2008), a sprawling exploration of addiction and the stigma that surrounds it. In his book, Maté wonders why we are so hostile to people suffering from addictions, when we all have some experience with this issue, either directly or indirectly:

> Maté sees addiction as existing along a continuum, and we are all on it. It's not just about "them"—the marginalized, desperate aliens who represent our stereotype of addiction—it's about all of us, Maté included.... "At heart, I am no different than my patients—and I sometimes cannot stand seeing how ... little heaven-granted space separates me from them." (Skinner 2008, 1325)

Maté notes that stress, powerlessness, emotional isolation, and social dislocation set the stage for substance abuse to occur, and these are conditions to which we are all vulnerable.

As we discussed at the beginning of this chapter, our moral frames shape our views of substance abuse, human behaviour, and what we value for ourselves and for those around us in a world of growing interdependence. If we see human problems as bad behaviour that requires punishment and derogation, then we will fall back to approaches to substance abuse that are age-old but increasingly out of place. If we recognize that we too have evolved, that we have the capacity to bring skills and abilities that are both compassionate and effective, then we can more constructively shape policy not just to reduce harm but to enhance well-being. And this recognition represents the evolutionary potential of healthier people living together in healthier worlds.

Appendix A: Major Approaches in Addictions Treatment

The following is a listing of addiction treatment models, each with a brief summary of its main premise and intervention techniques, and a reference for suggested further reading.

Cognitive Behavioural Therapy

Premise: Substance use problems are learned behaviours that can be "unlearned" via cognitive and behavioural techniques.

Coping skills training
Identification of relapse risk and relapse prevention strategies
Positive self-talk and "thought-stopping"
Role-playing and real-life practice of skills

Further reading: Herie, M., and L. Watkin-Merek. 2006. *Structured Relapse Prevention: An Outpatient Counselling Approach*. 2nd ed. Toronto: Centre for Addiction and Mental Health.

Motivational Interviewing

Premise: Enhancing motivation is key to changing substance use behaviour.

Facilitating exploration of ambivalence towards change (weighing the "pros and cons" of change)
Empathic reflection used strategically
Eliciting "change talk" via open questions and reflection

Further reading: Miller, W.A., and S. Rollnick. 2002. *Motivational Interviewing: Preparing People for Change*. 2nd ed. New York: Guilford Press.

Harm Reduction Psychotherapy

Premise: Not everyone is ready to stop using substances—programs must take a pragmatic and humane response to reducing drug-related harms.

Delivering education about safer ways of using substances, often in the person's own community via outreach
Providing clean syringes, condoms, dental dams, etc. (to reduce the risk of transmission of infectious diseases)
Addressing the person's own priorities (such as food, housing or money), as opposed to focusing on substance use

Further reading: Denning, P. 2000. *Practicing Harm Reduction Psychotherapy: An Alternative Approach to Addictions*. New York: Guilford Press.

Narrative Therapy

Premise: Each person has developed a personal "story" or narrative of his or her life; this story can be "re-authored" in a more positive way, engendering hope and uncovering new possibilities and strengths.

Re-authoring conversations, using a therapist "scaffold" of key questions (facilitating a point of entry into alternative story lines)

"Re-membering" conversations (exploring the perspectives and impacts of significant people in an individual's life)

Definitional ceremony (telling/performing life stories in front of an outside witness, who in turn retells the story, then is retold the story, etc.)

Further reading: Payne, M. 2006. *Narrative Therapy: An Introduction for Counsellors*. 2nd ed. London: SAGE Publications.

Solution-Focused Therapy

Premise: All people have untapped strengths and resources that can be mobilized to address their substance use problems. The focus is on discovering solutions as opposed to exploring problems.

Scaling questions (for example, "On a scale of one to ten, how would you rate your situation? What could you do to move one point higher on the scale?")

The "miracle question" ("If you woke up tomorrow and all of your problems were solved while you were asleep, what would be different?")

Looking for exceptions (when does the person not use drugs?)

Further reading: Miller, S.D., and I.K. Berg. 1995. *The Miracle Method: A Radically New Approach to Problem Drinking*. New York: W.W. Norton & Company.

Structural Family Therapy

Premise: Substance use problems are a symptom of a larger issue in the family system. Changing how family members function and relate to one another is key to resolving one member's substance use.

Joining with family members
Reframing perceptions about people and events, "unbalancing" family patterns/perceptions, and enactment of communication processes in sessions
Re-forming boundaries and restructuring the family system

Further reading: Hecker, L.L., and J.L.Wetchler, eds. 2003. *An Introduction to Marriage and Family Therapy*. New York: Haworth Clinical Practice Press.

Interpersonal Group Therapy

Premise: The group is a microcosm of each person's functioning in the broader social context; the group is a "laboratory" for exploring and developing new ways of communicating and interacting with others.

Interpersonal difficulties in the group are treated as opportunities for change
"Here-and-now" focus, (where the group attends to interactions as they are happening)
Facilitation of "corrective emotional experiences" (understanding of how others view and respond to us, and consolidation of new ways of relating to others)
Regular, structured monitoring of substance use and attention to relapse risks

Further reading: Yalom, I.D., and M. Leszcz. 2005. *The Theory and Practice of Group Psychotherapy*. 5th ed. New York: Perseus Books.

Mindfulness Meditation

Premise: Based on Buddhist principles and teachings; asserts that non-judgmental acceptance of personal experiences in the present leads to changed perceptions of self, and an increased sense of freedom, choice, and awareness.

Training in different types of meditation practice, aimed at being present to (and aware of) sensations, thoughts, and feelings
Includes "body scan," breath-counting, naming emotions (e.g., "angry mind," "despairing mind"), and other techniques

Further reading: Kabat-Zinn, J. 1994. *Wherever You Go, There You Are: Mindfulness Meditation in Everyday Life.* New York: Hyperion.

Self-Help or Self-Guided Treatment

Premise: People have the internal resources to recover on their own, especially when complemented by peer support. Note that self-help is frequently recommended as a useful adjunct to "formal" addiction treatment approaches.
These can be grouped into two broad categories:

Groups based on the 12-step approach, as set out by AA, which asserts that alcoholism/addiction is a disease requiring complete abstinence from all substances and lifelong recovery
Alternative approaches to AA, some of which reject the 12 steps but maintain a disease focus with a requirement of abstinence (such as Women For Sobriety); others take a more behavioural approach that allows for goal choice (such as Moderation Management, Rational Recovery, or Self Management And Recovery Training)

Further reading: Hamilton, B. 1995. *Getting Started in AA.* Centre City, MN: Hazelden.
Rotgers, F., M.F. Kern, and R. Hoeltzel. 2002. *Responsible Drinking: A Moderation Management Approach for Problem Drinkers.* Oakland, CA: New Harbinger Press.

Notes

Chapter 1

[1]The most recent revision of the manual is commonly identified as *DSM-IV-TR*. Here and throughout this book, we refer to this work as *DSM* for simplicity.

Chapter 2

[1]Alice Fleming's 1975 book, *Alcohol: The Delightful Poison*, gives a lively account of the origins, traditions, and impacts of alcohol on culture and society. Some highlights from her book are outlined in this chapter.

[2]An excellent overview of alcohol and its effects can be found at http://www.camh.net/About_Addiction_Mental_Health/Drug_and_Addiction_Information/alcohol_dyk.html.

[3]The Motherisk website, provided by the Hospital for Sick Children in Toronto, ON, contains a wealth of information and resources relating to alcohol and other drug use and pregnancy. See http://www.motherisk.org.

[4]To take the survey, visit http://alcoholhelpcenter.net.

[5]Project Amik is a project that provides affordable housing to individuals and families. See http://www.frontiersfoundation.ca/amik.

[6]For more information, see http://www.poundmaker.org.

Chapter 3

[1]Access to the collection is available online, and the entire database of documents is searchable by any key word. See http://www.cctc.ca/cctc/EN/industrywatch/internaldocuments/Guildford.

[2]For a comprehensive review of traditional tobacco among North American Aboriginal peoples, see Winter's *Tobacco Use by Native North Americans: Sacred Smoke and Silent Killer* (2000).

Chapter 4

[1]Chuvalo's website, "George Chuvalo's Official Fight Against Drugs," details his career and anti-drug work. See http://www.fightagainstdrugs.ca.

[2]*Cottonland* may be ordered from the National Film Board of Canada. See http://www.onf-nfb.gc.ca/eng/collection/film/?id=52109.

Chapter 5

[1]Alcohol prohibition has not entirely disappeared in Canada, with some communities who actively endorse and apply prohibitionist policies. For example, alcohol is prohibited on some First Nations' reserves as a way of protecting community members from the ravages of alcohol abuse.

Further Reading

Chapter 1

Alexander, Bruce. *The Globalisation of Addiction*. Oxford: Oxford University Press, 2008.

Crozier, Lorna, and Patrick Lane, eds. *Addicted: Notes from the Belly of the Beast*. 2nd ed. Vancouver: Greystone Books, 2006.

Herie, Marilyn, Tim Godden, Joanne Shenfeld, and Colleen Kelly. *Addiction: An Information Guide*. Toronto: CAMH Press, 2007.

Maté, Gabor. *In the Realm of Hungry Ghosts: Close Encounters with Addiction*. Toronto: Knopf Canada, 2008.

Internet Resources

Canadian Centre on Substance Abuse
http://www.ccsa.ca

Centre for Addiction and Mental Health
http://www.camh.net

Substance Abuse and Mental Health Services Administration
http://www.samhsa.gov

Chapter 2

Lane, Patrick. *There Is a Season: A Memoir*. Toronto: McClelland & Stewart, 2004.

Meyers, Robert J., and Brenda L. Wolfe. *Get Your Loved One Sober: Alternatives to Nagging, Pleading, and Threatening*. Center City, MN: Hazelden, 2004.

Rotgers, Frederick, Marc F. Kern, Rudy Hoeltzel. *Responsible Drinking: A Moderation Management Approach for Problem Drinkers*. Oakland, CA: New Harbinger Press, 2002.

Sanchez-Craig, Martha. *DrinkWise: How to Quit Drinking or Cut Down*. Toronto: Addiction Research Foundation, 1995.

Internet Resources

Alcohol Help Center
www.alcoholhelpcenter.net

Alcohol Policy Network
www.apolnet.ca

National Institute on Alcohol Abuse and Alcoholism
www.niaaa.nih.gov

Chapter 3

Carr, Allen. *Easy Way to Stop Smoking*. London: Penguin, 2006.

DeNelsky, Garland Y. *Stop Smoking Now! The Rewarding Journey to a Smoke-Free Life*. Cleveland: Cleveland Clinic Press, 2007.

Ivings, Kristina. *Free Yourself from Smoking: A Three-Point Plan to Kill Nicotine Addiction*. London: Kyle Cathie, 2006.

Keelan, Brian (2004). *Free at Last! Stop Smoking: How I did it, How You Can Do it Too*. Toronto: Hushion House.

Shafey, Omar, Michael Eriksen, Hanna Ross, and Judith Mackay. *The Tobacco Atlas*. 3rd ed. Atlanta, GA: American Cancer Society, 2009.

Internet Resources

Canadian Council for Tobacco Control
www.cctc.ca

Ontario Tobacco Research Unit
www.otru.org

Smokers' Helpline Online
www.smokershelpline.ca

Chapter 4

Marlowe, Ann. *How to Stop Time: Heroin from A to Z*. New York: Basic Books, 1999.

Reid, Stephen. Junkie. In *Addicted: Notes from the Belly of the Beast*, 2nd ed, ed. Lorna Crozier and Patrick Lane. Vancouver: Greystone Books, 2006.

Skinner, W.J. Wayne, Caroline P. O'Grady, Christina Bartha, and Carol Parker. *Concurrent Substance Use and Mental Health Disorders: An Information Guide*. Toronto: Centre for Addiction and Mental Health, 2004.

Internet Resources

Canadian Centre on Substance Abuse (Opioids)
http://www.ccsa.ca/Eng/Topics/SubstancesAndAddictions/Opioids/Pages/default.aspx

Canadian Harm Reduction Network
http://canadianharmreduction.com

Centre for Addiction and Mental Health (Do You Know ... Heroin)
http://www.camh.net/About_Addiction_Mental_Health/Drug_and_Addiction_Information/heroin_dyk.html

Centre for Addiction and Mental Health (Oxycontin: Straight Talk)
http://www.camh.net/About_Addiction_Mental_Health/Drug_and_Addiction_Information/oxycontin_straight_talk.html

Health Canada (Drug Prevention Publications)
http://www.hc-sc.gc.ca/hc-ps/pubs/adp-apd/index-eng.php#public_treatment

Chapter 5

Erickson, Patricia G., Diane M. Riley, Yuet W. Cheung, and Patrick O'Hare, eds. *Harm Reduction: A New Direction for Drug Policies and Programs*. Toronto: University of Toronto Press, 1997.
Heyman, Gene. *Addiction: A Disorder of Choice*. Cambridge, MA: Harvard University Press, 2009.
National Treatment Strategy Working Group. *A Systems Approach to Substance Use in Canada: Recommendations for a National Treatment Strategy*. Ottawa: National Framework for Action to Reduce the Harms Associated with Alcohol and Other Drugs and Substances in Canada, 2008. http://www.nationalframework-cadrenational.ca/detail_e.php?id_sub=10&id_top_sub=2.

Internet Resources

Canadian Foundation for Drug Policy
www.cfdp.ca

Canadian Harm Reduction Network
http://canadianharmreduction.com

City of Vancouver's Four Pillars Drug Strategy
http://vancouver.ca/fourpillars/fs_fourpillars.htm

Harm Reduction Journal
http://www.harmreductionjournal.com

References

AADAC. *See* Alberta Alcohol and Drug Abuse Commission.

Abrams, D.B., R. Niaura, R.A. Brown, K.M. Emmons, M.G. Goldstein, and P.M. Monti. 2003. *The Tobacco Dependence Treatment Handbook: A Guide to Best Practices*. New York: Guilford Press.

Adlaf, E.M., P. Begin, and E. Sawka, eds. 2005. *Canadian Addiction Survey (CAS): A National Survey of Canadians' Use of Alcohol and Other Drugs, Detailed Report*. Ottawa: Canadian Centre on Substance Abuse. http://www.ccsa.ca/2005%20CCSA%20Documents/ccsa-004028-2005.pdf.

Agic, B. 2005. *Culture Counts: Best Practices in Community Education in Mental Health and Addiction with Ethnoracial/Ethnocultural Communities*. Toronto: Centre for Addiction and Mental Health. http://www.camh.net/education/Resources_communities_organizations/culture_counts_jan05.pdf.

Ahmad, N., N. Poole, and C.A. Dell. 2008. Women's Substance Use in Canada: Findings from the 2004 Canadian Addiction Survey. In *Highs and Lows: Canadian Perspectives on Women and Substance Use*, ed. N. Poole and L. Greaves. Toronto: Centre for Addiction and Mental Health.

Alberta Alcohol and Drug Abuse Commission (AADAC). 2006. *Fact Sheet: The Truth About the Tobacco Industry*. http://www.aadac.com/documents/truth_about_tobacco_industry.pdf.

———. 2007. *Fact Sheet: The Truth About Spit Tobacco*. http://www.aadac.com/documents/truth_about_spit_tobacco.pdf.

Alberta Transportation. 2008. *Alberta Traffic Collision Statistics*. Edmonton: Alberta Office of Traffic Safety. http://www.

transportation.alberta.ca/Content/docType47/Production/2008AR.
pdf.

Alcohol Help Center. http://www.alcoholhelpcenter.net. Based on
K. Kypri, J. Langley, and S. Stephenson (2005). Episode-centred
Analysis of Drinking to Intoxication in University Students. *Alcohol
and Alcoholism* 40(5): 447–452.

Alcoholics Anonymous. 1976. *Alcoholics Anonymous: The Story of How
Many Thousands of Men and Women Have Recovered from Alcoholism*.
3rd ed. New York: Alcoholics Anonymous World Services.

———. 1984. *This Is A.A.: An Introduction to the A.A. Recovery
Program*. New York: Alcoholics Anonymous World Services. http://
www.aa.org/pdf/products/p-1_thisisaa1.pdf.

Alexander, B.K. 2001. *The Roots of Addiction in Free Market Society*.
Vancouver: Canadian Centre for Policy Alternatives. http://www.
policyalternatives.ca/documents/BC_Office_Pubs/roots_addiction.
pdf.

American Cancer Society. 2009. Child and Teen Tobacco Use:
Prevention and Early Detection. http://www.cancer.org.

American Psychiatric Association (APA). 2000. *Diagnostic and Statistical
Manual of Mental Disorders*. 4th ed. Text Revision. Arlington, VA:
American Psychiatric Association.

APA. *See* American Psychiatric Association.

Babor, T.F., J.C. Higgins-Biddle, J.B. Saunders, and M.G. Monteiro.
2001. *AUDIT—The Alcohol Use Disorders Identification Test: Guidelines
for Use in Primary Care*. 2nd ed. Geneva: World Health Organization.
http://whqlibdoc.who.int/hq/2001/WHO_MSD_MSB_01.6a.pdf.

Bader, P., P.W. McDonald, and P. Selby. 2009. An Algorithm for Tailoring
Pharmacotherapy for Smoking Cessation: Results from a Delphi
Panel of International Experts. *Tobacco Control* 18 (1):34–42.

Bateson, M.C., and R. Goldsby. 1988. *Thinking A.I.D.S.: The Social
Response to the Biological Threat*. New York: Addison-Wesley.

Bjartveit, K., and A. Tverdal. 2005. Health Consequences of Smoking
1–4 Cigarettes per Day. *Tobacco Control* 14:315–20

Blocker, J.S. 2003. *Alcohol and Temperance in Modern History: An
International Encyclopedia*. Santa Barbara, CA: ABC-CLIO.

Booth, M. 1996. *Opium: A History*. London: Simon & Schuster.

Boulos, D., P. Yan, D. Schanzer, R.S. Remis, and C.P. Archibald. 2006.
Estimates of HIV Prevalence and Incidence in Canada, 2005.
Canada Communicable Disease Report 32 (15).

Brands, B., ed. 2000. *Management of Alcohol, Tobacco and Other Drug
Problems: A Physicians' Manual*. Toronto: Centre for Addiction and
Mental Health.

Brands, B., B. Sproule, and J. Brands, eds. 1998. *Drugs and Drug
Abuse*. Toronto: Addiction Research Foundation.

British Columbia Centre of Excellence for Women's Health. 2005. *Women's Health Policy Brief*. http://www.cewh-cesf.ca/PDF/bccewh/policyBCCEWH.pdf.

Britton, J., ed. 2004. *ABC of Smoking Cessation*. Malden, MA: Blackwell.

Brook, D.W., J.S. Brook, C. Zhang, M. Whiteman, P. Cohen, and S.J. Finch. 2008. Developmental Trajectories of Cigarette Smoking from Adolescence to the Early Thirties: Personality and Behavioral Risk Factors. *Nicotine & Tobacco Research* 10 (8):1283–91.

Burroughs, W.S. 1953. *Junkie*. New York: Ace Books.

———. 1966. *Naked Lunch*. New York: Grove Press.

Callaghan, R.C., L. Taylor, and J.A. Cunningham. 2007. Does Progressive Stage Transition Mean Getting Better? A Test of the Transtheoretical Model in Alcoholism Recovery. *Addiction* 102:1588–96.

CAMH. *See* Centre for Addiction and Mental Health.

Canadian Broadcasting Corporation. 1995. Still Standing: The People's Champion George Chuvalo. Television Interview (5 December). http://archives.cbc.ca/sports/boxing/topics/907/.

Canadian Centre on Substance Abuse. 2005. *National Framework for Action to Reduce the Harms of Alcohol and Other Drugs and Substances in Canada*. Ottawa: Canadian Centre on Substance Abuse. http://www.nationalframework-cadrenational.ca/index_e.php?orderid_top=2.

Canadian Council for Tobacco Control. Guildford Depository of Tobacco Industry Internal Documents. http://www.cctc.ca/cctc/EN/industrywatch/internaldocuments/Guildford/.

Canadian Council for Tobacco Control. 2007. Backgrounder: Smoke-Free Legislation in Canada. http://www.cctc.ca/cctc/EN/mediaroom/backgrounders/backgrounderlegislation/at_download/file.

Canadian Criminal Justice Association (CCJA). 2006. Brief to the Standing Committee on Justice, Human Rights, House of Commons (15 February): On Amendments to the *Criminal Code of Canada* (Impaired Driving), Bill C-301. http://www.ccja-acjp.ca/en/c301en.html.

Canadian HIV/AIDS Legal Network. 2006. *Nothing About Us Without Us—Greater Meaningful Involvement of People Who Use Illegal Drugs: A Public Health, Ethical and Human Rights Perspective*. 2nd ed. Toronto: Canadian HIV/AIDS Legal Network.

Canadian Medicine. 2008. Tony Clement Takes Flak for Calling Doctors' Support for Harm Reduction Unethical. 19 August. http://www.canadianmedicinenews.com/2008/08/tony-clement-takes-flak-for-calling.html.

Cancer Care Ontario. Creation: A Relationship with Tobacco Begins to Emerge. http://www.tobaccowise.com/traditional/elders.

Carey, K.B. 1996. Substance Use Reduction in the Context of Outpatient Psychiatric Treatment: A Collaborative, Motivational, Harm Reduction Approach. *Community Mental Health Journal* 32 (3):291–306.

CCJA. *See* Canadian Criminal Justice Association.

CDC. *See* Centers for Disease Control and Prevention.

Centers for Disease Control and Prevention (CDC). 2005. Tobacco Use, Access, and Exposure to Tobacco in Media Among Middle and High School Students: United States, 2004. *Morbidity and Mortality Weekly* Report 54 (12):297–301.

———. 2007. Smoking and Tobacco Use. Centers for Disease Control and Prevention Online. http://www.cdc.gov/tobacco/data_statistics/Factsheets/smokeless_tobacco.htm.

Centre for Addiction and Mental Health (CAMH). 2002. CAMH Position on Harm Reduction: Its Meaning and Applications for Substance Use Issues. Toronto: Centre for Addiction and Mental Health. http://www.camh.net/Public_policy/Public_policy_papers/publicpolicy_harmreduc2002.html

———. 2007a. *Exposure to Psychotropic Medications and Other Substances during Pregnancy and Lactation: A Handbook for Health Care Providers.* Toronto: Centre for Addiction and Mental Health.

———. 2007b. *Harm Reduction: Its Meaning and Application for Substance Use Issues; Position Statement.* Toronto: Centre for Addiction and Mental Health. http://www.camh.net/Public_policy/Public_policy_papers/harmreductionposition.html

———. 2007c. *The Legal Sanctions Related to Cannabis Possession/Use: Position Statement.* Toronto: Centre for Addiction and Mental Health. http://www.camh.net/Public_policy/Public_policy_papers/cannabis.html.

———. 2008a. *Fact Sheet: Do You Know ... Alcohol, Other Drugs and Driving.* http://www.camh.net/About_Addiction_Mental_Health/Drug_and_Addiction_Information/alchohol_drugs_driving_dyk.html.

———. 2008b. *Fact Sheet: Do You Know ... Tobacco.* http://www.camh.net/About_Addiction_Mental_Health/Drug_and_Addiction_Information/tobacco_dyk.html.

———. 2008c. *Fact Sheet: Low-Risk Drinking Guidelines.* http://www.camh.net/About_Addiction_Mental_Health/Drug_and_Addiction_Information/low_risk_drinking_guidelines.html.

Cha, Y.M., Q. Qiang Li, W.A. Wilson, and H.S. Swartzwelder. 2006. Sedative and GABAergic Effects of Ethanol on Male and Female Rats. *Alcoholism: Clinical and Experimental Research* 30 (1):113–18.

City of Toronto. 2007. *The Toronto Drug Strategy: A Comprehensive Approach to Alcohol and Other Drugs.* www.toronto.ca/health/drugstrategy/pdf/tds_report.pdf.

Cocteau, J. 1957. *Opium*. Trans. E. Boyd. London: Peter Owen.

Collaborative Group on Hormonal Factors in Breast Cancer. 2002. Alcohol, Tobacco and Breast Cancer: Collaborative Reanalysis of Individual Data from 53 Epidemiological Studies, Including 58515 Women With Breast Cancer and 95067 Women Without the Disease. *British Journal of Cancer* 87 (11):1234–45. http://www.nature.com/bjc/journal/v87/n11/full/6600596a.html.

Commission for Distilled Spirits (Commissie Gedistilleerd). 2005. *World Drink Trends 2005*. Oxfordshire: World Advertising Research Council.

Cooney, N.L., A. Zweben, and M.F. Fleming. 1995. Screening for Alcohol Problems and At-Risk Drinking in Health-Care Settings. In *Handbook of Alcoholism Treatment Approaches: Effective Alternatives*, 2nd ed., ed. R.K. Hester and W.R. Miller. Boston: Allyn & Bacon.

Cornuz, J., S. Zwahlen, W.F. Jungi, J. Osterwalder, K. Klingler, et al. 2008. A Vaccine Against Nicotine for Smoking Cessation: A Randomized Controlled Trial. *PLoS ONE* 3 (6):e2547. http://www.plosone.org.

Cunningham, J.A. and F.C. Breslin. 2004. Only One in Three People with Alcohol Abuse or Dependence Ever Seek Treatment. *Addictive Behaviors* 29 (1):221–23.

Cunningham, J.A., K.N. Humphreys, K. Kypri, and T. van Mierlo. 2006. Formative Evaluation and Three-Month Follow-Up of an Online Personalized Assessment Feedback Intervention for Problem Drinkers. *Journal of Medical Internet Research* 8 (2):e5. http://www.jmir.org/2006/2/e5.

Cunningham, J.A., P.L. Selby, and T. van Mierlo. 2006. Integrated Online Services for Smokers and Drinkers? Use of the Check Your Drinking Assessment Screener by Participants of the Stop Smoking Center. *Nicotine and Tobacco Research* 8 (Suppl 1):S21–S25.

Cunningham, J.A., T. van Mierlo, and R. Fournier. 2008. An Online Support Group for Problem Drinkers: AlcoholHelpCenter.net. *Patient Education and Counseling* 70 (2):193–98.

Cussen, M., and W.E. Block. 2000. Legalize Drugs Now! An Analysis of the Benefits of Legalized Drugs. *The American Journal of Economics and Sociology* 59 (3):525–36.

Dackis C., and C. O'Brien. 2005. Neurobiology of Addiction: Treatment and Public Policy Ramifications. *Nature Neuroscience* 8 (11):1431–36.

DeBeck, K., E. Wood, T. Kerr, and J. Montaner. 2007. Harper's New Anti-Drug Strategy Is Not Anti-HIV. Editorial. *National Review of Medicine* 4 (15). http://www.nationalreviewofmedicine.com/issue/2007/09_15/4_editorial_15.html.

Denning, P. 2000. *Practicing Harm Reduction Psychotherapy: An Alternative Approach to Addictions*. New York: Guilford Press.

Department of Justice Canada. 2008. Backgrounder: National Anti-Drug Strategy. Ottawa: Government of Canada. http://justice.gc.ca/eng/news-nouv/nr-cp/2008/doc_32306.html.

Dole, V.P., and M.E. Nyswander. 1967. Heroin Addiction: A Metabolic Disease. *Archives of Internal Medicine* 120 (July):19–24.

D'Hondt, Jeff. 2008. *Spiderbones*. Trafford Publishing, www.trafford.com.

Dziegielewski, S.F., ed. 2005. *Understanding Substance Addictions: Assessment and Intervention*. Chicago: Lyceum Books.

Edmonton Journal. 2008. Tory Flyer Targeting Junkies Hits Sour Note. 16 August.

Edwards, J., M. Hinton, K. Elkins, and O. Athanasopoulos. 2003. Cannabis and First Episode Psychosis: The CAP Project. In *Substance Misuse in Psychosis: Approaches to Treatment and Service Delivery*, ed. H.L. Graham, A. Copollo, M.J. Birchwood, and K.T. Mueser. Chichester, UK: John Wiley and Sons.

Ellis, A., and W. Dryden. 2007. *The Practice of Rational Emotive Behavior Therapy*. 2nd ed. New York: Springer.

Erickson, P.G. 1998. Neglected and Rejected: A Case Study of the Impact of Social Research on Canadian Drug Policy. *Canadian Journal of Sociology* 23 (2-3):263–80.

Erickson, P.G., and G.F. Murray. 1986. Cannabis Criminals Revisited. *Addiction* 81 (1):81–85.

Fell, J.C., and R.B. Voas. 2006. The Effectiveness of Reducing Illegal Blood Alcohol Concentration (BAC) Limits for Driving: Evidence for Lowering the Limit to .05 BAC. *Journal of Safety Research* 37 (3):233–43.

Fingerhood, M.I. 2005. Comorbid Medical Disorders. In *The Treatment of Opioid Dependence*, ed. E.C. Strain and M.L. Stitzer. Baltimore: Johns Hopkins University Press.

Fiore, M.C., C.R. Jaén, T.B. Baker, et al. 2008. *Treating Tobacco Use and Dependence: 2008 Update*. Clinical Practice Guideline. Rockville, MD: US Department of Health and Human Services. Public Health Service. http://www.ncbi.nlm.nih.gov/books/bv.fcgi?rid=hstat2.chapter.28163.

First Nations and Inuit Health Committee, Canadian Paediatric Society. 2006. Use and Misuse of Tobacco Among Aboriginal Peoples: Update 2006. *Paediatrics & Child Health* 11 (10):681–85. http://www.cps.ca/ENGLISH/statements/II/FNIH06-01.htm.

Fischer, B., M. Firestone Cruz, and J. Rehm. 2006. Illicit Opioid Use and Its Key Characteristics: A Select Overview and Evidence from a Canadian Multisite Cohort of Illicit Opioid Users (OPICAN). *Canadian Journal of Psychiatry* 51 (10):624–34.

Fischer, B., J. Rehm, J. Patra., and M. Firestone Cruz. 2006. Changes in Illicit Opioid Use Across Canada. *Canadian Medical Association Journal* 175 (11):1385–1387.

Fischer, B., J. Patra, M. Firestone Cruz, J. Gittins, and J. Rehm. 2008. Comparing Heroin Users and Prescription Opioid Users in a Canadian Multi-site Population of Illicit Opioid Users. *Drug and Alcohol Review* 27 (6):625–32

Fleming, A. 1975. *Alcohol: The Delightful Poison.* New York: Delacorte Press.

Frieden, T.R., and M.R. Bloomberg. 2007. How to Prevent 100 Million Deaths from Tobacco. *Lancet* 369 (9574):1758–61.

Gartner, C.E., W.D. Hall, S. Chapman, and B. Freeman. 2007. Should the Health Community Promote Smokeless Tobacco (Snus) as a Harm Reduction Measure? *PLoS Medicine Online* 4 (7):e185. http://www.plosmedicine.org.

Giesbrecht, N., J. Patra, and S. Popova. 2008. *Changes in Access to Alcohol and Impacts on Alcohol Consumption and Damage: An Overview of Recent Research Studies Focusing on Alcohol Price, Hours and Days of Sale and Density of Alcohol Outlets.* Halifax: Nova Scotia Department of Health Promotion and Protection. http://www.gov.ns.ca/hpp/publications/Dr._Norman_Giesbrecht.pdf.

Giffen, P.J., S. Endicott, and S. Lambert. 1991. *Panic and Indifference: The Politics of Canada's Drug Laws.* Ottawa: Canadian Centre on Substance Abuse.

Glantz, S.A., J. Slade, L.A. Bero, P. Hanauer, and D.E. Barnes, eds. 1996. *The Cigarette Papers.* Berkeley: University of California Press. http://ark.cdlib.org/ark:/13030/ft8489p25j/.

Goldstein, A. 1994. *Addiction: From Biology to Drug Policy.* New York: W.H. Freeman & Co.

Golmier, I., J-C. Chebat, and C. Gélinas-Chebat. 2007. Can Cigarette Warnings Counterbalance Effects of Smoking Scenes in Movies? *Psychological Reports* 100 (1):3–18.

Granfield, R., and W. Cloud. 1999. *Coming Clean: Overcoming Addiction Without Treatment.* New York: New York University Press.

Grauerholz, J., and I. Silverberg. 1998. *Word Virus: The William S. Burroughs Reader.* New York: Grove Press.

Haddock, C.K., M.V. Weg, M. DeBon, R.C. Klesges, G.W. Talcott, H. Lando, and A. Peterson. 2001. Evidence That Smokeless Tobacco Use Is a Gateway for Smoking Initiation in Young Adult Males. *Prevention Medicine* 32 (3):262–67.

Hamilton, B. 1995. *Getting Started in AA.* Centre City, MN: Hazelden.

Hardwick, S., and L. King. 2008. *Home Office Cannabis Potency Study*, 2008. St Albans, UK: Home Office Scientific Development Branch. http://drugs.homeoffice.gov.uk/publication-search/cannabis/potency?view=Binary

Harrison, S., and E. Ingber. 2004. Working with Women. In *Alcohol and Drug Problems: A Practical Guide for Counsellors*, 3rd ed., ed. S. Harrison and V. Carver. Toronto: Centre for Addiction and Mental Health.

Hasin, D.S., and B.F. Grant. 2004. The Co-occurrence of DSM-IV Alcohol Abuse in DSM-IV Alcohol Dependence. *Archives of General Psychiatry* 61 (September):891–96.

Hatsukami, D.K., and H.H. Severson. 1999. Oral Spit Tobacco: Addiction, Prevention and Treatment. *Nicotine and Tobacco Research* 1 (1):21–44.

HCH Clinicians' Network. 2003. A Comprehensive Approach to Substance Abuse and Homelessness. *Healing Hands* 7 (5):1–6. Nashville, TN: National Health Care for the Homeless Council.

Health Canada. 1998. *Canada's Drug Strategy*. Ottawa: Health Canada. http://www.cicad.oas.org/Fortalecimiento_Institucional/esp/planes_nacionales/canada.pdf

———. 1999. *Best Practices: Substance Abuse Treatment and Rehabilitation*. Ottawa: Health Canada.

———. 2002. *Best Practices: Methadone Maintenance Therapy*. Ottawa: Health Canada.

———. 2003. Building and Sustaining Partnerships: A Resource Guide to Address Non-traditional Tobacco Use. Ottawa: Health Canada. http://www.hc-sc.gc.ca/fniah-spnia/pubs/substan/_tobac-tabac/2003_sust-maint_part/index-eng.php.

———. 2005. Frequently Asked Questions: Medical Use of Marihuana. Ottawa: Health Canada. http://www.hc-sc.gc.ca/dhp-mps/marihuana/about-apropos/faq-eng.php#a4.

——— 2007. Healthy Living: Rewards of Quitting. Ottawa: Health Canada. http://www.hc-sc.gc.ca/hc-ps/tobac-tabac/quit-cesser/ready-pret/reward-gratifiant-eng.php.

———. 2008. *Canadian Tobacco Use Monitoring Survey (CTUMS), Summary of Annual Results for 2008*. Ottawa: Health Canada. http://www.hc-sc.gc.ca/hc-ps/tobac-tabac/research-recherche/stat/_ctums-esutc_2008/ann_summary-sommaire-eng.php.

Hecker, L.L., and J.L.Wetchler, eds. 2003. *An Introduction to Marriage and Family Therapy*. New York: Haworth Clinical Practice Press.

Henningfield, J.E., C. Cohen, and J.D. Slade. 2009. Is Nicotine More Addictive Than Cocaine? *Addiction* 86 (5):565–69.

Herie, M., and L. Watkin-Merek. 2006. *Structured Relapse Prevention: An Outpatient Counselling Approach*. 2nd ed. Toronto: Centre for Addiction and Mental Health.

Heyman, G. 2009. *Addiction: A Disorder of Choice*. Cambridge, MA: Harvard University Press.

Hodge, J. 1996. *Trainspotting: The Screenplay*. London: Faber and Faber.

Homer-Dixon, T. 2006. *The Upside of Down: Catastrophe, Creativity, and the Renewal of Civilization*. Toronto: Knopf Canada.

Hubble, M.A., B.L. Duncan, and S.D. Miller. 1999. *The Heart & Soul of Change: What Works in Therapy*. Washington, DC: American Psychological Association.

Hughes, J.R., J. Keely, and S. Naud. 2004. Shape of the Relapse Curve and Long-Term Abstinence Among Untreated Smokers. *Addiction* 99 (1):29–38.

Humphreys, K. 2004. *Circles of Recovery: Self-Help Organizations for Addictions*. Cambridge: Cambridge University Press.

Insite Expert Advisory Committee. 2008. *Vancouver's INSITE Service and Other Supervised Injection Sites: What Has Been Learned from Research?* Ottawa: Health Canada. http://www.hc-sc.gc.ca/ahc-asc/pubs/_sites-lieux/insite/index-eng.php.

Jackson, M. 2002. *Pain: The Fifth Vital Sign*. Toronto: Random House Canada.

Jarvis, M.J. 2004. Why People Smoke. In *ABC of Smoking Cessation*, ed. J. Britton. Oxford: British Medical Journal Books, Blackwell Publishing.

Joy, J.E., S.J. Watson, and J.A. Benson. 1999. *Marijuana and Medicine: Assessing the Science Base*. Washington, DC: National Academy Press.

Kabat-Zinn, J. 1994. *Wherever You Go, There You Are: Mindfulness Meditation in Everyday Life*. New York: Hyperion.

Kahan, M. 2000. [Alcohol] Metabolism and Acute Effects. In *Management of Alcohol, Tobacco and Other Drug Problems: A Physicians' Manual*, ed. B. Brands. Toronto: Centre for Addiction and Mental Health, 71–86.

Kahan, M., and L. Wilson. 2002. *Managing Alcohol, Tobacco and Other Drug Problems: A Pocket Guide for Physicians and Nurses*. Toronto: Centre for Addiction and Mental Health.

Kalant, H., W. Corrigal, W. Hall, and R. Smart, eds. 1999. *The Health Effects of Cannabis*. Toronto: Centre for Addiction and Mental Health.

Kalivas, P.W., and N.D. Volkow. 2005. The Neural Basis of Addiction: A Pathology of Motivation and Choice. *American Journal of Psychiatry* 162 (August):1403–13.

Kalman, D., S.B. Morissette, and T.P. George. 2005. Co-Morbidity of Smoking in Patients with Psychiatric and Substance Use Disorders. *American Journal of Addiction* 14 (2):106–23.

Kaufman, J.F., and G.E. Woody. 1995. *Matching Treatment to Patient Needs in Opioid Substitution Therapy*. Rockville, MD: US Department of Health and Human Services.

Kerr, T., M.W. Tyndall, R. Zhang, C. Lai, J.S.G. Montaner, and E. Wood. 2007. Circumstances of First Injection Among Illicit Drug Users Accessing a Medically Supervised Safer Injection Facility. *American Journal of Public Health* 97 (7)1228–30.

Kessler, D.A. 1994. Statement on Nicotine-Containing Cigarettes, Speech to the US House Subcommittee on Health and the Environment, US Food and Drug Administration. http://www.fda.gov/bbs/topics/SPEECH/SPE00052.htm.

King, V.L., and R.K. Brooner. 1999. Assessment and Treatment of Comorbid Psychiatric Disorders. In *Methadone Treatment for Opioid Dependence*, ed. E.C. Strain and M.L. Stitzer. Baltimore: Johns Hopkins University Press.

Kishline, A. 1995. *Moderate Drinking: The Moderation Management Guide for People Who Want to Reduce Their Drinking*. New York: Three Rivers Press.

Klein, R. 1993. *Cigarettes Are Sublime*. Durham, NC: Duke University Press.

Kosten, T.R., and T.P. George. 2002. The Neurobiology of Opioid Dependence: Implications for Treatment. *Science & Practice Perspectives* 1 (1):13–20.

Kozlowski, L.T., R.J. O'Connor, and C.T. Sweeney. 2001. Cigarette Design. In *Monograph 13: Risks Associated with Smoking Cigarettes with Low Machine-Measured Yields of Tar and Nicotine*, ed. D.R. Shopland et al. Rockville, MD: National Cancer Institute. , pp. 13–38. http://cancercontrol.cancer.gov/tcrb/monographs/13/m13_2.pdf.

Krantz, M.J., and P.S. Mehler. 2004. Treating Opioid Dependence: Growing Implications for Primary Care. *Archives of Internal Medicine* 164 (3):277–88.

Kurtz, E. 1979. *Not-God: A History of Alcoholics Anonymous*. Center City, MN: Hazelden.

Lakoff, G. 2008. *The Political Mind: Why You Can't Understand 21st-Century American Politics with an 18th-Century Brain*. New York: Viking Penguin.

Lenton, S. 2003. Policy from a Harm Reduction Perspective. *Current Opinion in Psychiatry* 16 (3):271–77.

Leshner, A. 1997. Addiction Is a Brain Disease, and It Matters. *Science* 278 (5335):45–47.

Littell, J.H., and H. Girvin. 2002. Stages of Change: A Critique. *Behavior Modification* 26 (2):223–73.

Luty, J., and A. Lawrence. 2009. Preferred Activities of Opiate Dependent People. *Journal of Substance Use* 14 (1):61–69.

Mackay, J., M. Eriksen, and O. Shafey. 2006. *The Tobacco Atlas*. 2nd ed. Atlanta, GA: American Cancer Society.

MacPherson, D. 2001. *A Framework for Action: A Four Pillar Approach to Drug Problems in Vancouver*. http://vancouver.ca/fourpillars/pdf/Framework.pdf.

Marlatt, G.A., ed. 1998. *Harm Reduction: Pragmatic Strategies for Managing High-Risk Behaviors*. New York: Guilford Press.

Marlowe, A. 1999. *How to Stop Time: Heroin from A to Z*. New York: Basic Books.

Martin, G., B. Brands, and D.C. Marsh, eds. 2003. *Methadone Maintenance: A Counsellor's Guide to Treatment*. Toronto: Centre for Addiction and Mental Health.

Maté, G. 2008. *In the Realm of Hungry Ghosts: Close Encounters with Addiction*. Toronto: Knopf Canada.

Mattick, R.P., C. Breen, J. Kimber, and M. Davoli. 2009. Methadone Maintenance Therapy Versus No Opioid Replacement Therapy for Opioid Dependence. *Cochrane Database of Systematic Reviews* 2009 (1): Art. No. CD002209.

Mattick, R.P., J. Kimber, C. Breen, and M. Davoli. 2003. Buprenorphine Maintenance Versus Placebo or Methadone Maintenance for Opioid Dependence. *Cochrane Database of Systematic Reviews* 2003 (2): Art. No. CD002207.pub2.

Mayfield, D., G. McLeod, and P. Hall. 1974. The CAGE Questionnaire: Validation of a New Alcoholism Screening Instrument. *American Journal of Psychiatry* 131 (10):1121–23.

McCrady, B.S., and S.I. Delaney. 1995. Self-Help Groups. In *Handbook of Alcoholism Treatment Approaches: Effective Alternatives*, 2nd ed., ed. R.K. Hester and W.R. Miller. Boston: Allyn and Bacon.

McEwan, A., P. Hajek, H. McRobbie, and R. West. 2006. *Manual of Smoking Cessation: A Guide for Counsellors and Practitioners*. Oxford: Addiction Press, Blackwell Publishing.

Melendez, R.I., and P.W. Kalivas. 2008. The Basic Science of Addiction. In *Pain and Chemical Dependency*, ed. H.S. Smith and S.D. Passik. New York: Oxford University Press.

Miller, S.D., and I.K. Berg. 1995. *The Miracle Method: A Radically New Approach to Problem Drinking*. New York: W.W. Norton & Company.

Miller, W.M., and K.M. Carroll, eds. 2006. *Rethinking Substance Abuse: What the Science Shows, and What We Should Do About It*. New York: Guilford Press.

Miller, W.R., and R.F. Munoz. 2005. *Controlling Your Drinking: Tools to Make Moderation Work for You*. New York: Guilford Press.

Miller, W.A., and S. Rollnick. 2002. *Motivational Interviewing: Preparing People for Change*. 2nd ed. New York: Guilford Press.

Mueser, K.T., and R.E. Drake. 2003. Integrated Dual Disorder Treatment in New Hampshire (USA). In *Substance Misuse in*

Psychosis: Approaches to Treatment and Service Delivery, ed. H.L. Graham, A Copollo, M.J. Birchwood, and K.T. Mueser. Chichester, UK: John Wiley and Sons.

Mumenthaler, M.S., J.L. Taylor, R. O'Hara, and J.A. Yesavage. 1999. Gender Differences in Moderate Drinking Effects. *Alcohol Health and Research World* 23 (1):55–64.

National Alcohol Strategy Working Group. 2007. *Reducing Alcohol-Related Harm In Canada: Toward a Culture of Moderation.* Ottawa: Health Canada. http://www.ccsa.ca/2007%20CCSA%20Documents/ccsa-023876-2007.pdf.

National Cancer Institute. 2003. Smokeless Tobacco: Questions and Answers. The National Cancer Institute Online. http://www.cancer.gov/.

National Drug Intelligence Center. 2008. *National Drug Threat Assessment 2009: Marijuana*. Washington, DC: US Department of Justice. http://www.usdoj.gov/ndic/pubs31/31379/marijuan.htm.

National Institute on Alcohol Abuse and Alcoholism (NIAAA). 1999. Alcohol and Coronary Heart Disease. *Alcohol Alert* No. 45. http://pubs.niaaa.nih.gov/publications/aa45.htm.

National Institute on Drug Abuse (NIDA). 2008. Comorbidity: Addiction and Other Mental Illness. *Research Report Series*. Bethesda, MD: National Institutes of Health.

National Treatment Strategy Working Group. 2008. *A Systems Approach to Substance Use in Canada: Recommendations for a National Treatment Strategy*. Ottawa: National Framework for Action to Reduce the Harms Associated with Alcohol and Other Drugs and Substances in Canada. http://www.nationalframework-cadrenational.ca/uploads/files/TWS_Treatment/nts-report-eng.pdf.

Naylor, L. 2008. Creating Comprehensive Methadone Treatment for Women. In *Highs and Lows: Canadian Perspectives on Women and Substance Use*, ed. L. Greaves and N. Poole. Toronto: Centre for Addiction and Mental Health.

New York Times. 2007. In Guilty Plea, OxyContin Maker to Pay $600 Million. 10 May.

NIAAA. *See* National Institute on Alcohol Abuse and Alcoholism.

NIDA. *See* National Institute on Drug Abuse.

Nides, M. 2008. Update on Pharmacologic Options for Smoking Cessation Treatment. *The American Journal of Medicine* 121 (4 Suppl):S20–S31.

Ono, K., M.M. Condron, L. Ho, J. Wang, W. Zhao, G.M. Pasinetti, and D.B. Teplow. 2008. Effects of Grape Seed-Derived Polyphenols on Amyloid β-Protein Self-Assembly and Cytotoxicity. *Journal of Biological Chemistry* 283 (47):32176–87.

Ontario Medical Association. 2008. *Rethinking Stop Smoking Medications: Treatment Myths and Medical Realities*. Ontario Medical Review 75 (1):22–34. https://www.oma.org/Health/Tobacco/Myths_Realities2008.pdf.

Ontario Ministry of Health Promotion. 2006. *Fact Sheet: Costs of Tobacco Use and Tax Revenues*. http://www.mhp.gov.on.ca/english/health/smoke_free/fact_sheets/120208-tobacco_revenue.pdf.

Ontario Tobacco Research Unit. 2006. What Population Surveys Say about Smokeless Tobacco Use. *OTRU Update* (October). http://www.otru.org/pdf/updates/update_oct2006.pdf.

Payne, M. 2006. *Narrative Therapy: An Introduction for Counsellors*. 2nd ed. London: SAGE Publications.

Peachey, J.E., and H. Lei. 1988. Assessment of Opioid Dependence with Naloxone. *British Journal of Addiction* 83 (2):193–201.

Perkins, K.A., C.A. Conklin, and M.A. Levine. 2008. *Cognitive-Behavioral Therapy for Smoking Cessation: A Practical Guidebook to the Most Effective Treatments*. New York: Routledge.

Physicians for a Smoke-Free Canada. 2003. *Tobacco in Canada*. http://www.smoke-free.ca/pdf_1/tobaccoincanada2003.pdf.

———. 2008. *Backgrounder: Cigarillo Smoking in Canada*. http://www.smoke-free.ca/eng_home/2008-media/2008-news-release-background/Cigarillo-Q&A.pdf.

Picard, A. 2008. Clement's Insite Attack Leaves WHO Red-Faced. *The Globe and Mail*. 6 August. http://www.theglobeandmail.com/life/clements-insite-attack-leaves-who-red-faced/article701599/.

Pickett-Schenk, S.A., M. Banghart, and J.A. Cook. 2003. Integrated Treatment Outcomes for Homeless Persons with Severe Mental Illness and Co-occurring Substance Use Disorders. In *Substance Misuse in Psychosis: Approaches to Treatment and Service Delivery*, ed. H.L. Graham, A. Copollo, M.J. Birchwood, and K.T. Mueser. Chichester, UK: John Wiley and Sons.

Popova, S., J. Patra, S. Mohapatra, and B. Fischer. 2009. How Many People in Canada Use Prescription Opioids Non-medically in General and Street Drug-Using Populations? *Canadian Journal of Public Health* 100 (2):104–8.

Prochaska, J.O., and C.C. DiClemente. 1984. *The Transtheoretical Approach: Crossing the Traditional Boundaries of Therapy*. Malabar, FL: Krieger.

Prochaska, J.O., J.C. Norcross, and C.C. DiClemente. 1992. *Changing for Good: A Revolutionary Six-Stage Program for Overcoming Bad Habits and Moving Your Life Positively Forward*. New York: Avon Books.

Public Health Agency of Canada. 2001. What Determines Health? http://www.phac-aspc.gc.ca/ph-sp/determinants/index-eng.php.

Rabinoff, M., N. Caskey, A. Rissling, and C. Park. 2007. Pharmacological and Chemical Effects of Cigarette Additives. *American Journal of Public Health* 97 (11).

Raphael, D., ed. 2004. *Social Determinants of Health: Canadian Perspectives*. Toronto: Canadian Scholars' Press.

RCMP. *See* Royal Canadian Mounted Police.

Rehm, J., D. Baliunas, S. Brochu, B. Fischer, W. Gnam, J. Patra, S. Popova, A. Sarnocinska-Hart, and B. Taylor. 2006. *The Costs of Substance Abuse in Canada 2002*. Ottawa: Canadian Centre on Substance Abuse. http://www.ccsa.ca.

Reid, S. 2006. Junkie. In *Addicted: Notes from the Belly of the Beast*, 2nd ed., ed. L. Crozier and P. Lane. Vancouver: Greystone Books.

Roberts, B. 2007. *Inventions in the Tobacco Industry*. North Carolina Museum of History, Offices of Archives and History, NC Department of Cultural Resources. http://www.ncmuseumofhistory.org/collateral/articles/f06.inventions.in.tobacco.industry.pdf.

Rosenbaum, B., K. Valbak, S. Harder, P. Knudsen, A. Køster, et al. 2005. The Danish National Schizophrenia Project: Prospective, Comparative Longitudinal Treatment Study of First-Episode Psychosis. *The British Journal of Psychiatry* 186:394–99.

Rotgers, F., M.F. Kern, and R. Hoeltzel. 2002. *Responsible Drinking: A Moderation Management Approach for Problem Drinkers*. Oakland, CA: New Harbinger Press.

Royal Canadian Mounted Police. 2008. *Drug Situation in Canada: 2007*. Ottawa: Queen's Printer.

Russell, M. 1994. New Assessment Tools for Drinking in Pregnancy: T-ACE, TWEAK, and Others. *Alcohol Health & Research World* 18 (1):55–61.

Saladin, M.E., and E.J. Santa Ana. 2004. Controlled Drinking: More Than Just a Controversy: Brief History of the Controlled Drinking Controversy. *Current Opinion in Psychiatry* 17 (3):175–87.

Sanchez-Craig, M. 1995. *DrinkWise: How to Quit Drinking or Cut Down*. 2nd ed. Toronto: Addiction Research Foundation.

Sante, L. 2004. *No Smoking*. New York: Assouline.

Saunders, B., C. Wilkinson, and M. Phillips. 1995. The Impact of a Brief Motivational Intervention with Opiate Users Attending a Methadone Programme. *Addiction* 90 (3):415–24.

Selby, P., and C. Els. 2004. Tobacco Interventions for People with Alcohol and Other Drug Problems. In *Alcohol and Drug Problems: A Practical Guide for Counsellors*, 3rd ed., ed. S. Harrison and V. Carver. Toronto: Centre for Addiction and Mental Health.

Severson, H.H., and D. Hatsukami. 1999. Smokeless Tobacco Cessation. *Tobacco Use and Cessation* 26 (3):529–51.

Shafey, O., M. Eriksen, H. Ross, and J. Mackay. 2009. *The Tobacco Atlas*. 3rd ed. Atlanta, GA: American Cancer Society.

Sibbald, B. 2005. All Provinces Likely to Join Tobacco Litigation. *Canadian Medical Association Journal* 173 (11):1307.

Siegel, R.K. 2005. *Intoxication: The Universal Drive for Mind-Altering Substances*. Rochester, VT: Park Street Press.

Sieswerda, L.E., J.M. Starkes, and E.M. Adlaf. 2006. *Student Drug Use in Northwestern Ontario: Results of the Northwestern Ontario Student Drug Use Survey, 1997–2005*. Thunder Bay, ON: Thunder Bay District Health Unit. http://www.tbdhu.com/NR/rdonlyres/2C52E632-4AB7-414C-AAB2-66819228AD00/0/05NWOSDUSExecSummary.pdf.

Silversides, A., and R. Collier. 2008. Federal Health Minister Assails Ethics of InSite. *Canadian Medical Association Journal* 179 (6):521–22.

Singer, M. 2008. *Drugging the Poor: Legal and Illegal Drugs and Social Inequality*. Long Grove, IL: Waveland Press.

Single, E. 1995. Defining Harm Reduction. *Drug and Alcohol Review* 14 (3):287-90.

Skinner, W.J. 2008. Ghost-Busting Addictions: Book Review. *Canadian Medical Association Journal* 178 (10):1325–28.

Smart, R.G., and A.C. Ogborne. 1996. *Northern Spirits: A Social History of Alcohol in Canada*. Toronto: Addiction Research Foundation.

Smith, H.S., and S.D. Passik, eds. 2008. *Pain and Chemical Dependency*. New York: Oxford University Press.

Sobell, L.C., T.P. Ellingstad, and M.B. Sobell. 2002. Natural Recovery from Alcohol and Drug Problems: Methodological Review of the Research with Suggestions for Future Directions. *Addiction* 95 (5):749–764.

Sobell, M., and L. Sobell. 1993. *Problem Drinkers: Guided Self-Change Treatment*. New York: Guilford Press.

———. 1999. Stepped Care for Alcohol Problems. In *Changing Addictive Behavior: Bridging Clinical and Public Health Strategies*, ed. J.A. Tucker, D.M. Donovan, and G.A. Marlatt. New York: Guilford Press.

Srivastera, A., and M. Kahan. 2006. Buprenorphine: A Potential New Treatment Option for Opioid Dependence. *Canadian Medical Association Journal* 174 (13):1835–36.

Stepanov, I., J. Jensen, D. Hatsukami, and S.S. Hecht. 2008. New and Traditional Smokeless Tobacco: Comparison of Toxicant and Carcinogen Levels. *Nicotine and Tobacco Research* 10 (12):1773–82.

Stitzer, M.L., N. Petry, and K. Silverman. 2005. Contingency Management Therapies. In *The Treatment of Opioid Dependence*, ed.

E.C. Strain and M.L. Stitzer. Baltimore: Johns Hopkins University Press.

Strang, J., and G. Stimson, eds. 1990. *AIDS and Drug Misuse*. London: Routledge.

Tan, W.C., C. Lo, A. Jong, L. Xing, M.J. FitzGerald, W.M. Vollmer, S.A. Buist, and D.D. Sin. 2009. Marijuana and Chronic Obstructive Lung Disease: A Population-Based Study. *Canadian Medical Association Journal* 180 (8):814–20.

Thompson, S., C. Stich, and L. Johnston. 2008. *Tobacco Treatment for New Canadians in Waterloo Region*. Collaboration between the Ontario Tobacco Research Unit and the Program Training and Consultation Centre. http://www.otru.org/pdf/learn/LEARN_Tobacco_Treatment_for_New_Canadians.pdf.

Tschakovsky, K. 2009. *Methadone Maintenance Treatment: Best Practices in Case Management*. Toronto: Centre for Addiction and Mental Health.

Tsemberis, S., L. Gulcur, and M. Nakae. 2004. Housing First, Consumer Choice, and Harm Reduction for Homeless Individuals with a Dual Diagnosis. *American Journal of Public Health* 94 (4):651–56.

UNAIDS. 2008. *2008 Report on the Global AIDS Epidemic*. Geneva: Joint United Nations Programme on HIV/AIDS. http://data.unaids.org/pub/GlobalReport/2008/jc1510_2008_global_report_pp29_62_en.pdf

UNICEF. 2004. At a Glance: Canada. http://www.unicef.org/infobycountry/canada_statistics.html.

United Nations Office on Drugs and Crime. 2005. *World Drug Report, Volume 1*. Vienna: United Nations Office on Drugs and Crime. http://www.unodc.org/pdf/WDR_2005/volume_1_web.pdf.

US Department of Justice. 2006. Amended Final Opinion in Civil Action No. 99-2496 (GK), *USA v. Philip Morris Inc. et al.* http://www.usdoj.gov/civil/cases/tobacco2/amended%20opinion.pdf.

Valenzuela, C., and R.A. Harris. 1997. Alcohol: Neurobiology. In *Substance Abuse: A Comprehensive Textbook*, 3rd ed., ed. J.H. Lovinson, P. Ruiz, R.B. Millman, and J.G. Langrod. Baltimore: Williams & Wilkins.

Van den Brink, W., and C. Haasen. 2006. Evidence-Based Treatment of Opioid-Dependent Patients. *Canadian Journal of Psychiatry* 51 (10):635–45.

Vancouver Coastal Health. InSite—Safe Injection Site: Research Results. http://www.vch.ca/sis/research.htm.

Vancouver Province. 2007. Legalize It, Control It and Tax the Livin' Hell Out of It: Interview with Larry Campbell. 11 November.

Veen, N.D., J-P. Selten, I. van der Tweel, W.G. Feller, H.W. Hoek, and

R.S. Kahn. 2004. Cannabis Use and Age at Onset of Schizophrenia. *The American Journal of Psychiatry* 161 (3):501–6.

Volkow, N.D., and T-K. Lee. 2004. Drug Addiction: The Neurobiology of Behavior Gone Awry. *Nature Reviews Neuroscience* 5 (12):963–70.

Wakefield, M., C. Morley, J.K. Horan, and K.M. Cummings. 2002. The Cigarette Pack as Image: New Evidence from Tobacco Industry Documents. *Tobacco Control* 11 (Suppl 1):i73–i80.

Wardman, D., D. Quantz, J. Tootoosis, and N. Khan. 2007. Tobacco Cessation Drug Therapy Among Canada's Aboriginal People. *Nicotine & Tobacco Research* 9 (5):607–11.

Wayne, G.F., and G.N. Connolly. 2002. How Cigarette Design Can Affect Youth Initiation into Smoking: Camel Cigarettes 1983-93. *Tobacco Control* 11 (Suppl 1):i32–i39.

Webster, L.D., and B. Dove. 2007. *Avoiding Opioid Abuse While Managing Pain*. North Branch, MN: Sunrise River Press.

West, R., and S. Shiffman. 2007. *Fast Facts: Smoking Cessation*. Abingdon, UK: Health Press.

Westphal, J., D.A. Wasserman, C.L. Masson, and J.L. Sorenson. 2005. Assessment of Opioid Use. In *Assessment of Addictive Behaviors*, 2nd ed., ed. D.M. Donovan and G.A. Marlatt. New York: Guilford Press.

WHO. *See* World Health Organization.

Winnickoff, J.P., J. Friebely, S.E. Tanski, C. Sherrod, G.E. Matt, M.F. Hovell, and R.C. McMillen. 2009. Beliefs about the Health Effects of "Thirdhand" Smoke and Home Smoking Bans. *Pediatrics* 123 (1):e74–e79.

Winter, J.C., ed. 2000. *Tobacco Use by Native North Americans: Sacred Smoke and Silent Killer*. Norman, OK: University of Oklahoma Press.

Wood, E., T. Kerr, W. Small, K. Li, D.C. Marsh, J.S.G. Montaner, and M.W. Tyndall. 2004. Changes in Public Order After the Opening of a Medically Supervised Safer Injection Facility for Illicit Injection Drug Users. *Canadian Medical Association Journal* 171 (7):731–34.

Wood, E., M. Tyndall, C. Lai, J.S.G. Montaner, and T. Kerr. 2006. Impact of a Medically Supervised Safer Injecting Facility on Drug Dealing and Other Drug-Related Crime. *Substance Abuse Treatment, Prevention, and Policy* 1 (13):220–22.

Wood, E., M. Tyndall, R. Zhang, J. Stoltz, C. Lai, J.S.G. Montaner, and T. Kerr. 2006. Attendance at Supervised Injecting Facilities and Use of Detoxification Services. *The New England Journal of Medicine* 354 (23):2512–14.

World Health Organization (WHO). 2004a. *Global Status Report: Alcohol Policy*. Geneva: World Health Organization.

————. 2004b. *Neuroscience of Psychoactive Substance Use and Dependence*. Geneva: World Health Organization.

————. 2005. *Advisory Note: Waterpipe Tobacco Smoking; Health Effects, Research Needs and Recommended Action by Regulators*. Geneva: WHO Study Group on Tobacco Product Regulation (TobReg). http://www.who.int/tobacco/global_interaction/tobreg/ Waterpipe%20recommendation_Final.pdf.

Wright, J. 2003. *There Must Be More Than This: Finding More Life, Love, and Meaning by Overcoming Your Soft Addictions*. New York: Broadway Books.

Wyckham, R.G. 1999. Smokeless Tobacco in Canada: Deterring Market Development. *Tobacco Control* 8:411–20.

Yalom, I.D., and M. Leszcz. 2005. *The Theory and Practice of Group Psychotherapy*. 5th ed. New York: Perseus Books.

Zhou, X., J. Nonnemaker, B. Sherrill, A.W. Gilsenan, F. Coste, and R. West. 2009. Attempts to Quit Smoking and Relapse: Factors Associated with Success or Failure from the ATTEMPT Cohort Study. *Addictive Behaviors* 34 (4):365–73.

Index

Credits

Every possible effort has been made to trace the original source of text and visual material contained in this book. Where the attempt has been unsuccessful, the publisher would be pleased to hear from copyright holders to rectify any errors or omissions.

CPSIA information can be obtained
at www.ICGtesting.com
Printed in the USA
LVOW04s0106090216

474256LV00010B/33/P